SPEED IN

Style

Patrick Stephens Limited, a member of the Haynes Publishing Group, has published authoritative, quality books for enthusiasts for more than twenty years. During that time the company has established a reputation as one of the world's leading publishers of books on aviation, maritime, military, model-making, motor cycling, motoring, motor racing, railway and railway modelling subjects. Readers or authors with suggestions for books they would like to see published are invited to write to: The Editorial Director, Patrick Stephens Limited, Sparkford, Nr Yeovil, Somerset, BA22 7JJ.

SPEED IN Style

**The origins and development of the
Grand Touring Car**

JONATHAN WOOD

Patrick Stephens Limited

First published in 1990

British Library Cataloguing in Publication Data
Wood, Jonathan
Speed in style
The history and development of the grand touring car.
1. Sports & GT cars, history
I. Title
629.222

ISBN 1–85260–080–2

Patrick Stephens Limited is a member of the
Haynes Publishing Group P.L.C.,
Sparkford, Nr Yeovil, Somerset,
BA22 7JJ.

Typeset by Burns & Smith Ltd, Derby
Printed in Great Britain by J. H. Haynes & Co. Ltd.

1 3 5 7 9 10 8 6 4 2

Contents

Foreword

By Victor Gauntlett
Executive Chairman, Aston Martin Lagonda Ltd

AC, Aston Martin, Bentley, Ferrari, Jaguar, Lagonda, Lamborghini, Lotus, Maserati, MG — these are the very battle honours of the traditional sports car industry yet today not one of these companies remains independent. The battle has been unrelenting and the demands of vastly expensive development — not least to meet the ever-greater requirements of legislation — has, in the main, led to their loss of independence. That said, these companies are almost all vibrant, alive and still imbued with the spirit of their founding fathers, and so continue to produce both out-and-out sports cars and Grand Touring machinery of which every enthusiast dreams and which is fully worthy of their traditions.

In this book Jonathan Wood examines an area of the industry fascinating to all enthusiasts and highlights clearly that, whilst many companies have been in pursuit of similar goals, the results of these efforts have been immensely diverse and so have ensured the fuelling of our various enthusiasms and allegiances.

Sports and Grand Touring machinery has been my passion for the past 40 years and for the boy who watched Aston Martins at Goodwood and prayed for them at Le Mans it has been a wonderful experience to be deeply involved in Aston Martin Lagonda over the last ten years. My passion and my work has given me the enormous pleasure and privilege of coming into contact with some of the 'greats'. They range from Enzo Ferrari and W.O. Bentley, who in addition to founding the company that bears his illustrious name was — like Sir David Brown, Frank Feeley, Tadek Merak and John Wyer — a vital part of the Aston Martin and Lagonda story, to Sir William Lyons and Lofty England of Jaguar and Colin Chapman of Lotus. These are the standard-bearers both of motoring reality and legend, without whom this book would probably never have been written and without whom we would undoubtedly never have enjoyed such speed in such style.

Introduction

The idea for this book came from what Winnie the Pooh would have called 'a puzzlement'. And it is this: why is it that after the Second World War Britain, which possesses some of the worst weather in Europe, became the world's largest manufacturer of *open* two seater sports cars while Italy, renowned for its predictable, sunny climate, was the home of the *Gran Turismo*, which is a *closed* car?

The answer to this question is contained in the factors which led to the creation of what is known as the Grand Tourer in English and the GT the world over. But first it must be made clear that a GT is not necessarily a large car. As will become apparent, it can be, within reason, one of any particular size. This is because the Grand Tourer was born of two extremes, both geographical and automotive; from the big, long-legged French Grand Routiers of pre-war days and their contemporary small-engined Italian closed sports cars. The original Gran Turismo Alfa Romeo, it will be recalled, was a car of a mere 1750 cc. To illustrate these two all important diverse threads to the story, I can do no better than to quote the words of two respected motoring historians, one British and the other Italian.

In an absorbing *Autocar* account of Hugh Harben's magnificent restoration of his mighty, and very French, 6½-litre Speed Six Bentley coupé, once owned by Woolf Barnato, Ronald Barker wrote: 'He [Barnato] is said to have sketched the outline of its closed body on the back of an envelope and told Gurney Nutting to get on with it . . . All in all it was a pioneer GT in the true sense.' Angelo Tito Anselmi, in chronicling the 1930s origins of the Gran Turismo movement in Italy, describes the GT as: 'agile and potent but powered by a relatively *small* [my italics] engine, and capable of providing comfortable, long transcontinental journeys without compromising sheer driving pleasure.'

A third, and all important influence, is the sports coupé of the 1930s and its descendants can claim GT designation. It was the almost exclusive product of German and Italian manufacturers: a high performance closed car which was stimulated by the demands of sports car racing and the science of aerodynamics. The latter found a receptive climate amongst the automobile engineers of continental Europe, who benefited from a training which incorporated a strong theoretical element while their British counterparts relied, to a disproportionate degree, on practical experience and designed, in the main, reliable but mechanically unadventurous cars. Consequently Britain ignored the sports coupé and the technically demanding field of Grand Prix racing, which was almost an exclusively Continental preoccupation during the 1920s and 30s. This conservatism was also a factor, I believe, in the remarkable longevity of the traditional open two-seater British sports car, which appeared in the 1920s and endured for the next sixty or so years. Yet the open sports car also played a significant role, in its own right, in the development of the Grand Tourer.

So this is a story of birth and death. A story of the demise of the British sports car, which wilted and disappeared along with much of the country's motor industry for which it depended for so many of its component parts and the story of the arrival of the Grand Tourer, which succeeded it, an outward manifestation of the post-war growth and buoyancy of the Italian motor industry, which overtook British car production for the first time in 1970. Thence to the present day when it is the booming Japanese industry which espouses the mass produced GT with greatest enthusiasm.

But this is not just a story of the development of the Grand Tourer, it is also one of the dilution of the concept, and its GT initials, beginning in America in the 1960s with the arrival of the top selling Ford Mustang which, in turn, spawned its European GT for Everyman, the Capri, the progenitor of successive mass produced GTs.

What follows is what I consider to be a representative cross section of Grand Tourers. It makes no pretence to be a roll call for all available GTs. I am sure that there will be some who will disagree with my choice! Also I have set down, in greater detail, what I consider to be significant and innovative models which, I hope, will help to give the story form and pace. I have concentrated on road cars but have not included the so called 'homologation specials' and the many sports racing GTs, which surely deserve a book of their own.

So what is a Grand Tourer? Like many writers past and present, I wrestled for a long time to try to create the definitive GT formula and, in the end, have had to admit defeat. All I can say is that I think that I have identified the influences which have wrought the GT revolution and believe that the cars so identified in this book are Grand

Tourers. They therefore all embody, to a greater or lesser extent, elements of the sports car, the sports coupé, the Grand Routiers and the saloon car. If anyone can produce a concise description from these diverse ingredients, I'd be delighted to hear from them!

Jonathan Wood
Frensham, Surrey

CHAPTER ONE

Wind-cheating coupés

'The BMW team included a splendid aerodynamic Berlinetta, wind tunnel designed by German specialists, that was extremely fast at 135 mph ... I couldn't believe the speed of which these BMWs were capable'

Count Giovanni Lurani, a member of the BMW team in the 1940 Mille Miglia, in his *Mille Miglia 1927–1957*

When the 1951 Turin Motor Show opened its doors to the public on Wednesday 4 April, it was the Americans and British, with no less than twenty marques apiece, which dominated the proceedings. Italy, the host country, offered by contrast a mere nine marques but from a historical standpoint, by far and away the most important of these came from the innovative Lancia company. At Turin it introduced a handsome Pinin Farina coupé version of its Aurelia saloon of the previous year, which carried the *Gran Turismo* (Grand Touring) name. Just as the Aurelia's V6 engine had represented a world first, so the concept of the sports car combined with the comfort and wider appeal of the saloon, was effectively born, though as will be apparent, Lancia was not the first company to offer such a model. Nevertheless, the 100 mph (162 kmh) coupé did reflect the innovative climate then current in Italy and, above all, it provided the new concept with a name. Soon to be abbreviated to the simpler, and more memorable, GT initials, the theme was to revolutionize the concept of the performance road car, so that within two decades the traditional open two seater, a British bastion since the pioneering days of motoring, would be in retreat.

But what were the influences that wrought the GT revolution? There are three clearly discernible, with each to some extent interdependent on the others: firstly, the traditional open two seater sports car, secondly, its closed derivatives, and thirdly, the research into the benefits of aerodynamically acceptable bodywork, which so enlivened the motoring

A closed car, in this instance a Touring-bodied BMW 328, wins the 1940 Mille Miglia at an average speed of 104.2 mph (167.6 kmh), driven by von Hanstein and Baumer. 328s also come in third, fourth and sixth with Alfa Romeo upholding Italian laurels in second place.

scene on continental Europe during the inter-war years.

First, the sports car proper. Definitions of this delightful open form of transport are many and varied, but I don't think I can improve on the description applied by that colourful figure, Rodney Walkerley, sports editor of *The Motor*, from 1934 until 1959. Writing under the pseudonym of *Grande Vitesse*, he opined: 'A sports car is a motor car designed primarily for the driver to enjoy driving fast'. It does, of course, depend what you mean by 'fast' and certainly the model which could claim to be the ancestor of the modern sports car was capable of a mere 47 mph (75 kmh). This was the exquisite 1.3-litre overhead camshaft FENC Isotta Fraschini of 1909, a production version of the car that had run in the Grand Prix des Voiturettes in the previous year. Although the little Isotta Fraschini was the first four-cylinder car home (in eighth place) it was to have an influence far beyond the confines of the race's Dieppe circuit.

The Italian company decided to market a road going version of the FE, which duly went on sale in 1909 with a slightly larger capacity 1.3-litre engine to offset the extra weight required to equip the model for the road. Significantly, the bodywork was open and doorless in the manner of all competition cars of the day and a contemporary Italian magazine was moved to comment: 'Although the small Isotta car may have the appearance of an attractive plaything, it is a masterpiece of precision . . . agile and light but compact and robust. This small, swift vehicle induces a feeling of intoxication in the driver . . .' The Milan firm manufactured a respectable 100 FEs from 1909 and the model was available until the outbreak of the First World War in 1914.

Meanwhile other small four-cylinder racing *voiturettes* followed in the wheeltracks of the FE. Two years later, in 1910, a 2.6-litre T head four-cylinder Hispano-Suiza won the event and this evolved into the 3.6-litre Alphonso model of 1911, with a top speed of 77 mph (123 kmh).

Although the FE Isotta Fraschini was an important model in its own right, it is also significant for what it inspired because that extraordinary artist engineer, Ettore Bugatti, based his celebrated 1.2-litre Type 13 of 1910 on the Isotta, although it endured for much longer, until 1925. Here was a delectable small sports car, well built and responsive and with excellent handling.

But performance motoring was not confined to low capacity cars. The foundations of the larger sports models were laid in the Bavarian Herkomer Trials, which began in 1905, and led to the Prince Henry Trials of 1908, so named after Prince Heinrich of Prussia, who was the brother of the

Kaiser. Although larger cars were supposed to be handicapped in favour of smaller ones, a 7.8-litre Benz was victorious in the first year though a 2.1-litre Opel won in 1909. Then, in 1910, came a one, two, three victory for the Vienna-based Austro-Daimler company, with Ferdinand Porsche, the designer, at the wheel of the winning car. Like the Isotta Fraschini and Bugatti, this 5.7-litre car boasted an overhead camshaft engine and about 200 examples of the appropriately named Prince Henry model were built.

Another participant in the 1910 Prince Henry Trial came from the British Vauxhall company. For this event, chief engineer Laurence Pomeroy prepared three special cars and two of these 3-litre cars completed the course. Like Austro-Daimler, Vauxhall also offered a Prince Henry model, which was almost identical to the Tour car, and offered for 'fast travelling or speed work'. From the Prince Henry sprang the legendary 30/98 of 1914. This followed Pomeroy's enlarged $4\frac{1}{2}$-litre hill climb car produced for Joseph Higginson, inventor of the Autovac petrol pump. This was a 100 mph (160 kmh) side valve model though overhead valves arrived in 1923 and the model lasted until 1927.

The outbreak of the First World War brought sports car development to a temporary halt though, afterwards, just as its origins were to be found on the race tracks of the pre-1914 era, so the momentum was perpetuated in the post-war years. In 1922 a new 2-litre racing formula was introduced, which had a demonstrable effect on the sports car's appearance as well as its mechanical specifications. In 1914 Mercedes had dominated Grand Prix racing but, in the early post-war years, with a defeated Germany banned from participating in international events, the innovative baton passed to the Italian Fiat company and the Type 804/404 car of 1922 was not only to profoundly affect the appearance of racing car bodywork for the next twelve or so years but was to similarly alter the appearance of the European sports car. The bonnet closely followed the shape of the radiator and there was a two-seater doorless body, open of course, while the distinctive wedge-shaped tail concealed the chassis members. The underside of the wind tunnel tested body was contained within an undershield.

This model won the prestigious French Grand Prix of 1922 and later, in its definitive 405 form, it set the seal on its distinctive bodylines and introduced the supercharger to racing cars, where it remained for the next thirty years. It would also not be long before it found its way on to the more expensive sports cars of the inter-war years.

It was the French who first took up the Fiats' rakish body

lines, as these were cheap and easy to copy, in contrast to the sophisticated mechanicals. It was, incidentally, in about 1921, that the term *sports car* first appeared. The 900 cc C4 Amilcar of 1922 mirrored the appearance of that year's Grand Prix Fiat, with added wings and stepboards and introduced the concept of the cheap, small sports car to the European market while the 1100 cc Salmson was not far behind. The lines were also elongated for larger four-seater road cars. One such was the 3½-litre Lorraine-Dietrich which won the Le Mans 24-hour race in 1925. But the car that is synonymous with the 24-hour classic was the Bentley from Britain; a greater contrast to the diminutive Amilcar is difficult to imagine.

In 1919 Walter Owen Bentley introduced the new make that bore his name, a car in the spirit of the 30/98 Vauxhall but with a smaller capacity 3-litre overhead camshaft engine. Although W.O. conceived the Bentley as a sporting car with rakish, open bodywork, many customers insisted that it be fitted with commodious and heavy saloon coachwork. In 1926 came a 6½-litre six-cylinder model, while Bentley reverted to his four-cylinder theme with his 4½-litre car of 1927. These cars were to dominate the Le Mans 24-hour race during the 1920s.

The race had been born in 1923 when Charles Faroux, of the French motoring magazine, *La Vie Automobile*, received a visit from his old friend, George Durand, who was keen to organize a motor race centred on the town of Le Mans in the Department of Sarthe. Quite coincidentally, Emile Coquille, who was otherwise best remembered for having introduced the Rudge-Whitworth knock-off wheel to France, was also keen to establish a new type of motor race for the sole reason, he stated, 'of making manufacturers perfect their electrical equipment'. This meant running through the hours of darkness and he had given the Le Mans based Automobile Club d'Quest 10,000 francs (£4,000) to stage the event.

So the world's first significant 24-hour race was born. The first race was held in 1923 and was won by a French Chenard Walcker, but Bentleys, clad in their traditional four-seater open coachwork, won in 1924, 1927, 1928, 1929 and 1930, a reminder that reliability was a cornerstone of W.O.'s design philosophy.

The Bentley did have its French equivalents, such as the superlative 6½-litre H16 Hispano-Suiza, with which it shared a fixed head, single overhead camshaft engine. This was an expensive 85 mph (136 kmh) car but rather cheaper were the fast touring *Les Grand' Routiers* models with either four but more usually six-cylinder pushrod or overhead camshaft engines, capable of about 70 to 75 mph (112 to 120 kmh) and able to cruise all day at around 60 to 65 mph (96 to 104 kmh). These appeared in France from the early 1920s and were ideally suited for those fast, straight roads, so beloved of the Continentals. This breed is perhaps typified by the new Ballot make; the 2-litre overhead camshaft, 2LT of 1921, was a 75 mph (120 kmh) car, as was the pushrod engined 6-litre GL Delage of 1926 while the 2.3-litre sleeve valve C11 Voisin of the same year represents a more idiosyncratic interpretation of the same theme. Faster, pricier and more exclusive was the Type 50 of 1930 Bugatti, a 115 mph (185 kmh) supercharged 4.9-litre car, the first twin-overhead camshaft model from Molshiem, which would point the way to the even more popular 3.3-litre Type 57 of 1934.

The arrival of the Type 50 represented a shift in emphasis for Bugatti away from the delectable sports and grand prix cars of the 1920s. The firm's influence had waned in this area in the following decade in the face of sure-footed opposition from Alfa Romeo and, later, the revolutionary Mercedes-Benz and Auto Unions from Germany. From the mid 1930s however, it concentrated its resources on sports car racing and, in 1937 and 1939, Bugattis won at Le Mans. In both instances, Jean-Pierre Wimille, at the wheel of the famous open bodied Type 57 'tanks', took the chequered flag. However, in the latter year, there came an all important pointer to future trends, in that the BMW 328, placed fifth in the 1939 event, was not an open car but a closed one, with a stylish coupé body, the work of the Milan-based Touring coachbuilding concern. In many ways this 2-litre car, which came in only 103 miles (165 km) behind the winning 3.3-litre Bugatti, encapsulated the development of the sports coupé on continental Europe during the inter-war years, which was largely concentrated in Germany and Italy. It was this type of car that was to pave the way to the *Gran Turismo* models of the post-war years and was developed because it was recognized that *a closed car, designed to aerodynamic principles, is more efficient than its open equivalent,* and is consequently faster. Therefore it will be seen that the evolution of the new science of aerodynamics lies at the very heart of the creation and evolution of the sports coupé.

When Benz and Daimler created the motor car in 1886, they were far more concerned with mechanicals than bodywork, such as it was. However, flourishing coachbuilding businesses producing a wide variety of bodies, from the most basic to ones of great elegance and proportion, had grown up by the outbreak of the First World War.

But their products almost exclusively betrayed their carriage antecedance and there was little awareness of the advantages of aerodynamically efficient bodywork.

Having said that, some knowledge did exist in France and Germany in the late nineteenth century of the worth of wind cheating bodywork. This was all too apparent, on 4 March 1899, when the Comte de Chasseloup-Laubat, in a celebrated battle with the Belgian Camille Jenatzy, took the world land speed record at 57.6 mph (92.6 kmh) in an electric vehicle fitted with a 'windcutting' nose, undertray and pointed tail. Jenatzy responded with another electric powered vehicle, which he christened *La Jamais Contente* ('The Never Satisfied'). The aluminium cigar-shaped body, designed by Leon Auscher of Rothschilds of Paris, who built it, must have caused a sensation in its day even if the driver, perched on rather than in the vehicle, must have caused havoc with the airflow. Aerodynamics therefore played a formative role in the conception of one-off Land Speed Record cars and were to do so from thereon.

So much for the unorthodox. But what of mainstream car bodywork? As already noted, most car bodies were all too conventional, but as the vast majority of cars were bodied by separate coachbuilders, there were opportunities for experimentation. The open Austro-Daimler which Ferdinand Porsche drove to victory in the 1910 Prince Henry trials revealed aerodynamical awareness in its side profile. The same year a Gregoire was fitted with a closed body by Alin and Liautard with an obviously balloon-shaped rear. Perhaps the most celebrated example of the art came from Italy where Count Marco Ricotti, an engineer who was deeply interested in both automobiles and aeronautics,

Record cars have long reflected the benefits of aerodynamic research and, during the 1930s, Germany was pre-eminent in this respect. This Mercedes-Benz of 1936 was daringly innovative in that its wheels were enclosed in an aerodynamic shell. It took a clutch of records in October 1936, wind tunnel testing at the Zeppelin works at Friedrichshafen having confirmed a Cd of 0.25.

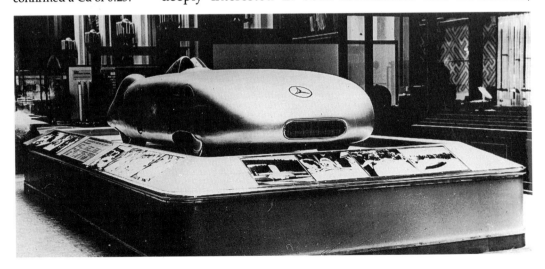

designed a teardrop shaped body, its futuristic appearance being accentuated by the introduction of portholes along its sides. Built by Castagna, it was mounted on a standard 50 hp ALFA chassis which, in conventional form, was capable of about 55 mph (88 kmh). However, once fitted with its new body, it apparently recorded a top speed of 87 mph (140 kmh). But this body was unique and was never put into production. It may also have produced something of a claustrophobic effect on its occupants because, in 1911, much of the top was removed, though the distinctive front remained. (A replica of the original rendering can be seen today in the Alfa Romeo Museum in Milan.)

These three examples, and there were others, all reveal that stylists and engineers were looking skywards for their inspiration, not to aircraft, but to rigid and non-rigid airships. It was the French who pioneered the latter, with the flight of *La France* in 1884, and the body of Jenatzy's 1899 Land Speed Record vehicle reflects this influence. But in Germany, Count Ferdinand von Zeppelin effectively created the rigid airship with the arrival of the *LZ1* in 1900 and, by the outbreak of the First World War, 22 examples of these lighter-than-air craft had been constructed.

One year into the war, in 1915, a 26-year-old Austro-Hungarian arrived at the Zeppelin works at Friedrichshafen. His name was Paul Jaray, who was destined to be the formative influence on the aerodynamics of car body design in the inter-war years. Born in Vienna, capital of the Austro-Hungarian empire, Jaray (1889–1974) had Hungarian parents. His father was a sculptor but young Paul attended a Viennese technical college where he became an assistant to Dr R. Doerfl, a pioneer in the science of aerodynamics, who introduced his young pupil to the subject. Jaray graduated with a degree in mathematics in 1910 and, in the following year, got his first job, with EAG, a Prague-based company which built cranes and similar heavy engineering equipment. He subsequently transferred to Austro-Daimler but, in 1914, moved to Germany for a job with Flugzeugbau at Friedrichshafen, which was the Zeppelin company's seaplane offshoot. Although he worked on the FF17 and FF21 'planes, Jaray did not enjoy his assignment and switched to airships. The first he was involved with was the *LZ 38*, launched in 1915, and was responsible for the aerodynamic calculations that determined its shape. Jaray considered that the early airships had been too thin and the *LZ 62* of 1916 was the first which reflected his influence, differing from its predecessors in having a blunted nose and slim tail.

At this time, Zeppelin possessed no wind tunnel, so Jaray arrived at his shapes by mathematical calculation, but he was keen to have one to check the accuracy of his work. In 1916 he built a small 3.2 ft (960 mm) diameter tunnel but, in the following year, he supervised the construction of a much larger one, which at 9.5 ft (2,890 mm) was Germany's largest. Although initially used for his airship work, Jaray was to employ it subsequently for his experiments into the shape of automobile bodywork.

After the end of the war in 1918, Germany was initially banned from participating in aircraft manufacture by the terms of the Treaty of Versailles, so Jaray suggested to the Zeppelin management that instead of building airships it might consider the manufacture of aerodynamically efficient car bodywork. His inspiration came from a fellow countryman, Edmund Rumpler, who had completed the designs of his Tropfen Auto (Teardrop Car) in 1919. Rumpler (1872–1940), was also Vienna born and, after education at the city's technical college, obtained his first job at the Nesselsdorfer Wagon Works at the age of 24 in 1897. The company finally emerged as Tatra in 1923, and set up a car division. However, in 1898, he left and moved to Germany, first working for Allgemeine Motorwagen Gesellschaft in Berlin and then, in 1900, with Daimler at Marienfelde.

By 1902, he had moved again to become technical director of Adler in Frankfurt. Not only was Rumpler responsible for what was thought to be the first L, as opposed to T-head, engine in Germany in 1903, but in the same year was responsible for patenting the swing axle, though it would not attain production status until the 1920s. Rumpler remained at Adler until 1906 when he moved back to Berlin to set up his own consultancy, which soon diversified into the design of aircraft engines. Soon he became associated with Igo Etrich, and Rumpler's company produced the *Taube* (Dove) monoplane, which gained a formidable reputation for itself during the First World War.

With his grounding in automobile and aviation engineering, Rumpler had been contemplating applying the science of aerodynamics to car bodywork. In 1919 his company was liquidated, because it was an aircraft manufacturer, but the Tropfen-Auto, which followed the contours of a falling drop of liquid, was announced at the 1921 Berlin Motor Show and was, by all accounts, 'the star of the show,' and fairly bristling with individuality. The chassis was effectively a metal tub displaying the familiar teardrop contours, but this demanded a centrally located engine, a purpose built 2.6-litre radial six-cylinder unit, manufactured by Siemens and Halske. Rumpler's own swing axle featured at the rear. The standard two-door saloon's body echoed those of the tub and, accordingly, had a distinctive curved windscreen.

An open version was also listed but there were few takers for either car, despite the fact that the Rumpler saloon was capable of 68 mph (109 kmh), which reflected its impressive drag coefficient, the measurement of aerodynamic attainment. This was confirmed in testing by the Aerodynamic Research Institute's Gottingden wind tunnel in 1922.

Drag coefficient, written as Cd, is the number that expresses a car's aerodynamic efficiency. The lower the number, the greater that efficiency. In the 1920s, the average angular saloon car had a Cd of around 0.60. In 1979 a surviving Rumpler, owned by the Deutches Museum in Munich, was tested in Volkswagen's climatic wind tunnel and recorded an impressive Cd (drag coefficient) of 0.28, which was considerably better than the rival Jaray designs which usually recorded a Cd of over 0.30.

One factor in the Rumpler's commercial failure was its unconventional appearance, a problem that has haunted designers of aerodynamically efficient vehicles from thereon, coupled with the fact that the car's launch came at a time of economic recession. Rumpler countered with a more conventional long wheelbase open version in 1924 but it was only listed for another year. An attempt by Benz to manufac-

An example of Edmund Rumpler's extraordinary Tropfen Auto (Tear drop car) of 1921, though it only lasted until 1924. Not surprisingly there were few takers. Note the central steering and curved windscreen, the unconventional 'bonnet' being made possible by the use of a mid-mounted engine. All this combined to produce an astonishingly low Cd of 0.28.

ture a racing car based on Rumpler's patents suffered for the same reasons and the concept did not attain success until the arrival of Ferdinand Porsche's mid-engined Auto Union P-Wagen of 1934. With the rise of Hitler in 1933, Edmund Rumpler emigrated to America but later returned to Germany and died in 1940.

Early in 1922, the year after the appearance of Rumpler's car, Paul Jaray began experimenting with models in the Zeppelin wind tunnel. Initially he used open and closed designs but soon what can be considered as the distinctive Jaray look emerged. This was an aerofoil shaped saloon, less radical than Rumpler's car because it retained a conventional located front engine, and represented a much reduced top half of an airship, with a rounded windscreen, pointed tail and an underframe. These experiments were transformed into a full size car on a Loreley chassis and the resulting curious, high, narrow two-door saloon showed a 29 per cent fuel saving over a conventionally bodied example even though it was 1.37 in (3,480 mm) longer and 199 lb (90 kg) heavier.

In 1923 Jaray left Zeppelin for Switzerland, where he established the Jaray Streamline Carriage Company in Zurich and continued his experiments there with the design of a racing car on another Loreley chassis. His recognition of the importance of closed bodywork was reflected by this competition car having a roof. 'Everyone laughed when I did the Ley racer as a closed car' remembered Jaray, though he eventually had to let the driver's head stick out. But the car's performance — it was capable of 80 mph (128 kmh) from a 26 hp engine — confirmed the soundness of his theories. He continued his experiments on Audi and Dixi chassis though, in the meantime, the thread of aerodynamic research had moved from Germany, which remained in the grip of economic recession for much of the decade, and switched to France.

Like Germany, France had pursued aerodynamics studies in the pre-First World War era, much of which was centred on an aerodynamics laboratory and wind tunnel established by Alexander Gustave Eiffel, in 1909–10, near the base of the tower which bore his name, and the previously mentioned Parisian coachbuilders, Alin and Liautard, were responsible for producing bodywork created with the aid of these facilities.

However, at the end of the war, a new full size wind tunnel at the Issy-les-Molineux aerodrome became available for the use of the French car makers. Aerodynamic influence did not, in the first instance, have any noticeable effect on

French production cars though it did in the more esoteric racing sector. A stimulus occurred with the introduction of the *Grand Prix de Tourisme*, staged for the first time at the French Grand Prix at Strasbourg in 1922, and held prior to the race proper. Although the winning car's average speed was a factor in the results, a crucial element was that overall fuel consumption was also to be a major factor, thus giving an incentive for manufacturers to adopt wind-cheating bodies to improve their fuel consumption figures. This first event was won by an aircraft manufacturer, Gabriel Voisin, who entered a team of sleeve valve 18CV models. The rules had specified a minimum body width of 4.2 ft (1,300 mm) and Voisin responded with an open body only 2.11 ft (900 mm) wide, with streamlined bulges accounting for another 2.11 ft. Voisin was deterred from entering the following year's event by a rule which specified that all cars should carry a large rectangular panel at the rear which negated any aerodynamic benefits. He responded by entering a quartet of cars for the pukka 1923 French Grand Prix at Tours. Drawing on aircraft technology, he created four narrow wedge-shaped racing cars, of innovative semi-monocoque construction, which weighed only 83.5 lb (37.8 kg). All but one, alas, failed to finish but the surviving car was placed fifth, and last, arriving five hours behind Henry Segrave's winning Sunbeam. Bugatti fielded a trio of aerodynamically aware 'tank' bodied cars in this event, one of which was placed third. This was the third of Bugatti's aerodynamically inspired cars. The first, with bulbous circular bodywork, had appeared at the previous year's French Grand Prix and was similar to that fielded by Ballot. By the time of the 1923 Indianapolis 500-mile Race these bodies had been dispensed with and replaced by a far neater single-seater one by Bechereau and aerodynamicists at the SPAD aircraft company.

Although Voisin was back at the *Grand Prix de Tourisme* at Lyon in 1924, the event was won by a Peugeot, boasting a sleeve valve engine in the Voisin manner, and the open bodywork which revealed attention having been given to improve its wind cheating properties, with cowled radiator and front apron and carefully faired front wings. But the aerodynamic advantages of closed bodywork had not escaped the Austrian Steyr company, which entered a Type V1 model with lofty Weymann body and pointed tail though it did not figure in the results.

What was to prove to be the last *Grand Prix de Tourisme* was held at the newly opened Montlhery circuit in 1925 and was, once again, won by Peugeot who followed Steyr's example and entered a light, fabric-bodied saloon, which was built under Weymann patents by Lagache and Glazmann of Paris. The windscreen had a pronounced V and there were only two doors but no rear window and streamlined tail. Careful attention was given to the underside of the car which was contained within an undershield. There were no intrusive headlights to interfere with the air flow, but they were concealed within the sides of the scuttle and could be extended when required. Unfortunately the *Grand Prix de Tourisme* did not prove popular with the car makers as, by 1925, it was being overshadowed by the Le Mans 24-hour race which had already inspired a similar event at Spa in 1924. Alas, these endurance events took no account of the entrants' fuel consumption and the stimulus to streamlined body design from that particular source lapsed.

But the move towards closed bodywork was given an added fillip by the mass producers when, in 1925, Andre Citroen introduced the cheap American pressed steel saloon body to the European market. This development coincided with a marked rise in the popularity of closed Weymann coachwork in France. Charles Torres Weymann was a versatile French inventor and industrialist who had Nivex petrol gauges and Jaeger instruments (both of which graced the instruments panels of high quality Continental cars) to his credit. In 1920 he had began work on a quiet, light and durable alternative to the traditional wood/aluminium construction. The result of these labours were first seen at the 1922 Paris salon, mounted on a Talbot-Darracq. Instead of the usual metal panelling, there was a visually pleasing fabric covering concealing a wooden frame which was part of an integrated support structure, with a 4 mm gap between the timbers, which were separated by metal plates. This added up to a light, rigid structure which, above all, did not creak and absorbed mechanical sounds. Even more significantly, although there were Weymann tourers, it was a structure which particularly lent itself to closed coachwork. The Weymann soon gained considerable popularity in France. *The Autocar's* distinguished Continental correspondent, W.F. Bradley, probably spoke for many when he said: 'The fact that I have reduced weight and eliminated all noise has resigned me, an open car enthusiast, to a saloon.' By 1927 it was claimed that no less than 85 per cent of closed cars built in France were manufactured under Weymann patents and, by the following year, over 50,000 Weymann bodies were in use.

From about 1925 the Weymann began to replace the open tourer in popularity among the long-legged Grand

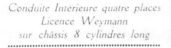

Conduite Intérieure quatre places
Licence Weymann
sur châssis 8 cylindres long

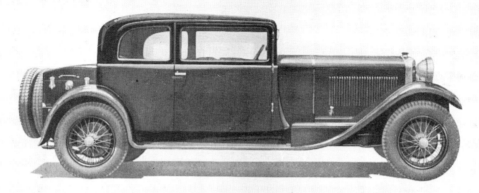

From the mid 1920s, until the early 1930s, the Weymann saloon became an increasingly popular feature of French high-speed tourers. This is a 3-litre straight-eight Ballot illustrated in the firm's 1930 catalogue.

Routiers models, as customers opted for comfort and protection from the weather on their long trans-Continental journeys. The lofty, swaying saloon body was soon replaced by lower, more elegant lines and, by the early 1930s, the concept of the long-bonneted, low-roofed coupé or saloon had arrived, and these lines were soon being magnificently but conventionally interpreted by some of France's best bespoke coachbuilders.

The Weymann phenomena disappeared as quickly as it had arrived. Although the fabric body looked smart and presentable when new, it did not weather well and looked tired and shabby when old. It was also difficult to repair satisfactorily and there were plenty of cheap imitations on the market which devalued the originals. But, above all, the increasing popularity of the pressed steel body eliminated practically all the shortcomings of the coachbuilt one and did not require a skilled workforce to manufacture it. By the mid-1930s, the Weymann had all but disappeared from the Continental motoring scene.

But the Weymann phenomenon had not been confined to its native France. In 1923 Weymann Motor Body was established in Britain, where fabric bodies enjoyed considerable vogue. In Italy, the Weymann licence was held by the old established Alessio coachbuilding concern and, in 1926, the rights to build the system in Lombardy were purchased by the newly formed Carrozzeria Touring of Milan, perhaps the greatest Italian coachbuilding house of the inter-war years.

Touring had been established by Felice Bianchi Anderloni, a former law student who had joined Isotta Fraschini in

1904, and quickly showed his worth by testing cars. He soon headed the test department and later became a racing driver for the firm. After a spell in the army and service in the First World War, Anderloni rejoined Isotta Fraschini where he remained until 1924, when he transferred to the Italian branch of the French Peugeot company, which also came within the Isotta orbit. During the winter of 1925, Anderloni decided on a new career. With the help of a lawyer friend, Gaetano Ponzoni, he bought a controlling interest in the small Milan coachbuilding company of Carrozzeria Falco, which was run by Vittorio Ascari, whose brother Antonio had already made his name as a racing driver for Alfa Romeo. The talented Anderloni took over responsibility for styling while Ponzoni looked after the commercial side of the firm which changed its name to the English sounding one of Touring. The business grew and prospered and, during the 1930s, Anderloni produced a range of distinctive bodies of great subtlety of line and proportion, which have never been surpassed.

Initially Touring bodied a wide variety of cars, and produced coachwork for such companies as Isotta Fraschini, Lancia and OM but, from the early 1930s, its association

It was Alfa Romeo which bought the *Gran Turismo* name to prominence, as the firm's 1930 catalogue reveals. The 1750 range is shown here and note than *Gran Turismo* was initially applied to the Touring bodied four-door saloon in the centre, while its chassis was also used for the 2/4 seater roadster on the left.

with the Alfa Romeo company, which was also Milan based, was highly significant and the vast majority of Touring's output found its way onto Alfa Romeo chassis. Its founders' express intention had been to establish a sporting marque and ALFA began building cars in 1910. Just after the First World War, in 1920, industrialist Nicole Romeo took the firm over and added his name to that of Alfa. The first of the legendary post-war Alfa Romeo sports cars was the 3-litre pushrod engined RL series of 1920, though the new 1½-litre 1500 of 1927 was a very different proposition. It had been designed by the masterly Vittorio Jano, who had been wooed from Fiat's racing department in 1923 by none other than Enzo Ferrari. Jano had initially produced the all conquering P2 Grand Prix car of 1924 but the 1500 was his first sports model for his new employers. Available in single and twin overhead camshaft Sport and Super Sport forms, it remained in production until the arrival of the definitive 1750 version in 1929.

The bottom of the 1750 range was the single cam *Turismo* (Touring) model, while its more potent twin overhead camshaft derivative was the *Gran Turismo* (Grand Touring), the initials of which would become instantly identifiable with closed performance motoring in the post-war years. The 1929 series was available with a variety of both open and closed four-seater coachwork, unlike the top line supercharged twin overhead camshaft Gran Sport, which was only offered in open two-seater form. Then, in 1931, with the arrival of the Fifth series 1750 came a supercharged *Gran Turismo* and although factory coachwork was available, the most memorable examples were bodied by Touring. By far the most significant of these were some special 'Aerodynamic' coupés built by the Milan coachbuilder for Alfa Romeo to run in the 1931 Mille Miglia, and these can be considered as the true ancestors of the post-war GT.

It had been the creation of the Le Mans 24-hour race in 1923 that inspired a group of Italian enthusiasts to stage this larger and more impressive event. The 'four musketeers', as they were known, were Aymo Maggi, Franco Mazzotti, Giovanni Canestrini and secretary of the Brescia Automobile Club in northern Italy, Renzo Castagneto. Like the Le Mans event, they planned to run the race on public roads, from Brescia to Rome and back in a figure of eight form, with Bologna as the crossing point. The distance was approximately 994 miles (1,600 km), which was the equivalent of one thousand old Roman miles, or *miglia*, which gave the race its title, The Mille Miglia (The 1,000 Miles).

The first race was held in 1927, and was won by OM but, in the following year, Alfa Romeo took the chequered flag and from thereon dominated the event until Italy entered the war, failing to win only in 1931 and 1940. The race was to play a key role in the development of the GT, for up until 1930, practically all cars entered in the race were open ones. But that year the organizers introduced an additional *Turismo* (Touring) class for four-seater saloons, with the hope of attracting more entrants.

Alfa Romeo did not compete in this new class in 1930 but, for the 1931 event, entered a trio of Gran Turismos. Touring created, specially for the race, a body which it diplomatically described as an 'aerodynamic sports saloon' because the race regulations specified a four-seater body. Concessions to aerodynamics were the sloping windscreen and gently arched roof while the boot contained the spare wheels, as they would otherwise have contributed to turbulence if mounted outboard. Although Weymann bodywork was fast becoming unfashionable, Touring reverted to it for these works cars in the interests of lightness though the lines were also offered, in conventional metal form, and known as the Coupé Royal. In the race the three unsupercharged Gran Turismos all finished and dominated their class, which they won, and the victorious car was also placed eighth overall. This was some compensation for Alfa Romeo because the event was won by Caracciola in an SSKL Mercedes-Benz.

In the following year (1932) Alfa Romeo was taking no chances and its cars took the first seven places. For the saloon class, Touring had prepared new aerodynamic bodies, refinements of the previous year's offerings but with steeper inclinations to the windscreens and with the battery boxes on the wings carefully faired in to improve air flow. The cars were lighter than the previous year's and Touring even adopted railway carriage type window pulls to raise and lower the glass, in place of the conventional mechanism, to save a few precious kilos. One of these cars not only won its class but was also placed fourth overall in the event proper.

For all their attention to detail, these 'Aerodynamic' coupés were essentially conventional bodies which featured wind cheating refinements of an all-too empirical nature. But, once again, it was the arrival of the pressed steel body which dispensed with traditional wooden framework, and so freed stylists from its boxy, angular constraints. Consequently, during the 1930s, many so called 'Aerodynamic' bodies appeared though, with some notable exceptions, most had more to do with fashionable 'streamlining' and

The genesis of the sports coupé: the Weymann-bodied 1750 Alfa Romeo, by Touring, one of the three cars which the firm entered for the 1931 Mille Miglia. An example was placed eighth.

had never been near a wind tunnel. Cars which had been specifically designed for aerodynamic efficiency were very much the exception though, in 1934, two such models entered production on either side of the Atlantic: Chrysler's Airflow and the Tatra Type 77 from Czechoslovakia.

The American car was relatively short-lived and its radical lines were hastily revised for 1935 when an Airstream derivative was also introduced. But only 25,103 Airflows had been built by the time the model was discontinued in 1937. By contrast, the rear-engined Type 77 Tatra endured in Type 87 guise until 1950. Prophetically *The Autocar* greeted it with the headline 'This Year, Next Year, Some Time?' and although Hans Ledwinka was responsible for the car's overall design, he worked closely with aerodynamicist Paul Jaray on the styling of its radical bodywork. The mass producers, in the main, eschewed wind cheating bodywork, simply because the resulting car's inevitably unconventional appearance was a disincentive to potential customers and, in those days of cheap petrol, the fuel saving advantages were negligible.

Nevertheless, much research work into aerodynamically efficient bodywork did manifest itself in the 1930s, not on touring cars but on the racing sports coupé, which was generally not available for public sale, and where the advantages of superior aerodynamics, against its conventionally styled open-bodied opponents, were more apparent. As Germany had been in the forefront of such research, it was wholly appropriate that this revived interest in the subject was carried out by the Stuttgart based FKFS (Research Institute for Motor Transport and Motor Vehicles Engines), established in 1930, and only a few yards from the west gate of the Daimler-Benz plant at Unterturkheim. FKFS's head, Dr Wunibald Kamm, built on the foundations so assiduously laid by Rumpler, Jaray and others.

Wunibald Irmin Erich Kamm (1889–1966) was born in Basel, Switzerland but had studied at the Stuttgart technical college and graduated in 1922 with a degree in aeronautics. He subsequently joined Daimler as a design engineer and worked on the engine of the 1924 Grand Prix Mercedes. In 1926 he left Stuttgart and joined the German Aviation Test Institute in Berlin-Adlerhof, as head of the power transmission section. When he returned to the city in 1930, he was therefore well versed in the twin disciplines of motor vehicle engineering and aeronautics.

Initially, in the terrible depression years of 1931–2, the Institute's research facilities were relatively modest but, in 1933, a small wind tunnel for model testing was built. That year Adolf Hitler became Germany's chancellor and, following Mussolini's example of constructing purpose-built motor roads, initiated the autobahn programme. This, in its turn, stimulated aerodynamic research in both countries because the high speeds they made possible meant that cars with 'slippery' bodies would be faster, and more economical than their more conventionally bodied counterparts.

Kamm's speciality was the effect of wind resistance on moving vehicles and, as early as 1933, he was lecturing on the aerodynamic advantages of a distinctive cut off rear: the so called Kamm Tail, a profile which flew in the face of Jaray's tapering rear end. However, when Adler tested an experimental vehicle to determine the shape of its new Adler Autobahn model, tests showed that they both had similar coefficients of drag and the Jaray look won the day because it appeared more conventional.

Kamm's work was reflected in the publication of two books, *The Motor Vehicle*, in 1936 and, two years later, *Testing and Measuring in the Field of Motor Vehicles*, destined to become the standard works on the subject. His researches culminated in his constructing a car (in 1938), with bodywork built according to his theories. BMW contributed a pre-production example of its $3\frac{1}{2}$-litre Type 335 model. The K1, as it was subsequently designated, was a two-door saloon, built by Vetter of Stuttgart, with cowled radiator, wheels and undertray while the wind-up windows, which were flush with the body sides, were contributed by Professor Emil Everling, who had undertaken similar work in Berlin. With a drag coefficient of 0.23, K1 was found to be capable of averaging 87 mph (147 kmh). Kamm's researchers were aided by the construction of a full sized wind tunnel at the Institute in 1940 and, subsequently, three more experimental K cars were built during the war, two (K2 and K3) on Mercedes-Benz 170V chassis while the BMW 335 based K4 was constructed for a high ranking SS officer with an interest in unusual vehicles.

But German motor manufacturers, in the main, did not succumb to aerodynamics, as far as the bodywork of their cars was concerned. Inevitably, the Mercedes-Benz and Auto Union racing cars, which appeared in 1934, reflected the benefits of such influences but certainly as far as the conservative Daimler-Benz was concerned, this was not transferred to production cars, with the exception of the short-lived 150HY Volkswagen look-alike of 1934.

That particular project had been initiated by Adolf Hitler soon after he came to power in 1933 and had been conceived, like the autobahns, when he was imprisoned in Lansberg Castle in 1923-4. The task of designing and developing what was named the KdF-Wagen ('Strength through Joy' car) in 1938, was entrusted to the Stuttgart-based Porsche design bureau. Though the body shape, the work of Porsche's Erwin Komenda, was subjected to wind tunnel testing, it recorded a less than particularly impressive Cd of 0.49, before the shape was finalized. However, the outbreak of the Second World War prevented what we now know as the Volkswagen from entering production until after hostilities.

Of greater relevance, as far as the development of the GT is concerned, was Porsche's development of a sports version of the KdF-Wagen, which was specially built for a projected 1939 race, between the twin fascist capitals of Berlin and Rome and back. As long sections of autobahn were included in the route, Komenda came up with an aerodynamic sports coupé with a 91 mph (145 kmh) top speed. As it happened, the outbreak of the Second World War in 1939 meant that the event was cancelled, but three cars were built and Ferdinand Porsche used one himself on those empty wartime autobahns. The Type 64 represents the first stirrings of the Porsche marque, which would emerge as the Type 356, though like the parent KdF-Wagen project, it would not come to fruition until the post-war years.

Although the big battalions of the German motor industry eschewed aerodynamically efficient bodywork, the smaller Frankfurt-based Adler company did market its Autobahn saloon, as will have already been apparent, in 1938. The firm's main significance, in the evolution of the Grand Tourer, came with the arrival of a generation of sports coupés, the first of which were first seen at the Le Mans 24-hour race. The competition programme had been initiated by sports car enthusiast and Adler's junior manager, Erwin Kleyer, who had instigated the construction of a closed, single-seater version of Adler's front-wheel-drive Trumpf model, which broke thirteen international records in 1935.

Kleyer sought advice from Kamm and aerodynamicist Richard Koenig-Fachensfeld, who had read engineering and economics at Stuttgart and, from 1931 onwards, designed 'streamlined' bodywork for private motorists, coach-building companies and motor manufacturers, based on Jaray patents. However, in 1936, following wind tunnel tests on models of buses, he applied for a patent for 'K' type abbreviated rear end.

In the event, the resulting sports coupé, was more 'Jaray' than 'Kamm', and ran at Le Mans for the first time in 1937. Adler entered no less than three examples of this 1.7-litre car and two of them succeeded in attaining fifth and sixth place, so introducing to the 24-hour classic the concept of the racing sports coupé. Adler continued to refine these cars, so that by 1939 they had achieved a Cd of .20 though in that particular year both coupés were unsuccessful. Their appearance began something of a fashion for closed coachwork and, in 1938, there were two Talbots and a Touring-bodied Alfa Romeo, in addition to the Adlers, one

A closed car nearly won Le Mans in 1938 when this Touring-bodied Alfa Romeo 2900B, driven by Sommer and Biondetti, led the 24-hour race from the third lap until early on the Sunday afternoon, at which point it dropped a valve. It was not until 1952 that a coupé finally took the chequered flag at the Sarthe circuit.

of 1.7 litres and the other 1.5, and, once again, the cars finished in fifth and seven places respectively, the larger capacity car winning the Biennial Cup. The Touring-bodied Alfa Romeo coupé nearly won in 1938, enduring until the 22nd hour, when it withdrew while in the lead because of a dropped valve. But Adler stopped building cars at the outbreak of the Second World War and subsequently concentrated on its established business as a typewriter manufacturer.

If Adler made some impression in international sports car racing, then the German firm which was in the forefront of such initiatives was the BMW company, which had only begun car production in 1929, having started building motor cycles in 1923. From the early 1930s, BMW had been experimenting with aerodynamic bodywork, with a view to improving the performance of its sports car. This initially revealed itself in the 315 and 319 models of 1935 which, in turn, paved the way to that technological *tour de force*, the 328 of 1937. In its customary open two-seater form, it revealed such aerodynamic features as cowled radiator grille, integral headlamps and spatted rear wheels. However, the 328 would have been more aerodynamically efficient if it had been produced in coupé form and a lesser known factory approved accessory was a streamlined hardtop, with curved Plexiglass screen, produced by Vereinigte Werkstatten of Munich.

BMW had watched with interest the activities of the Reutlingen based Wendler coachbuilding company, which built a number of aerodynamic coupé bodies on the BMW 326 and 328 chassis to the designs of Koenig-Fachensfeld, who was keen that BMW produce a vehicle to his specifications. Although the firm was to keep its options open, one of his Wendler-built cars was in the forefront of the firm's own research and one of his bodies did feature in BMW's stand at the 1938 Berlin Motor Show.

The arrival of the 328 saw BMW initiate its own aerodynamic research which was undertaken by Dr Beissbach and Fritz Fiedler, using models which were tested in Kamm's Stuttgart wind tunnel. However, the 328 coupé placed fifth at Le Mans in 1939 was not BMW's own, but was by Touring, and almost identical to the design that had graced the 2.9-litre Alfa Romeo, which had come close to winning the event in 1938.

In 1940 BMW completed six special 328s which it entered for that year's Mille Miglia, scheduled for April, despite the fact that Germany had been at war since the previous September. There were two coupés, both with distinctive

This car perhaps embodied the innovative spirit prevalent in Germany in the 1930s. It is one of the two Kamm-tailed factory-bodied BMW 328s built for the 1940 Mille Miglia, the other car was not entered. Bearing race number 73, it proved to be the fastest in practice having exceeded 135 mph (217 kmh) but it dropped out early in the race with carburettor and lubrication troubles.

Kamm tails, along with three open cars. All were designed and bodied by BMW, apart from a Touring-bodied coupé, with a tail in the Jaray manner, which may have been the 328 run at Le Mans in 1939. But before looking at the outcome of that extraordinary Mille Miglia, this is an appropriate moment to pause and consider the considerable contribution made by Italy to the development of the sports coupé in the 1930s.

It will be recalled that Alfa Romeo and Touring had been in the forefront of the coupé's conception, though Alfa was a relatively small company, which was bankrupted in 1933, and saved by the Italian government. Alfa Romeo was to remain in state ownership until 1987. Fiat, by contrast, was a bastion of private enterprise, a fifedom controlled by the formidable Giovanni Agnelli, and *was* the Italian motor industry. Although a firm of great technical competence, for most of the inter-war years its designs followed simple, conventional mechanical lines in the American manner. But the arrival of the 1500 in 1935 was an up-to-date European offering with an overhead, rather than side, valve engine, backbone chassis, independent front suspension while aerodynamic influences were reflected in its sloping radiator and faired in headlamps.

Next of the new generation of Fiats was Dante Giacosa's revolutionary 500, at only 569 cc the smallest four-cylinder car in the world. Its cowled radiator echoed that of the 1500 and this was also the common factor with the 508C 1100 Ballila, which entered production in 1937. This model was to form the basis of the 508C MM of the same year, the first series production sports coupé in the world.

The MM (Mille Miglia) came about through a curious combination of empirical and scientific principles. While the famous 500 was under development in 1936, the design team built an experimental van version which, to its surprise, turned out to be faster than the production car! As the two vehicles had identical mechanical specifications, it therefore followed that the van's aerodynamics were superior to those of the car and the only demonstrable difference was the appearance of their respective rear ends.

Faced with this intriguing conundrum, Dante Giacosa, Fiat's design maestro, 'immediately thought of using this factor in the design of the 1100 sports coupé.' Fiat's new 1100 cc, the 508C, was due to appear in 1937 and an aerodynamically significant derivative would provide the firm with excellent publicity. Consequently a number of 1:5 scale models were produced and tested in the Turin Polytechnic's wind tunnel at the Castle of Valentino.

However, the Fiat team was constrained by the need to use the 508C's chassis and mechanicals, and as it was not possible to lower the front of the body appreciably, the use of aerodynamic bodywork meant that interior accommodation had to be reduced somewhat and rear visibility was also restricted. The abruptly cut-off tail reflected the principles enunciated by the redoubtable Professor Kamm in Stuttgart. Only a small production was envisaged, so construction of the car's body was entrusted to the Savio brothers, Antonio and Guiseppe, and their Turin coachbuilding establishment.

In its original form, the Ballila was powered by a 1089 cc 32 bhp overhead valve four-cylinder engine, which made it a 68 mph (109 kmh) car. The MM boasted 42 bhp, with raised compression ratio, which resulted in an 87 mph (140 kmh) top speed though in a later form, 95 mph (152 kmh) was recorded, even if the lack of rear visibility and a noisy interior came in for contemporary criticism. The 508C MM remained in production until 1940.

The model received an impressive baptism in the 1938 Mille Miglia though the cars had only been completed ten days prior to the event. The 1100 class attracted no less than 37 entries, all of them Fiats, but the aerodynamic coupé proved its worth and Piero Taruffi drove a tremendous race, beating all the other 1100s by a considerable margin.

There was no Mille Miglia in 1939, because the previous year's event had been marred by an accident at Bologna when a Lancia Aprilia went into the crowd, killing ten people outright, many of whom were children, and injuring a further 23. So Fiat entered an MM, with modifications to

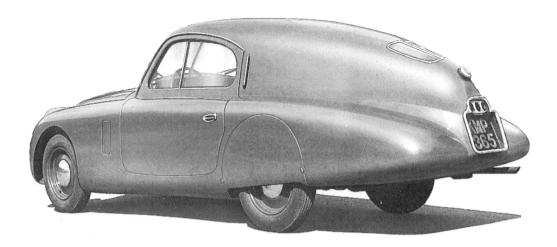

What the other drivers saw. This picture graphically demonstrates the problem facing the company which wanted to market an aerodynamically efficient car. This rear end belongs to a Fiat 508CMM, introduced in 1938. Rear visibility clearly left something to be desired!

both its front and rear, in that year's 908-mile (1,461-km) Tobruk-Tripoli race. It averaged 74.49 mph (119 kmh) for a class win, 3 mph (4.8 kmh) faster than the quickest Lancia Aprilia of 1.3 litres capacity.

Lancia had been founded in Turin by former Fiat racing driver Vincenzo Lancia, in 1906, and the firm grew to be Italy's second largest car maker though in productive terms it was a long way behind Fiat. Up until 1922, Lancias were conventional, high quality cars but, that year, the firm introduced the Lambda, which was probably the most technically advanced car of its day, with its unitary body, independent front suspension and V4 engine. The V8-engined Dilambda of 1929 was a development of this theme, while the small 1932 Augusta also represented a restatement of this innovative momentum and was Europe's first unitary construction saloon. In 1937 Lancia introduced its Aprilia, intended as a light, small capacity car with superlative road holding. Its body reflected aerodynamic research at the Turin Polytechnic though, perhaps fortunately, plans for a long Jaray type tail were abandoned. Alas, Vincenzo Lancia died, aged only 55 in 1937, the year of the Aprilia's announcement and he never saw one of his most famous designs into production.

As the Aprilia boasted unitary construction, a special version, with a platform chassis, was produced for the use of specialist coachbuilders, of which the most significant was Battista 'Pinin' Farina. In much the same way that Touring had special relationship with Alfa Romeo, so it was between Lancia and Pinin Farina. Both Vincenzo and Pinin were firm friends and Lancia had encouraged him to go into business on his own account in 1930. He had been born on the outskirts of Turin in 1893, the tenth child of a poverty stricken family or eleven; hence his nickname of 'Pinin' which means 'baby of the family'. Fortunately for posterity, Giovanni, one of his older brothers, was apprenticed to a Turin coachbuilder named Marcello Alessio. It was while going to meet his brother from work that young Pinin decided that he was also going to a coachbuilder. As it happened, in 1910, Giovanni set up in business on his own account, along with his brothers Carlo and Battista when the latter was just 17. Stablimenti Farina was established in Turin: it was to remain in business until 1953.

Pinin soon found himself in charge of design for the company and, during the next 20 years became acquainted with all the leading figures in the Italian motor industry, which was exclusively concentrated in the north of the country, in and around the cities of Turin and Milan. Pinin had long harboured the desire to found his own business and, encouraged by Vincenzo Lancia, who offered him a bodywork contract for his new Dilambda model, Carrozzeria Pinin Farina was established in Turin's Corso Trapani in June 1930. His first important assignment was the Dilambda's series of factory approved designs. These first cars were elegant, restrained offerings and Pinin soon built up an impressive client list, which included the Queen of Romania, the King of Iraq and the Prince of Drago, all of whom ordered Lancia's new V8, which underlines the prestige accorded to the marque.

Later came the Aprilia and Farina's interest in the world of aerodynamics was reflected by his adventurous production, between 1937 and 1939, of five experimental aerodynamic coupés in the Jaray manner. These were Aprilia-based

The Italian coachbuilding house of Pinin Farina was in the vanguard of aerodynamic research, as this special bodied Lancia Aprilia based coupé, built on Jaray principles, reveals. The Turin-based company built no less than five examples between 1937 and 1939.

research vehicles but Pinin Farina also built a handsome 'Aerodynamic coupé' with concealed headlamps on the Aprilia chassis and, from then onwards, his work displayed a marked aerodynamic awareness.

Meanwhile, in 1938, Lancia had received an illustrious recruit in the shape of 47-year-old Vittorio Jano, as head of the experimental department. Despite his outstanding work for Alfa Romeo, which included the fabled P2 monoposto racing car, he was dismissed from the Milan company on the grounds that he was 'too old'. This followed the failure of his V12 engined racing car, when its rear axle mounted gearbox gave trouble in the 1937 Italian Grand Prix. But Alfa Romeo's loss would be Lancia's gain, though the results of Jano's work would not become apparent until after the Second World War.

No less than 12 Lancia Aprilias were entered for the Mille Miglia, which was revived in 1940 after a year's absence on a new 104 mile (167 km) triangular circuit, between the towns of Brescia, Cremona and Mantua. Alfa Romeo, which had won the event on ten occasions since its 1927 inception, clearly had high hopes of perpetuating this success. Managed by former Bugatti driver and team manager, Meo Costantini, its entry consisted of four 2½-litre six-cylinder cars, all of which were Touring bodied and one of which was a stylish coupé. The open cars had a top speed of 115 mph (185 kmh) but the superior aerodynamics of the closed car meant that it was faster and was capable of 122 mph (196 kmh). All these cars benefited from a new form of lightweight body construction that Touring had introduced in 1937. Felice Anderloni's motto had been, 'weight is the enemy and aerodynamic drag the obstacle' and his *Superleggera*

Touring, perhaps the greatest of the Italian *carrozzeria* in the inter-war years, perfected its light, strong, Superleggera method of body construction in 1937. This 2900 B Alfa Romeo coupé of 1938 clearly anticipated the *Gran Turismo* cars of the post-war years though the name had not yet become generic.

(Superlight) system of body construction consisted of a lattice of load bearing tubes, onto which the aluminium bodypanels were attached.

It will be recalled that a Touring coupe was one of the six 328 BMWs from Germany entered for the event and although these 2-litre cars were of a smaller capacity than the rival Alfa Romeo, they were a good 6 cwt (304 kg) lighter. The fastest BMW was one of the Kamm-tailed coupés, which was found to be capable of 135 mph (217 kmh), with the open cars being good for 125 mph (201 kmh). The rest of the field was made up of a bevy of privately entered Alfa Romeos, and there were also Fiat and Lancia entries and a small number of foreign entrants. Enzo Ferrari, who had previously managed Alfa Romeo's racing team, anonymously entered a pair of cars under the 815 name.

The event took place on 28 April, only 12 days before the German army rolled into Holland. The German cars soon showed that they were faster than the Alfa Romeos and although one of the Kamm-tailed coupés dropped out with fuel troubles, the Touring-bodied coupé was soon lapping the 104-mile course in less than an hour. . .

This BMW, driven by Huschke von Hanstein and Walter Baumer, won the event in perfect weather at an average speed of 104.2 mph (167.6 kmh). One of the open Alfa Romeos was second but 328s took third, fifth and sixth places. The $1\frac{1}{2}$-litre class was won by a Lancia Aprilia at an average speed of 78.9 mph (126.9 kmh), but once again the smaller capacity 508C MM Fiat coupés proved faster. They dominated the 1100 cc class and the winning car averaged 83 mph (133 kmh). Incidentally, neither of the Fiat-based 'Ferraris' finished the race: the punishing course proved too much for the unproven $1\frac{1}{2}$-litre cars.

The 13th Mille Miglia thus gave a considerable fillip to both the German motor industry, in the shape of the winning BMWs, and the growing stature of the sports coupé with its aerodynamic superiority to its open counterpart. It was a message not to be overlooked by the Italians in the post-war years.

Two cars entered for the race, though neither completed it, were a pair of French Delages, driven by Italian drivers, though the two countries would be at war seven weeks after the Mille Miglia. These cars were traditional open two seaters, which appeared positively archaic beside the BMWs and Alfa Romeos, though their cowled radiators and integral headlamps did reflect the work of Jean Andreau, the leading French aerodynamicist of his day. Andrea began his career in the French army, after attending the Saint Cyr military college. He then joined the army technical services when he undertook a notable study on the effects of artillery and aviation during the First World War. After hostilities, he foresook his military career and switched to the motor industry when he established a technical consultancy, specializing in chassis and suspension work, near Bordeaux. In this capacity, his clients included Citroen and Bonnet but, in 1932, he left to join the Laboratories Chausson, which also built bodies. The results of scale model wind tunnel tests he undertook there were taken up by Peugeot, France's third largest car maker which, it will be recalled, had successfully fielded an aerodynamic saloon in the 1925 *Grand Prix de Tourisme*.

The outcome of these experiments was the 402 Peugeot saloon of 1936, with its distinctive, deeply curved radiator grille in the manner of the Fiat 1500 of the previous year, also containing the headlamps, and possessed a Cd of 0.38, at a time when most mainstream European models seldom fell below the 0.5 figure. This was followed by the similar, but smaller 302 of 1938 and the following year's 202. Peugeot's interest and commitment to aerodynamics appeared in a more extreme manifestation in the shape of a 402-based futuristic four-door saloon, complete with rear stabilizing fin, which featured on the firm's stand at the 1936 Paris Motor Show. Heralded as 'the car of 1940', it achieved a Cd of 0.28. Andreau was also responsible for the lines of the Paulin-built open 402 DS Peugeots, which attained seventh and eighth places at Le Mans in 1937 and one scored a more creditable fifth in 1938, so beating the Alder coupé from Germany, which was seventh.

Figoni and Falaschi was also responsible for the body of this Type 57 Bugatti, built for Lord Cholmondley in 1939. Although a four-door four-seater, it nevertheless encapsulates the spirit of the *Grand Routiers*.

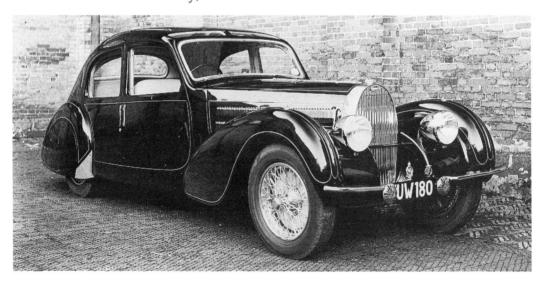

The Figoni and Falaschi coachbuilding concern was responsible for bodying some of the most memorable Grand Routiers of the 1930s. This one graces a 1939 4-litre Talbot Lago Special though similar examples were also fitted to Delahaye chassis.

In addition to his work for Peugeot, Andreau undertook similar work for Delahaye, and Delage which it had taken over in 1935. He also undertook overseas commissions and was responsible for the lines of George Eyston's land speed record car, *Thunderbolt*, which took the record for Britain in 1937 and 1938.

Andreau's work was reflected in a new generation of Grand Routiers, as some of France's leading coachbuilders began to interpret his ideas magnificently, resulting in some of the most visually exciting sports bodies to appear on European roads in the 1930s. There was the new D8 from Delage, which was often endowed with the latest offering from Letourney and Marchand, Saoutchik or Henri Chapron, while the Type 135 Delahaye and $4\frac{1}{2}$-litre Talbot could be specified with daring renderings by Figoni and Falaschi, which imbibed them with a sense of movement, even when they were stationary. Then there was Bugatti. From about 1930 Ettore Bugatti's son, Jean, took over a greater stylistic role and his talents were reflected in Profilee bodies, with inclined windscreens and sharply cut off rears, on the Type 50 chassis. This led, in turn, to the Ventoux Type 57 saloon, the Atlante coupé and, in 1936, its 57S Atlantic derivative, perhaps the most exquisite and memorable Bugatti body designs of the inter-war years, even though only three examples were built.

Some of these Gallic developments did trickle over to Britain though, for the most part, the country remained aloof from all these European initiatives. This was despite the fact that Britain had the distinction of having played host to what was probably the world's first wind tunnel — in 1871. But aerodynamic research of the type so popular on the

The Singer Airstream of 1934 was Britain's answer to the ill-fated Chrysler Airflow and was equally unsuccessful. Based on the 1½-litre Eleven, sales of 750 were anticipated though the majority were completed in conventional form.

Continent, apart from its role on the bodies of LSR and Brooklands cars, was virtually ignored. This was undoubtedly a reflection of the fact that European engineers placed a much greater emphasis on theoretical studies than their British counterparts, who were brought up in a nineteenth century-rooted environment which venerated practical experience, and while this tended to produce sound, reliable designs, they were seldom innovative ones. Consequently Britain played virtually no part in the technically demanding field of Grand Prix racing in the inter-war years and, significantly, the Sunbeam that Henry Segrave took to victory in the 1923 French Grand Prix was designed by a duo of Italian engineers. It was dubbed unkindly, but perceptively, 'a Fiat in green paint'.

Without the competititve bedrock seen on the Continent, new British initiatives in the field of aerodynamics were virtually nil, so the sports coupé that resulted from it remained an exclusively Continental concept. The 1920s were practically bereft of such ideas though it is not difficult to see that manufacturers mainly fought shy of aerodynamics, because of the unconventional-looking vehicles that resulted from such experimentation. One of the few such was the Putney built North-Lucas of 1923, inspired by Rumpler's Tropfen-Auto of two years previously, though it never attained series production. One project that did just reach manufacturing status was the Burney of 1930. It was the work of Sir Dennistoun Burney, designer of the *R100* airship, who had established Streamlined Cars Ltd, for the purpose. Here again the inspiration was probably Continental because his rear-engined design bore a striking visual resemblance to the car which French aerodynamic Emile Claveau unveiled at the 1927 Paris salon. The Burney, alas, only lasted until 1933, despite the Prince of Wales ordering one. Only 12 were built.

By contrast, the Singer Airstream of 1934 attracted slightly more customers though this was a desperate attempt by a once frontline car company to boost its flagging sales. Designed by Irishman Captain D.F.H. Fitzmaurice's Airstream company, this version of the Singer Eleven resembled a scaled-down Chrysler Airflow and was just as unsuccessful. By all accounts, 750 were laid down but the majority of chassis ended up with conventional bodies. Singer dropped the model in 1936, the year in which the firm was reconstructed. There were less extreme manifestations by individual coachbuilders but these 'Airline' and 'Speedline' bodies did little more than reflect the streamlined look of the day and there was little attempt to produce genuine wind-cheating bodywork.

But by this time, across the English Channel in France, the new generation of elegant Bugattis, Delahayes and Delage Grand Routiers were appearing and, as John McLellan has pointed out: 'Enshrined in a Players cigarette card, the Delahaye Mouette came to represent to a whole generation of youngsters in England all that was advanced.'*

It was French initiatives such as these, triggered as they were by Jean Andreau's work, that eventually stirred Rolls-Royce to set aside a small annual sum for wind tunnel work for, as an aero engine manufacturer, it would have been

* *Bodies Beautiful* (David & Charles 1975)

The Bentley Speed Six of 1930 was built for Woolf Barnato, the firm's chairman, with Gurney Nutting coupé fabric body in the French idiom. In the same year Barnato beat The Blue Train from Monte Carlo to London with four hours to spare.

more aware than most of the benefits of aerodynamically efficient coachwork. It followed a visit by general works manager E.W. Hives and his assistant, W.E. Robotham, to Brooklands in April 1936 to examine an aerodynamic saloon, with rear-mounted Ford V8 engine, and a Cd of .30, created by Andreau for Andre Dubonnet. What impressed the two engineers was that it was capable of 109 mph (175 kmh) from an 80 hp engine though it appeared to have been 'made in a back yard'. This visit was to result in the creation of the most famous British 'Grand Tourer' of the 1930s, the so-called 'Embiricos Bentley' of 1938.

By their very nature, Rolls-Royce's own cars would not lend themselves to such attention but Bentley, with its sporting traditions, was a more appropriate candidate. Also, in 1930, Bentley chairman Woolf Barnato had taken delivery of a Speed Six on which coachbuilders Gurney Nutting had produced a memorable fabric-bodied coupé, which accurately mirrored the fashion of the contemporary French Grand Routiers of the day.

The new, post-1931 generation of Bentleys were Rolls-Royce-based though the sporting ambience was maintained. By 1936, however, Walter Sleator, Rolls-Royce's Paris representative, was complaining that the performance of the Bentley was falling behind those of its French rivals; he cited Bugatti, Talbot and Delahaye as examples. In August

Le Streamline, the Paulin-styled, Pourtout-bodied 4¼-litre Bentley of 1938, which led to the Corniche prototype of the following year. After the war it was run at Le Mans in 1949/50/51 and is seen here at a British race meeting.

Lagonda par excellence. A 1939 short chassis V12 with aerodynamic coupé body by Lancefield. This could have formed the basis of a production model, the Lagonda Continental, had not the Second World War intervened.

1936, Robotham wrote to managing director Arthur Sidgreaves, pointing out that although Bentleys were not as fast as their Continental contemporaries, British road conditions were somewhat different. However, he complained that the cars' 'conversative appearance are about as bad as any we know for lack of streamlining' and to illustrate his point he revealed that wind tunnel experiments at Bristol with a saloon 'showed that the standard Bentley would go 15 mph [24 kmh] faster. . . if it was driven backwards.' He thought that a further 30 hp could be obtained by producing a car with a frontal appearance similar to that of a contemporary Fiat.

A copy of Robotham's letter was sent to Walter Sleator in Paris and he approached one of his best customers, Andre Embiricos, who agreed to buy a $4\frac{1}{4}$-litre Bentley and have a streamlined lightweight body built for it at his own expense. Although George Eyston, who had been called in for advice, had suggested Andreau as aerodynamic consultant, it was a Paris based rival, M. Paulin, who got the job and the work was undertaken by the Pourtout coachbuilding company, which happened to be his next door neighbour! The two-door coupé, nicknamed *Le Streamline* by the factory, was duly completed in mid 1938 and subsequently recorded a top speed of 120 mph (193 kmh) which was 13 mph (20 kmh) faster than the usual $4\frac{1}{4}$. In his quest for cleaner body lines

British conservatism on land and air: a 1933 MG K3 Magnette open two seater, a world away from aerodynamic developments in Europe, with a contemporary Avro Tutor biplane providing an appropriate background.

Paulin had dispensed with the traditional Bentley radiator grille and replaced it with a cowl, which no doubt raised eyebrows at Derby! However, later in 1938, when a second car in the spirit of *Le Streamline* was built by the Parisian Van Vooren company for Major Eric Loder, it uneasily retained the customary radiator grille.

The lessons learnt on the Paulin Bentley were a sufficient encouragement for Rolls-Royce to press ahead with a new Bentley, named Corniche, though with four rather than two doors. The prototype, with bodywork by Van Vooren, was duly completed in mid-1939 and, like Embiricos's car, boasted a cowled radiator. Regrettably the car had to be abandoned in France at the outbreak of war after all-important testing on the German autobahns. So ended Rolls-Royce's aerodynamic adventures. Its post-war Bentleys initially reverted to more traditional lines.

A model in a similar spirit to *Le Streamline* was a special-bodied V12 Lagonda, which appeared in 1939. This was the short chassis Rapide model, with four carburettors in the manner of the cars that ran at that year's Le Mans race, when V12s were placed third and fourth. The chassis was dispatched to Lancefield, the London coachbuilders, which made a speciality of aerodynamic coachwork and had been the first British firm to apply for a Jaray patent. It produced a very French lightweight coupé, in the manner of the Paulin Bentley, with cowled radiator, integral headlamps, and flush-fitting door handles. Chairman Alan Good wanted to offer the car as a factory model. There were thoughts of calling it the Lagonda Continental: with a 120 mph (193 kmh) top speed it would have cost £400 more than the standard short chassis V12, but the car was not completed until August 1939, the month before the Second World War broke out and what would have been Britain's first series production 'Grand Tourer' became a tantalizing 'might have been'.

Forsaking the aerodynamic style seen in Europe then, Britain emerged in the 1930s as the world's largest manufacturer of the traditional *open* sports cars which had come of age in the previous decade. In 1929, MG had introduced its first cheap sports car in the shape of the £175 Midget and, in 1932, came the J2. Its delightfully proportioned bodywork, later flared wings doubled humped scuttle, cutaway doors and bolster tank represented, for many, the quintessence of the open two-seater. It was a shape that, incredibly, endured until 1955. Singer also followed in MG's wheel tracks and a scatter of smaller manufacturers, such as Aston Martin, HRG, Lagonda and Morgan, all produced visually charming though, in a European context, dated, open two-seaters. Many would continue to do, in even greater numbers after the Second World War. It was, however, the Continental countries, and Italy in particular, which would build on their pioneering sports coupés of the 1930s to produce the Grand Touring car, a style of vehicle which would ultimately contribute to the demise of the traditional, and all too British, open two seater.

CHAPTER TWO

Italy takes the lead, 1945-63

'One of the most important exhibits at the Turin Show, which opened last week, was a new Lancia Aurelia Gran Turismo streamlined two door coupé . . . the manufacturer's claim for a speed in excess of 100 mph seems well-founded.'

The Autocar, 13 April 1951,
on the occasion of that year's Turin Motor Show.

The 1950s was Italy's decade. From being a relatively poor country during the inter-war years, it emerged after the war as a major force within the European motor industry. In productive terms, the country's output soared from a mere 11,000 or so cars in 1946 to a then record 1.1 million in 1963. It was the same story in the field of Grands Prix, with the blood red single-seaters from Italy dominating the motor racing circuits of the world. So it was too in the field of performance road cars. The innovative momentum of the pre-war years was maintained with the concept of the sports coupé flowering as the GT of the 1950s, with the epochal Lancia Aurelia Gran Turismo of 1951 representing a starting point for the breed. These years were also coupled with a growth of the Italian coachbuilding houses and, if the 1930s belonged to Carrozzeria Touring, then it was Pinin Farina which emerged as the leading stylistic force of these post-war years, with Bertone, Ghia and Zagato all making their individual contributions.

However, it was Ferrari, the most famous of post-war marques, which dominated Formula 1. Along with Pinin Farina, Ferrari set the pace with a sensational series of GT cars to support a costly racing programme. In 1958, Maserati, having ceased its participation in Formula 1, followed suit and also began producing GTs in earnest. Pre-war, Alfa Romeo had been a relatively small manufacturer of specialist sports cars but, with state backing, it emerged as a mainstream car maker, to challenge the might of Fiat, though its competitive roots were always apparent and this Milan company produced an impressive variety of smaller GTs. Pinin Farina meanwhile encapsulated the innovative spirit of post-war Italy. The Pinin Farina bodied Cisitalia coupé of 1947 contained the stylistic excellence and innovative mechanical competence for which Italy is today famous.

During the Second World War (1943) Piero Dusio established the firm of Consorzio Industriale Sportivoa Italia, better known as Cisitalia, in Turin. An enthusiastic racing driver, Dusio had campaigned Alfa Romeos and had driven into third place in the 1938 Millie Miglia. He also briefly drove a Grand Prix Maserati. Dusio was intent on Cisitalia joining the ranks of Italy's racing car manufacturers but wartime conditions meant it had to concentrate on the production of machine tools and garage equipment until December 1944 when, with the prospect of peace a more possible reality, Dusio approached, via an intermediary, Dante Giacosa, renowned for his design of the Fiat 500 and the 508C MM sports car coupé. Dusio was keen that his new racing car be based on Fiat 500 and 1000 components and thought him the man for the job. Giacosa agreed to undertake the work, accepted the assignment on a freelance basis and designed the car after he had completed his day's work at Fiat. The plans were completed in August 1945, and this

How the ugly duckling became a swan. The 1950 Lancia Aurelia (left) was a technically sophisticated though undistinguished four-door saloon. It effectively gave birth to the GT movement by forming the basis of the 1951 Pinin Farina bodied B20 *Gran Turismo* coupé.

cheap single-seater for the enthusiast, which sold for about £1,000, went on sale in 1946. The cars were initially very popular and competitions featuring them provided popular curtain raisers at Formula 1 events.

However, Dusio was keen for there to be a two-seater version of the design and, on a summer afternoon in 1946, Giacosa laid out the lines of a car, which was designated 'Project 202.' The racing car had an innovative tubular chassis, Giacosa having been inspired by the frame of the Beltram bicycle that Dusio also manufactured. The single-seater's framework was modified for the road car and he extended this for a coupé body. This was duly constructed by Rocco Motto and was similar in concept to the 508C MM Fiat coupé, with Giacosa as the link between the two projects. But, with the coming of peace, Dante returned full time to Fiat and the project was handed over to Giovanni Savonuzzi, who joined Dusio in August 1945.

Savonuzzi, who had formerly been employed in Fiat's aero engine testing department, produced a second coupé. This was dominated by two large rear wings, introduced for directional stability, and the outcome of much experimentation in the Turin Polytechnic's wind tunnel. It was built by Stablimenti Farina and Dusio was so delighted with the results, that he presented Alfredo Vignale, who had supervised the project, with a bonus which was a sufficient inducement for him to leave Farina and set up his own styling house. This 1100 cc car, completed in April 1947, subsequently achieved a speed of 122 mph (196 kmh) on the Turin to Milan autostrada and a second aerodynamic coupé with a 1200 cc engine was also built along with an open version of the design with bodywork by Garella.

Impressive as these coupés were, their lines did not lend themselves to quantity production. Dusio had told Savonuzzi that he wanted a car 'that is wide like my Buick, low like a Grand Prix car, comfortable like a Rolls-Royce and light like our single-seater.' Savonuzzi produced a number of sketches to this brief and Dusio choose one, with the hope of producing 400 of them. Savonuzzi therefore approached Farina, Pinin Farina, Touring and Vignale, though it was Pinin Farina which got the job. He skilfully interpreted the lines submitted by Savonuzzi, which closely followed those of his aeorodynamic coupé, with the front of the body being virtually identical to it though lacking its dominating fins, replacing them with simpler, though integrated, rear wings.

The Cisitalia made its debut in September 1947, on the evening of the Italian Grand Prix, held in the town of Milan, but its official launch as the Gran Sport Cisitalia came at the

No car more typifies the new spirit of post-war Italy than the 1089 cc Cisitalia coupé of 1947 with supremely elegant Pinin Farina bodywork. Its modest production ran until 1952 and only about 170 examples were built. The spoked wheels were fitted with discs in the interests of aerodynamic efficiency.

Paris Motor Show the following month. Performance was still impressive. The little car had a top speed of 99 mph (160 kmh) though it possessed the comfort of a saloon. Here was the essence of the GT concept though the Gran Turismo Lancia B20 coupé was a good four years away. . .

Production did not begin until 1948 and Pinin Farina built them of 12 mm Itallumag aluminium, the complete car weighing only 15.3 cwt (780 kg) but, after about the 100th shell had been completed, Pinin's involvement ceased and production was then divided between Farina and Vignale. Ironically, it was Pinin Farina which reaped most of the benefit from the Cisitalia for, in 1951, the New York Museum of Modern Art staged an exhibition entitled *Eight Great Automobiles* and the Gran Sport was featured under the title of 'self moving sculpture' as the very embodiment of the new innovative spirit awakened in post-war Italy. It also brought Pinin's name to an international audience even though the essence of the coupé's lines had been Savonuzzi's.

Piero Dusio was less lucky. In late 1946, he unwisely permitted himself to be diverted into producing a costly, complicated and innovative mid-engined 360 Grand Prix racing car, with optional four-wheel drive, the design work being undertaken in Turin by the then peripatetic Porsche Bureau. Dusio departed for the Argentine in 1948 in the wake of financial problems and alas, lost interest in the lovely little Cisitalia coupé. Production ceased in 1952 after a mere 170 or so had been built.

Back at Fiat, Dante Giacosa produced an updated version

of his pre-war 508C MM aerodynamic coupé. Savio was once again responsible for the bodywork and the result was the 1100 S coupe of 1947. Twin Weber carburettors and a 51 bhp engine, coupled with advances in aerodynamics, meant that it was faster than its original predecessor, with a top speed of 93 mph (150 kmh). It was produced for the 1947 Mille Miglia, the first to be held since the war, and took from fifth to ninth places. It did even better in the 1948 race when examples achieved second, third and fourth positions behind the winning Ferrari, which was the new make's first Mille Miglia victory. Like its predecessor, the 1100S was also available for public sale and 401 examples had been built by the time production ceased in 1950.

Fiat took the next step on the road to producing the definitive GT, with the 1949 arrival of the 1100 S Pinin Farina coupé. Although it retained its predecessor's mechanical components, the bodywork was completely new and, effectively, a larger interpretation of the Cisitalia coupé. But there was one significant difference: the coupé was a rudimentary two-plus-two, with room for children in the back.

As the model was somewhat heavier than its predecessor, performance was inferior to it though it was capable of 87 mph (140 kmh) still, it should be noted, from a 1100 cc engine. Demand for this attractive, though expensive, model was inevitably limited and production ceased in mid-1951 after only about 50 had been sold.

But the big event of 1951 came at that years's Turin Motor Show when Lancia unveiled its Pinin Farina-bodied Gran Turismo B20 coupé version of the firm's Aurelia saloon introduced the previous year. This outwardly conventional saloon bristled with technical innovation and ingenuity, in which the masterly hand of Vittorio Jano is apparent. It will be recalled that he had joined Lancia from Alfa Romeo in 1938 and work on what was considered to be a replacement for the Aprilia had begun during the war. It was then that Francesco de Virgillio, a young Lancia engineer, decided to extend the concept of the long running V4 Lancia engine and extend it as a V6. It finally appeared in 60-degree 1794 cc form in the Aurelia, with short pushrods taking the place of the traditional Lancia overhead camshafts. The Aurelia was thus the first series production car in the world to be powered by a V6 engine and, although this was remarkable in itself, the innovation did not stop there.

Power was transmitted via a two-piece propellor shaft to a differential which also incorporated the four-speed gearbox. This had been a feature of Jano's 1936 12 C monoposto for Alfa Romeo, a 1937 derivative of which had triggered his departure from Portello. Brakes were also carried inboard, which was another Aprilia inheritance. A further innovation, and yet another world first, was the independent semi-trailing arm rear suspension, while at the front of the car, Lancia's traditional sliding pillars were perpetuated.

This exciting mechanical package was cloaked in a rather dull pillarless four-door saloon which, although it featured aluminium doors, bonnet and boot lid, still turned the scales at 21 cwt (1,080 kg) and although road holding was up to the usual Lancia standards the model was no great performer. Production lasted only until 1955 by which time 30,000 or so had been built. By contrast, its coupé derivative lasted a further three years, until 1958, and represents the starting point of the definitive Grand Tourer.

Producing a Pinin Farina coupé version of an existing saloon was standard Lancia practice and Farina came up with a masterpiece of timeless elegance in which all the lessons of his work in the 1947-50 era were combined to produce a single, unified design which combined the performance of the sports car with the comfort of the saloon. In the B20 are the elements of the Cisitalia of 1947, coupés which Pinin undertook on a 6C Alfa Romeo and Maserati A6 in 1948, along with the Fiat 1100 S coupé, with its rear accommodation for children. The original B10 Aurelia saloon had been underpowered and, in 1951, the V6 was enlarged to 1991 cc, which was also extended to the coupé, though in 75 rather than 70 bhp form as the B20 was developed as a sporting model in its own right. In addition the B20 had a shorter (8 ft 8¾ in–2,600 mm) wheelbase and higher rear axle ratio, making it a 100 mph car (160 kmh). Lancia chose the Gran Turismo name for its new model and the suggestion could only have come from Vittorio Jano himself for had he not been responsible for the original 1750 Alfa Romeo of the same name back in 1929?

In 1952 the model's power was upped to 80 bhp while 1953 saw capacity increased to 2451 cc and the model fittingly renamed the GT 2500. On the fourth series of 1954 a simpler de Dion rear axle replaced the semi trailing arms. From thereon the model's weight increased and performance diminished, a not unusual state of affairs, before production ceased in June 1958.

The model did enjoy some competition success. In 1953 a GT 2500 won its class in the 1953 Alpine Rally and, in the following year, an example gave Lancia its first Monte Carlo Rally victory. There had been success in the Sestriere Rally and an appropriate win in the GT category in the Giro d'Italia the same year and first and second places in the

The B20 Aurelia also had a distinguished competition career. Not only did it win the 1954 Monte Carlo Rally but had previously put up a good showing in the 1952 Targa Florio event, shown here, when Lancias took the first three places.

Monza Inter Europe Cup. But the reality was that the Aurelia coupé was a low production model, only 3,641 examples having been built of this high cost car.

Meanwhile, there were corporate changes taking place within Lancia. Vincenzo's son, Gianni had pursued a costly racing programme, which culminated in the family losing control of the firm in 1955. The new owner was Carlo Pesenti, a wealthy cement manufacturer, and he appointed Professor Antonio Fessia, an ardent advocate of front wheel drive, who was to become the firm's chief engineer. The first new car of his generation was the Pinin Farina-styled Flaminia saloon, which perpetuated the Aurelia's $2\frac{1}{2}$-litre V6 engine. Fessia discarded the sliding pillar independent front suspension for the first time on a Lancia since 1922 and replaced it with more conventional wishbones. Only about 2,600 of these big saloons had been sold by 1961 and production continued in limited 2.7-litre form until 1965.

As with the Aurelia, there were derivatives, which took over from the B20 GT. The first, on the short GT chassis, arrived for 1959 and were Touring-bodied coupé and open cars, with the latter available with a sturdy hardtop. Both $2\frac{1}{2}$ and 2.8 litre engines were to be on offer. There were also two more Flaminia coupés and these cars, as often was the way with Lancia, looked rather better than the parent saloon; there was the short chassis Zagato-bodied Flaminia Sport and, above all, a handsome Pinin Farina coupé, based on the one-off Lancia Floride II of 1957, which was a 105 mph (168 kmh) car. All lingered on until 1969 and another corporate reconstruction.

The second generation of Fessia designs appeared in 1961, with the arrival of the Flavia powered by a $1\frac{1}{2}$-litre horizontally-opposed four-cylinder engine, which was Italy's first series production front wheel drive car. There was a good looking Pinin Farina coupé with capacity soon increased to 1.8 litres, which meant 105 mph (168 kmh). Zagato was also responsible for the rarer Flavia Sport of 1963–67 though only 726 were built. The arrival of the 2000 in 1969 represented the ultimate version of the model, this 1990 cc derivative developing 131 bhp, appearing with a new Pinin Farina bodyshell, which lasted until 1975.

Lancia had produced a two-tier model line-up since pre-war days and, in 1953, the long-running Ardea was replaced by the 1089 cc Appia saloon, which with 90,000 or so built was the best selling Lancia of the decade. There were the inevitable closed derivatives, from Pinin Farina, Vignale and Zagato.

Lancia had been building cars since 1906 and owned the *Gran Turismo* name, but it was the more memorable GT initials which soon attained international popularity and it was a new make, Ferrari, which was responsible for bringing them to a world wide audience. For Ferrari was first and foremost a manufacturer of racing cars, who began to dominate Europe's race tracks during the 1950s. To generate much needed finance, he also produced a sensational series of road cars. So it was that during the decade the by then fabled GT initials were synonymous with the blood red Pinin Farina-bodied coupés from Modena.

One of the truly legendary figures of the post-war era, Enzo Ferrari (1898-1988), was the second son of Alfredo, a structural engineer, from Modena. The young Ferrari was soon attracted to motor racing as a spectator in pre-First World War days. Having served in the Italian army during the conflict, he approached Fiat following the Armistice, armed with a letter of introduction from his colonel. He had no luck there but soon got a job delivering lorries to be bodied in Milan, where he gravitated to bars, in particular the Vittori Emmanuele, which were frequented by racing drivers of the day. In 1919 he briefly became a test, and then a racing driver, for the new CMN concern but, soon afterwards in 1920, he managed to get a job as a driver with the Alfa Romeo racing team and that year Ferrari was placed second in the Targa Florio. He drove for the Turin company unti 1924, when he seems to have experienced some sort of breakdown and established a garage, with an Alfa Romeo agency, in his native Modena, though he resumed racing in 1927.

It was two years later, in September 1929, that Enzo set up the Modena-based Scuderia Ferrari, which campaigned Alfa Romeos in tandem with the works team. Vittorio Jano's magnificent Type B monoposto of 1932 gave the firm a fresh racing impetus, though from 1934 there was a formidable German challenge in the shape of state-sponsored Auto Union and Mercedes-Benz racing cars. A bankrupted Alfa Romeo came under state control in 1933, and Ferrari continued to uphold its racing programme, though the Teutonic opposition was such that, in 1937, he initiated the design of a new racing car intended for the less competitive voiturette formula. This was designed for him by Giacchino Colombo and was a $1\frac{1}{2}$-litre supercharged model, designated the Type 158 Alfetta, and delivered to Alfa Romeo in 1938. The car, and its 159 derivative, was also to successfully challenge Ferrari's own racing cars in the early post-war years.

However, in 1939, Alfa Romeo decided to direct its own racing programme and Alfa Corse (Alfa Racing) was established at the firm's factory in Portello, Milan. Although Ferrari moved there for a brief period, he soon left after a disagreement and returned to Modena, having agreed to refrain from motor racing under his own name for a period of four years. But it was not long before he was back in the fray having produced the aforementioned 815s, anonymously because of his agreement with Alfa Romeo, for the 1940 Mille Miglia.

During the war, Ferrari built machine tools from his small Modena factory but, late in 1943, he decided to establish a manufacturing base 12 miles (21 km) to the south at Maranello where he already owned land, for Ferrari had decided to produce racing cars under his own name. And, like Alfa Romeo had done in pre-war days, he needed to market sports cars to finance his competitive operations. Ironically, this first example appeared in 1947, ahead of the first of the single-seaters which did not arrive until the following year. The new Formula 1, operative from 1946, specified cars with $1\frac{1}{2}$-litre supercharged or $4\frac{1}{2}$-litre supercharged engines and, in pre-war tradition, Ferrari opted for a $1\frac{1}{2}$-litre 'blown' engine but took the daring decision of deciding on a V12, a configuration which was then being produced by one other manufacturer, Lincoln, across the Atlantic in America, a pre-war anachronism which ceased production in 1948. Every road-going Ferrari was V12-powered until 1967 and the configuration still features in the Ferrari model line up at the time of writing (1989). Ferrari was to claim subsequently to have been much impressed by the V12 Packard used by the Americans as staff cars during the First World War but he would also have had first-hand observation of the V12 Auto Union and Mercedes-Benz racing cars of the 1937–9 era.

Ferrari's first V12, a 60-degree unit, with single overhead camshafts per bank, was designed by Colombo, who had proved his worth with the 158 Alfetta, and was intended to power both the racing and road cars. From the very outset the formula was established with the smooth, understressed unit and five-speed gearbox mounted in an oval section tubular chassis. Transverse leaf independent front suspension featured, though there was a cart sprung rear. The combination of sophisticated power unit and relatively crude chassis represented a perfect expression of Enzo Ferrari's famous dictum that: 'I build engines and attach wheels to them'.

The first car was the 1½-litre 125 Sport, and the method of calculating the model name was thereafter applied to all road-going Ferraris, 125 being the displacement, in cubic centimetres, of one of its 12 cylinders. In 1947 Ferrari introduced its 2-litre 166 Sport successor and followed this with the 166 Inter of 1948. Introduced at that year's Turin show, Touring was responsible for the lovely barchetta (open) version, along with a handsome coupé. Although open cars were produced, the majority of the 38 or so 166s were closed ones with Farina, Vignale, Ghia and Bertone all contributing variations to the closed theme and the 166 can thus be considered as the first of the Grand Touring Ferraris.

An Allemano-bodied 166 coupé gave Ferrari its first Mille Miglia win in 1948 and the make was to be victorious every year apart from 1953–4, until the event ceased in 1957. The

Enzo Ferrari built road cars to finance his Formula 1 activities though only about 38 examples of the 166 Inter were produced between 1948 and 1951. This Touring-bodied example also features a Plexiglas roof.

following year of 1949 was even more successful with 166s taking the chequered flag once again not only in the Mille Miglia and Targa Florio but also at Le Mans, giving Ferrari its first win at Sarthe, and the Belgian 12-hour race. In addition, the 166 and its derivatives were soon to dominate the Coppa Inter Europe, held at Monza in May 1949, the first race to be specifically restricted to what we now know as Grand Touring cars, though the phrase was not then current. The 166 was followed in 1951 by the 2.3-litre 195 Inter though this only endured for a year and was succeeded by the 212 Inter of $2\frac{1}{2}$ litres which lasted until 1953.

As will have been apparent, this first generation of Ferrari road cars, although unblown, were directly related to the supercharged V12-engined racing cars. But Colombo departed in 1949 and he was replaced as Ferrari's chief engineer by young Aurelio Lampredi. In the effort to break the stranglehold of Alfa Romeo, he designed an enlarged $4\frac{1}{2}$-litre *unsupercharged* V12 engine, which first appeared in 1951, and such was its success that it effectively ended the use of the supercharger in Grand Prix racing.

This so called 'long block' V12 soon found its way to the road-going Ferraris, the first of which was the 4.1 litre 340 America of 1951, so called because Ferrari was becoming aware of the potential of transatlantic sales. This low production series (no two are exactly alike) evolved via the more refined 342, to the 375 of $4\frac{1}{2}$ litres to the 4.9-litre Superamerica 410 series of 1956 which endured until 1959. But these, and the Colombo-engined cars, were still being produced in penny numbers; the entire 340/342/375 family, for instance, accounted for only about 40 cars. Between 1949 and 1954 production of road cars, such as it was, amounted to about 200 cars, which compared with approximately 250 sports racers built over the same period.

A turning point in Ferrari's affairs came in 1954, with the arrival of the 250 GT which is significant to our story for a number of reasons. It was the first Ferrari to use the GT initials in its title and was also the first Maranello road car to employ coil and wishbone independent front suspension. But, above all, it was the first 'production' Ferrari and by the time it was discontinued in 1964, Ferrari was building about 670 cars a year. Not only this. It formalized an agreement between Ferrari and Pinin Farina, who had been responsible for bodying the model's 250 Europa and 375 America predecessors.

This followed a celebrated meeting between the autocratic Ferrari, who hated travelling, and Farina. In Pinin's own words: 'Ferrari . . . let it be known that he would like to have

The 250 GT series, which arrived in 1954, was the first Ferrari to be produced in anything like quantity production. This is a 1958 Pinin Farina coupé built for Prince Bertil of Sweden.

a meeting with me at Modena. Without a moment's thought, I answered: "I am perfectly willing to meet him, but I would like him to come here first, to Turin".' But he was told 'Ferrari never leaves Maranello.' The deadlock was only resolved when the redoubtable duo agreed to meet on neutral ground, at a restaurant in Tortona, though it should be said that the town is closer to Farina's Turin than Ferrari's Maranello. But the matter was swiftly resolved. Farina would produce bodywork for Ferrari on a regular basis, a state of affairs that continues to this day and some of his styling house's finest renderings have found their way on to Ferrari's chassis.

The 250 Europa GT, as it was called, was launched at the 1954 Paris Motor Show. It was directly derived from the 250 Europa of the previous year and represented the usual Ferrari mechanical formula of an oval section tubular chassis, the improved independent front suspension and live rear axle. However, the 2.9-litre V12 engine was a reaffirmation of the Colombo rather than the Lampredi design and a four-speed all-synchromesh gearbox also featured. These solid, handsome cars, almost all styled by Pinin Farina, and the bodies sometimes built in nearby Modena by Scaglietti, suffered from heavy steering and a harsh ride, but the superbly tractable race-bred engine and impressive handling ensured that Ferrari was soon serving the needs of a small, discriminating but growing clientele.

Further standardization for the 250 series came in 1956 with the Boana-built, but Pinin Farina-designed, coupé. It should be noted that the GT was also available in open forms though the Boana-built coupé was replaced by a new Pinin Farina design in 1958, this rather undistinguished GT

PF lasting until 1962. Then there was the GT Berlinetta of 1959–62, a short wheelbase competition-orientated 250. This chassis also formed the basis of the 250 GT Berlinetta Lusso (luxury) of 1962. It was fitted with a superbly proportioned Pininfarina[*] body which probably accounted for about 350 examples built by the time that production ceased in 1964. Disc brakes were fitted all round.

Most of these cars in the 250 series were uncompromising two seaters but, in 1960, Ferrari unveiled his first model which at least offered the owner rear accommodation for his children. The 250 GTE 2+2 of 1960, which endured until 1963, retained the usual 250 chassis length but the engine was moved forward eight inches (203 mm) to accommodate the rear seats. Bodywork was once again by Pinin Farina and in 1963, the final year of production, the 2+2 was available with a new 4-litre engine. Sales of about 950 units were a record for the day and ensured that a 2+2 would remain a feature of the Ferrari model range from thereon.

Far more exclusive and expensive was the 400 Superamerica of 1960. Unlike its 410 Superamerica predecessor, which employed the 5-litre Lampredi V12, its successor used the Colombo unit of 4 litres. The fitment of overdrive was another departure from previous practice. Most were Pinin Farina bodied though not perhaps one of the happiest and a mere 48 or so built reflected Ferrari's pre-1954 approach to road car manufacture.

Not only did all these cars enhance the GT name with a flair and allure which endures to this day, but Ferrari was also responsible for making the GT a much larger car than it had been; the Lancia Aurelia, it will be recalled, was of a mere 2-litre capacity.

In the late 1950s, however, Ferrari had toyed with producing a small GT, the *Ferrarina* ('baby Ferrari'). Originally of 850 cc, the light alloy single overhead camshaft four-cylinder engine had grown to 1032 cc when it appeared on the Bertone stand at the 1961 Turin Show. It was effectively a scaled down version of the the sports racing Testa Rossa with tubular chassis, coil and wishbone independent front suspension and live coil sprung rear axle, though it was not badged a Ferrari. The body was a coupé by Bertone but Ferrari decided not to produce it himself and the design was taken up by the de Nora family, with electrical and chemical interests, who established the Autocostruzioni Societa per Azioni in Milan and marketed the car under the ASA initials

---

[*] In 1960 Battista 'Pinin' Farina changed his surname to Pininfarina (one word) and the firm's name was altered accordingly.

This 1947 Pinin Farina-bodied A6 Maserati contains some of the elements also found in the contemporary Cisitalia. Note the progressive Plexiglas roof, shared with the Touring-bodied Ferrari 166 shown earlier. The Turin carrozzeria was responsible for bodying all sixty cars in the series, which endured until 1950.

from 1962. Although it looked right, performed well, with top speed of about 115 mph (185 kmh), the ASA 1000 was expensive and demand was accordingly limited; only 52 cars were delivered in 1964. Output continued intermittently until 1967 after a 1.3-litre six-cylinder glassfibre-bodied derivative failed to save the day.

Ferrari's great Italian rival on the race tracks in the 1950s was Maserati, which had been building racing cars since 1926. Up until 1937 the Bologna-based firm was owned by the Maserati brothers but, that year, it was taken over by Orsi industrial combine with steel mills in nearby Modena, which was where the firm moved to in 1938. The brothers agreed to remain for ten years and accordingly departed in 1947, the year in which the A6-1500, the first true road-going Maserati, appeared at the Geneva Motor Show. Powered by a 1488 cc six-cylinder overhead camshaft engine, production was sporadic. Bodies, both open and closed, were by Pinin Farina so these Maseratis were in the very vanguard of the evolution of the GT. But it was a low production model, the engine was enlarged to 1954 cc and the car redesignated the A6G in 1950, but only 16 examples had been built by 1953. It was followed, in 1954, by the A6G 2000, with a 1985 cc twin overhead camshaft engine rooted in the A6G CS sports racer. As Pinin Farina was, by that time, deeply committed to Ferrari, Allemano built some good looking coupés but on-ly 59 of these Grand Tourers had been built by the time that production ceased in 1957.

The reason for this low production run lies in Maserati's

Maserati followed in Ferrari's wheel tracks with its 3500 GT in 1957. The engine was a 3482 cc twin overhead camshaft six and, although most cars had Touring coachwork, this splendid rendering is by Bertone.

deep commitment to Formula 1, an area where it found itself initially outclassed by Alfa Romeo and Ferrari, though it was more successful in Formula 2 events from 1951. Two years later, in 1953, Maserati became the personal property of Adolpho Orsi, and his son Omer, and they recruited the famous Gioacchino Colombo to design a new Formula 1 racing car for the 1954 season. The resulting 250F lived up to all its expectations and remained competitive until 1957, a golden year when this all conquering single-seater won no less than seven international events. But the financial storm clouds were gathering, for, in addition to Formula 1, the Orsis had embarked on a costly sports racing programme and they realized that, although its reputation was greatly enhanced by successes on the race track, if Maserati was to survive, it would have to follow in Enzo Ferrari's wheel tracks and begin the series production of road cars.

Named the 3500 GT, the model made its debut at the 1957 Geneva Motor Show. Its engine was a detuned version of Maserati's 350S six-cylinder 3485 cc twin overhead camshaft power unit with tubular chassis, coils and wishbones at the front and a cart sprung rear. The handsome two-plus-two bodywork was by Touring and the 135 mph (217 kmh) car was to sell well, with close on 2,000 examples being built by 1964. The model had been steadily refined with disc brakes standardized in 1960, a five-speed gearbox being added the following year and a fuel injected engine arriving in 1962.

That year Maserati introduced a supplementary model in the shape of the Sebring, named after Maserati's victory in the 1957 American 12-hour event, with a shortened 3500 GT chassis powered by the standard engine and with two-plus-two coupé bodywork by Vignale. The engine was enlarged to 3694 cc in 1964 though this had been further increased to 4014 cc by the time that production ceased in 1966.

No doubt inspired by the initial success of the 3500 GT, and also having a small stock of V8 engines left over from its sport racing programme, in 1960 Maserati introduced a new, more expensive model in the shape of the 5000 GT, selling for 7,500,000 lire, which put it on a par with a Rolls-Royce Silver Cloud II. It was, in effect, the 3500 GT chassis fitted with the 4.9-litre V8, with twin overhead camshaft per cylinder bank, of the type that had powered the firm's ill-fated 450S sport racer and Allemano produced an appropriately purposeful two-door bodywork. This was a 160 mph (257 kmh) GT although the engine's noisy gear-driven camshafts were soon replaced by quieter chains. Just 32 examples were built over a four year period.

If the 5000 GT Maserati typified the exclusive end of the GT spectrum, then Alfa Romeo represented the opposing end of this increasingly popular market. As will have been apparent, pre-war Alfa Romeo had been a small, specialist manufacturer of exquisite sports and racing cars. But after the war, with governmental support, Alfa Romeo joined the ranks of the mass producers, though its sporting origins were still very obvious and up until the arrival of the Alfasud in 1972, every Alfa Romeo was powered by a twin overhead camshaft engine, a feature of the marque since 1929.

As the first new post-war Alfa Romeo would not appear until 1950, from 1946 the firm continued to produce its pre-war 6C 2500, with all independent suspension, introduced in 1939. Relevant, as far as the development of GT is con-

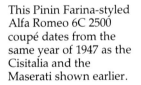

This Pinin Farina-styled Alfa Romeo 6C 2500 coupé dates from the same year of 1947 as the Cisitalia and the Maserati shown earlier.

cerned, was the 90 bhp Sport version and its 110 bhp Super Sport derivative, produced until 1952 and 1951 respectively and bodied by specialist coachbuilders. Perhaps the most memorable rendering on the Super Sport chassis was Touring's 'Villa d'Este' coupé of 1949.

Only 1.830 6c 2500s had been built by the time that the model finally ceased production in 1952. By then Alfa Romeo's all important new model, the 1900 saloon of 1950, had appeared. It was an all new car, with unitary construction four-door saloon bodywork, an 90 bhp 1884 cc four-cylinder engine, coil and wishbone independent front suspension and a live, coil sprung rear axle with radius arms and A brackets. This undistinguished boxy saloon was also produced in more potent 100 bhp TI (International Touring) form and fortunately its engine was fitted in an exciting derivative, the lighter and faster 1900 Sprint. Five inches (127 mm) was removed from the saloon's wheelbase and Alfa Romeo, in the well established Italian tradition, produced a platform chassis for the use of the coachbuilding fraternity. The Sprint was Touring-bodied and was effectively a scaled down version of the exquisite Villa d'Este lines that the styling house had produced for the larger 2500 model. Introduced in 1951, the 113 mph (181 kmh) Sprint only lasted until 1953 when it evolved into the Super Sprint with enlarged 1.9-litre 115 bhp engine. This was also Touring-bodied though it lacked the visual flair of its predecessor and lasted until 1958 when the 1900 ceased production. Pinin Farina had already introduced a cabriolet version of the 1900 Sprint and, in 1952, it also produced its own coupé, as did Castagna.

Spiritual successor to the pre-war Alfa Romeo 2900B, the low production Touring-bodied Villa d'Este coupé of 1949. Based on the ten-year-old 6C 2500 Super Sports chassis, it lasted until 1952, but Alfa Romeo was changing, its mass produced 1900 saloon having arrived in 1950.

A popular GT, the Bertone-styled 1300 cc Alfa Romeo Giulietta Sprint of 1954 lasted until 1962, by which time close on 30,000 examples had been built. A four-door saloon followed the Sprint in 1955.

All these variations were low production, pricey models; the best selling of the 1900 variants, the Super Sprint, had sold a mere 854 examples and total 1900 production was just 21,304 cars. However, in 1954, the firm introduced a much more successful model, the 1290 cc Giulietta, which lasted until 1965, by which time 177,690 had been produced. In this instance it was the sporting derivative of 1954 that appeared before the four-door saloon, which was not announced until the following year.

The restained but well-proportioned Bertone-styled Giulietta Sprint lasted until 1962 and sold 24,084 examples, which compared with a total of 1,796 1900 Sprints and Super Sprints. However, the Giulietta was about half its price. It was a 100 mph (160 kmh) car with an 80 bhp 1290 cc twin overhead camshaft wet liner alloy engine, with Weber carburettor, four-speed all-synchromesh gearbox with coil and wishbone independent front suspension and coil sprung live rear axle. In 1956 came the more powerful 90 bhp Sprint Veloce and this was replaced in 1957 by the fast, good looking short chassis 100 bhp Sprint Speciale, with five-speed gearbox. This time Bertone came up with a visually more daring package for use on both road and track. Top speed was an impressive 125 mph (200 kmh). It lasted until 1962 and was concurrent with the more bulbous and less popular Zagato-bodied SZ.

If the Giulietta can be regarded as a success then the 2000, which replaced the 1900 in 1958, was less so and only lasted until 1961 after a mere 2,804 were built. A coupé version did not appear until 1960 when Bertone produced its Sprint, which was clearly related to the contemporary and still successful Giulietta.

In 1962 Alfa Romeo introduced its new six-cylinder model of the post-war years, a 2584 cc twin-cam, and once again there was a Sprint, with 145 rather than 130 bhp engine, which was entrusted to Bertone and lasted until 1966. In 1964 came the 130 mph (209 kmh) SZ, a purposeful rendering by Zagato, which shared the same short chassis as the Sprint and lasted until 1968 when the 2600 was discontinued in favour of the new four-cylinder 1750 family.

The popular Giulietta range was replaced with the Giulia one in 1962. This was mechanically similar to its predecessor, though the twin-cam four was enlarged to 1600 cc, and there was a new boxy four-door saloon body. The Bertone-styled Sprint had, by then, become a well established tradition but the initial rendering was essentially that of the Giulietta which only lasted for three years. The 1600 engine was discontinued in 1964, and replaced by a 1300 one, as the larger engined version clashed with the new Sprint GT which had been introduced in the previous year.

This was a completely new body shell which, once again, was destined for a long production life, surviving an impressive 16 years, ultimately in 1600 form, until 1979. In its original guise it was the 106 bhp Sprint GT, neat, well mannered and lively 106 mph (170 kmh), and equally at home in the mayhem of Italian traffic or on the autostrada. In view of its long production life the Sprint GT was available in a bewildering number of variations though during the first two years of production, which fall within this chapter, it was only available in 1600 cc form.

The revitalized Alfa Romeo concern meant that Fiat, as by far and away Italy's largest car maker, had a challenger in the mass production market place, but throughout the 1950s it continued to serve successfully the needs of the Italian in the street, though it did produce some exciting offerings which fall within the Grand Touring orbit. The role of the Pinin Farina-bodied 1100S coupe of 1949 in the evolution of the GT has already been noted and Fiat sprang a surprise at the 1952 Geneva Show in the shape of the 8V sports coupé. This curious title was chosen as Ford owned the rights to the V8 name and that indeed was what powered this 118 mph

An unexpected offering from Fiat, the 8V coupé of 1952/54. Not only was it the first Fiat to be offered with all independent suspension, its 2-litre overhead valve V8 engine was never used in another car.

(190 kmh) car. Its 1996 cc pushrod V8 was matched with four- or sometimes five-speed all synchromesh gearbox and all independent coil and wishbone suspension, courtesy of the contemporary 1100 model. The wind tunnel-tested bodywork was usually built by Fiat though there were some memorable offerings by Ghia, Zagato and Vignale. Alas, the 8V only lasted for two years and was discontinued after only 114 had been built. Plans to use its unique power unit in a luxury saloon were also shelved.

Fiat introduced its first six-cylinder car of the post-war years in 1959 with the arrival of 1.8 and 2-litre six-cylinder saloons with torsion bar independent front suspension, the first Fiat models to employ this facility, and quarter elliptic/coil spring rear layout. Ghia took the standard 2-litre floor pan and designed a smart two-plus-two coupé body, which it exhibited at the 1960 Turin Show. Fiat liked what it saw and the model was given official status. When the 2300 coupé entered production in 1961, the saloon's capacity had been increased to 2279 cc though the 1.8 litre car continued unchanged and conventional half elliptic rear springs were introduced. The good-looking 108 mph (175 kmh) coupé lasted until 1964, when it was replaced by the supplementary 150 bhp 2300s version, which compared with the 136 bhp of the basic model. As flagship of the Fiat range, there was more than a hint of truth in the jibe that this coupé was a 'poor man's Ferrari' because Aurelio Lampredi, who was responsible for the engine, which featured inclined overhead valves in a cross flow cylinder head, had, prior to joining Fiat in 1955, been responsible for Ferrari's fabled $4\frac{1}{2}$-litre engine of 1951. This good looking coupé lasted until 1968.

CHAPTER THREE

Britain accepts the challenge, 1945–63

'The DB2 was a very good looking car and many people thought it must have been designed in Italy, but we had an excellent body designer named Frank Feeley and he styled the car — with my help.'

Sir David Brown, chairman of Aston Martin in *Racing with the David Brown Aston Martins* by Chris Nixon

Aston Martin was effectively reborn after the Second World War, following David Brown's purchase of the company in 1947. This is a 1953 DB2, so competently styled by the company's Frank Feeley.

If Italy gave birth to the Grand Tourer, of all the other European countries which took up the concept, it was Britain which eventually did so with the greatest enthusiasm. There were a number of reasons for this state of affairs. Compared with its Continental contemporaries, its industry had sur-

vived the rigours of the Second World War relatively unscathed and, in productive terms, it was European's largest (although it was to cede this pole position to West Germany in 1956). Pre-war, Britain had boasted a strong sporting tradition even though when it came to the Grand Tourer, its car makers had mirrored Italian practice with the GT essentially a low production, high-cost performance car with the most significant examples of the new breed, Aston Martin and Bristol, either indirectly or directly influenced by Continental precedent.

It was a different story when it came to the traditional open two-seater, which was effectively reborn after the war, as America discovered the delights of open air motoring. Austin Healey, Jaguar, MG and Triumph all responded to this transatlantic demand by marketing purpose-designed, mass-produced roadsters, with the result that Britain maintained its position as the world's leading manufacturer of open sports cars.

Of the other European countries, France seemed largely content to perpetuate its pre-war Grand Routier themes, while Germany was rebuilding its industry after the devastation of war. But just as Ferrari had emerged as Italy's newest marque after the Second World War, so Porsche joined the ranks of the car makers in Germany. Its first model, the 356 of 1949, was much more in the traditions of the stark pre-war European sports coupé. But Britain's newest make, the Healey, which appeared in 1946, was

Although wind tunnel testing was well-established continental pre-war practice, such procedures were rare in Britain during the early post-war years. Bristol, with its aeronautical parentage, was very much the exception to this rule and here a model of a Bristol 401 is tested in Bristol University's wind tunnel and exposed to blasts of paraffin smoke to determine the air flow. The result was the most aerodynamically efficient British car of its day.

more in the spirit of the Grand Routiers.

Donald Mitchell Healey was an enthusiastic, single-minded Cornishman, who became a car manufacturer at the age of 48. During the 1920s he became a keen participant in British rallies though, in 1930, he raised his horizons and entered the Monte Carlo event, in a Triumph Super Seven, and was placed seventh. In the following year, 1931, in a $4\frac{1}{2}$-litre Invicta, he won and became the second Briton to do so. (The first had been the Hon Victor Bruce, in an AC in 1926). He was second the following year but, by this time, he had left his native Perranporth for the Riley company in Coventry and two years later, in 1933, he joined Triumph as an experimental engineer. But Triumph's finances were seldom stable and, in 1939, the bank called in the receiver and Donald was out of a job.

By this time the war had started and Healey joined Humber's armoured car division and also found the time to become a member of the Royal Air Force Volunteer Reserve. It was there that he met James Watt, a friend from his Triumph days. At this stage Healey and Watt planned to buy the moribund Triumph company from the then owners, the Thomas Ward company. In 1942 Watt wrote a specification of the sort of car they had in mind. It would have been a 10 hp model intended to compete with contemporary Rovers and Sunbeam-Talbots. But Thomas Ward refused to sell it to them and Watt and Healey had to think again.

This resulted in a change of strategy and the car's profile changed accordingly. Healey now swung towards a 100 mph (160 kmh) model in the spirit of the $4\frac{1}{2}$-litre Invicta, though he hoped the handling would be better than that of the original! He already had a suitable engine in mind. In 1939 Lord Nuffield had bought the Riley company, for which Healey had once worked, and he thought that its $2\frac{1}{2}$ litre unit would be ideal to power the new car. At Humber he met up with stylist Ben Bowden while AC 'Sammy' Sampietro was to have responsibility for engineering the model.

By the summer of 1945, the Healey operations were concentrated at The Cape, Warwick and, at the beginning of 1946, the Healey car made its appearance with a sturdy box-section chassis, with trailing link independent front suspension. The engine was the aforementioned Riley unit and an open version, by Westland, in the best pre-war traditions, was perhaps inevitable. But what makes the model of particular interest is the fact that as a trained engineer, Healey was well aware of the aerodynamic advantages of a closed performance car. The result was the Elliot saloon, a scale model of which had been wind tunnel tested, and, in

The 2½-litre Riley-powered Healey Elliot of 1946 was the fastest closed car of its day, pictured during a record breaking run at Montlhery in October 1948 when it covered 103.76 miles (166.98 km) in one hour.

December 1946, he took one to Italy where it managed 104.6 mph (168.3 kmh) over the flying quarter-mile on the Milan-Como autostrada, making it the world's fastest saloon of its day.

The Elliot Healey was by far and away the more popular of the two body styles and by 1950 101 had been sold, compared with 64 Westlands, despite the fact that the closed car was more expensive at £1,597 at the time of its introduction, compared with £1,566 for the open one. In 1950 Tickford took over manufacture of the Healey saloon. It was to prove more popular than the Elliot and 224 had been built by the time that model ceased production in 1951. Although Donald Healey toyed with Nash, Cadillac and Alvis-engined variants, he realized that, as a small scale manufacturer, he would soon go out of business unless he produced a smaller, lighter, cheaper car. The outcome was the Austin-engined Healey 100, introduced at the 1952 Motor Show, which BMC financed and the model became the Austin Healey overnight, though this was a mass-produced open two-seater, aimed foursquare at the American market and the original Healey, which was effectively Britain's first Grand Tourer, came to the end of the road.

The Bristol, by contrast, was much more enduring and this Grand Touring line thankfully survives to this day. The marque came into being largely through the efforts of two men: George White, who wanted the Bristol Aeroplane

Company, of which he was a director, to diversify into car manufacture, and H.J. Aldington, the pre-war manufacturer of Frazer Nash cars, who had imported BMWs into Britain from 1934 onwards. In July 1945, while serving as a Lieutenant-Colonel in REME, he sought out BMW's bombed Munich factory and its personnel. There he discovered the special bodied open 328, which had been placed third in the 1940 Mille Miglia and returned to Britain with it. Aldington's plan was to build a post-war Frazer Nash-BMW in Britain using the talented BMW design team of Fritz Fiedler, Rudolph Schleicher, who had developed the 328's ingenious cross pushrod engine, and key personnel Ernest Loof, von Rucker and Alex von Falkenhausen.

Aldington's brother, Donald, had worked for the Ministry of Supply during the war and, in the course of his work, had established contact with Bristol, which wanted to create a car division. Bristol agreed to take a majority shareholding in Aldington's company, AFN Ltd, along with the manufacturing rights of the Frazer Nash and Frazer Nash-BMW cars with the new, post-war model to be called the Frazer Nash-Bristol. The aircraft company would also supply parts to Aldington, who would continue to produce Frazer Nash cars at Isleworth.

Then things started to go wrong. There were ministerial protests at so much German talent being exported to Britain and eventually only Fiedler came to the United Kingdom and he was more concerned with developing the post-war

The BMW-based Bristol was the most sophisticated British GT of the early post-war years. A new make, its life began with the 400 Series of 1947, was followed by the 401 in 1949. An example of the latter poses in front of the company's Brabazon airliner at Filton.

Manufacturers check the aerodynamic efficiency of a car's body by attaching tufts of wool to it. The car is then driven and photographed to check the distribution of the air flow. Here a Bristol 401 is pictured during tests on the two-mile (3.2 km) long Brabazon runway.

Frazer Nash. But by the time the car made its debut at the 1947 Geneva Motor Show, it had become the Bristol 400, as the Bristol/AFN liaison had been unscrambled in April 1947.

Bristol engineers, with Fiedler as consultant, had come up with an impressive automotive cocktail, for the 400 was, in effect, the BMW 327 Autenrieth-built two-door coupé, mounted on a 326 chassis and powered by the legendary 2-litre 328 engine. There was a robust box-section chassis, with transverse leaf spring independent front suspension. The rear was unusual, with a semi-floating axle and longitudinal torsion bars, running along the line of the frame, in conjunction with double-acting hydraulic bumpers, plus a central located A-bracket to check any sideways movement.

The cars were carefully built by hand and, apart from such proprietory items as wheels, tyres, carburettors and electrics, Bristol made practically everything themselves to demanding aircraft industry standards and an average of 150 cars *per annum* were produced during the first 18 years of manufacture. Consequently the 400 was not cheap, selling for £2,723 on its announcement, but it was an impressive 90 mph (144 kmh) performer.

The 400 was an undisguised Germanic pre-war car but in 1948 came the supplementary 401 which was perhaps what the 400 should have been in the first place. This was mechanically similar to the 400 but with a new, wind-cheating body, the lines of which had begun life with Touring in Milan, although the shape was greatly refined by Bristol engineers Dudley Hobbs and Denis Sevier in the

Filton wind tunnel and boasted such aerodynamic refinements as unobtrusive spring-loaded door locks and sturdy alloy body-hugging bumpers. The body was built according to improved Touring Superleggera principles and the 401's superior aerodynamics meant that it was faster than its stablemate, good for 100 mph (160 kph) and with better high speed acceleration. Meanwhile the 400 continued to be built and lasted until 1951, by which time 700 had been made, with the 401 enduring a further two years.

The next closed Bristol was the 403 of 1953, the 402 having been a drophead coupé derivative in the best Italian traditions. The 403 was externally similar to the 401 but beneath the surface there were suspension, brake and gearbox modifications and engine output was boosted from 85 to 100 bhp.

It was replaced in turn for 1954 by the short-chassis 404, with a completely new body. Up until then Bristol cars had retained the pre-war BMW radiator grille but, instead, this model featured an air intake, which echoed the leading edge of the Bristol Brabazon airliner's wing, while at the rear were vestigial tail fins. The use of a timber-framed body was curious, as was the location of the spare wheel because of the non-opening boot: it was accordingly positioned beneath the nearside front wing. Here was a Grand Tourer in the best Italian traditions, good for 110 mph (177 kmh) but costing £3,542. Only 40 were built. Its 405 four-door derivative, the only occasion on which Bristol strayed from two doors, was somewhat more successful and 297 found customers. The 406 of 1958, a restatement of the 404 theme, had an enlarged 2.2-litre engine, though it was the last model to be BMW powered, and endured until 1961.

The potent and finely engineered BMW 328-derived Bristol engine found its way under the bonnet of AC, Lister, Cooper and Lotus cars for road and track. The G-type ERA, a Formula 2 car, was also Bristol-engined and this formed the basis of the sports racing 450 coupés, initially with twin dorsal tail fins, which in 1954 and 1955, were placed seventh, eighth and ninth at Le Mans. On both occasions the 450 coupé won the 2-litre class but the firm withdrew from racing in the later year.

Clearly the BMW-derived six could not go on indefinitely and in 1952 work began on the Type 160, a purpose-designed aluminium 2987 cc twin overhead camshaft six-cylinder engine, along with a new chassis, which carried the Type 220 designation. But 1954 was a dark year for the British aircraft industry. Two de Havilland Comets crashed, as did Bristol's own prototype Britannia, though, fortunately, without loss of life. In response the government introduced rigorous new fatigue testing procedures for aircraft, which proved expensive to implement. A casualty of this increasing financial burden to Bristol was the 220 car and its Type 160 engine, by then increased to 3.6 litres capacity to cater for an intended automatic transmission system then under development. As a money-saving measure, Bristol subsequently adopted an American V8 engine in the manner of the French Facel Vega.

Meanwhile Bristol had been experiencing corporate upheavals. Bristol Cars was created in 1956 when the firm's Aircraft and Aero Engine divisions were similarly established, but in 1959 Bristol Aero Engines merged with Armstrong Siddeley to form Bristol-Siddeley Aero Engines and in 1960, Bristol Aircraft became part of the Bristol Aircraft Corporation. This left the cars out on something of a limb and Bristol Cars Ltd was established as a private company with George White becoming chairman and managing director, while Anthony Crook, a Bristol stalwart since 400 days, became a director. This association was to be consolidated as a partnership in 1966.

The BMW-derived six had reached the limit of its development, so the 407 of 1962, visually identical to its 406 predecessor, was powered by a 5.1-litre V8 engine by Chrysler of Canada. This engine was scrupulously rebuilt by Bristol with high-lift camshaft and mechanical tappets in place of the hydraulic ones to permit higher revving, while its attendant Torqueflite automatic transmission also featured. There were also suspension and steering changes. The long running transverse leaf suspension was replaced by more conventional coil springs and wishbones while the original rack and pinion steering gear was replaced by a worm gear unit. Top speed and refinement were noticeable improvements on the earlier cars and the 407 had a top speed nudging 120 mph (193 kmh). Suspension and steering shortcomings were rectified in the 408 of 1963 which lasted until 1965.

Even though the Bristol was in the forefront of British Grand Tourers, as will have been apparent, its Germanic roots were undisguised. However, the Aston Martin DB2, which appeared at the 1949 Motor Show, was clearly British, with a 2.6-litre twin-overhead camshaft six-cylinder engine, designed by none other than W.O. Bentley and styled and built by the Aston Martin works at Feltham, Middlesex. The firm had been selling traditional open two-seaters since 1922, but, in 1947, was bought by David Brown, chairman of David Brown and Sons, gear manufacturers of Hud-

dersfield, Yorkshire. At this stage Aston Martin merely consisted of its name and a Claude Hill-designed experimental
Atom saloon of 1939, a rare instance of a small British firm
interesting itself in a closed performance car in the pre-war
Continental manner. Brown drove it but considered its four-
cylinder 2-litre pushrod engine underpowered. Nevertheless he bought the firm for £20,000 and work was soon
underway on improving the Atom, though Brown felt that it
should have open bodywork in the pre-war Aston Martin
spirit. The car duly appeared at the 1948 Motor Show but, at
£2,331, there were few takers and only 15 examples were
built.

The model's coachwork had been designed by the same
Frank Feeley who had styled the LG6 and V12 Lagondas of
the immediate pre-war years, for Brown also bought that
firm (for £52,500) in 1947. W.O. Bentley had joined Lagonda
as technical director in 1935, and had been responsible for
the V12, but during hostilities had developed a 2.6-litre
engine, which was considered more appropriate for the
post-war years. This powered a prototype saloon, with all
independent suspension, and David Brown was excited by
the possibility of combining Bentley's engine with Hill's
chassis.

The deal did not include Lagonda's Staines factory so production was centred on Aston Martin's Feltham works and
Brown began planning his next model. He decided that, instead of perpetuating an open car he would opt, in the latest
Italian traditions, for a closed one and Frank Feeley was
soon studying the latest design trends. The cars were
ready for the 1949 Le Mans 24-hour race. There were three
examples, two fitted with the pushrod engine and one with
the Lagonda six, though this soon retired with water pump
trouble. One of the fours crashed but the remaining car
finished seventh. However, it would be the Spring of 1950
before the car became a production reality, with the announcement of the £2,331 DB (David Brown) 2. The model
represented a stylistic triumph for Frank Feeley, and David
Brown subsequently recalled that there were many who
believed that the car had been styled in Italy. In fact, Feeley
had been inspired by the coupés of the type which Pinin
Farina had created for Lancia and Maserati but he still
managed to give the car a uniquely British flavour. Powered
by the Bentley designed 2.6-litre twin-cam six, the DB2 was
a 110 mph (177 kmh) car, while the chassis was built up from
sections of straight lengths of square section steel tube.
Front suspension was by trailing arms and coil springs,
while the live rear axle was coil sprung and located by radius

arms. In 1951 came a more powerful 125 bhp Vantage engine though the standard 105 bhp six was perpetuated.

In its original form the DB2 had just two seats but, with the arrival of the DB2/4 in 1953 after 309 examples had been built, two token rear ones were introduced, along with a sensibly positioned back opening door. This was probably a factor in its proving more popular than the original DB2 and, from 1954, there was a race-bred increase in engine capacity — to 3 litres. A Mark II version, with Tickford coachwork, Brown having bought this Newport Pagnell-based company in 1955, appeared for 1956. The series lasted, in DB Mark III form, until mid 1959 by which time the engine was developing 162 bhp.

By this time Aston Martin had a new car, the DB4, arguably the most visually impressive British GT ever produced. Work on the car had begun in 1954, as the days of the Bentley-designed six were clearly numbered. Tadek Marek was recruited from Austin to design a completely new engine, which was originally to have had a cast-iron cylinder block like its predecessor, but as no suitable foundry could be found, it ended up with an aluminium one! Although Frank Feeley had done an outstanding job in styling the DB2 series, John Wyer, who had become Aston Martin's general manager in 1950, believed that the new car should be styled in Italy. In 1956 *The Daily Mail* had offered a Touring-bodied

The line that had begun with the DB2 in 1949 effectively came to the end of the road in 1958 when it was replaced by the all-new Touring-styled 140 mph (225 kmh) DB4. The initial result was a fragile car though arguably one of the best-looking British GTs ever produced. In 1963 came the 4's DB5 successor, an example of which is shown here.

DB2/4, one of two built, as a prize for one of its competitions and Wyer had been most impressed with the design.

Chief engineer Harold Beach produced a prototype, with Marek's new 3.6-litre twin-overhead camshaft engine and a perimeter chassis frame, which was dispatched to Touring in Milan, whereupon it informed Feltham that it required a platform one, which was speedily provided. The completed car was returned to Feltham in July 1957, and the results were sensational. Clearly the masters of Milan had not lost their touch. Aston Martin took out a licence for the Superleggera body construction and the car was unveiled at the 1958 Motor Show visually intact. Independent front suspension was by more conventional coils and wishbones but Beach's idea for a de Dion rear axle had to be abandoned because the David Brown-built gearbox transmitted too much noise to the chassis mounted differential, so a coil sprung, four-trailing link live rear axle, with Watts linkage, was employed.

Regrettably this 140 mph (225 kmh) Grand Tourer proved, in the first instance, to be a fragile performer, though at £3,976 it was the most expensive Aston Martin ever produced! Troubles were mostly associated with the engine and gearbox. Overheating was cured by progressively enlarging the size of the sump, although the gearbox problems were not resolved until the arrival of the 4's DB5 successor in 1963, when a five-speed ZF one replaced the David Brown unit. No matter. The DB4 was the best-selling Aston Martin of its day: 1,040 examples had been built by the time it ceased production in 1963.

Although the DB4 represented the quintessence of the Grand Touring concept, the GT initials were noticeably absent from its title. These were reserved for a similar but lighter short wheelbase GT derivative and DB4 GT Zagato, which weighed 25 cwt (1,270 kg) against the standard model's 26.5 cwt (1,346 kg), and was powered by a 314 bhp engine, with 12-plug head and Weber carburettors. Twin 30-gallon (136-litre) fuel tank and lightweight Borrani wheels were further departures from standard. These chunky, no-nonsense sports racers were, unlike the DB4, bodied in Italy, and although some left-hand drive examples remained in Europe, the British specification cars were returned to Aston Martin for completion. A mere 19 of these 150 mph (241 kmh) exotics were built.

Consequently, this variant was not offered on the DB4's DB5 successor, with a 4-litre engine. The DB4 had been available with a more powerful Vantage engine and this was perpetuated on the DB5 while, for the first time on an Aston

Martin, Borg-Warner automatic transmission was available as an optional extra. The DB5 proved as popular as its predecessor and the firm could have undoubtedly sold more, had it had the capacity to build them, following the construction of a special car for the James Bond film *Goldfinger*.

During 1964 Aston Martin left Feltham, its home since the 1920s, with production centred on the former Tickford works at Newport Pagnell. The DB4 had been built there from the outset, with staff being progressively transferred over the ensuing six years.

There was also a change of manufacturing location for Britain's most illustrious marque from 1946, when Rolls-Royce production was moved from Derby, its home since 1908, to Crewe, as the original factory was to be used exclusively for aero engine manufacture. As will be recalled, just before the war, Rolls-Royce had experimented with the Pourtout-built aerodynamic $4\frac{1}{4}$-litre Bentley, though this work was sidelined during hostilities and the sole post-war Bentley model was the 4.2-litre Mark VI saloon, with standardized Pressed Steel four-door bodywork. It appeared in 1946 and was fitted with an enlarged $4\frac{1}{2}$-litre unit in 1951. The following year came the lengthened R-type, which was when Rolls-Royce introduced its H.J. Mulliner-bodied two-door Contintental, which revived Bentley's pre-war sporting image. But whereas both Bristol and Aston Martin had turned to Germany and Italy for their respective inspirations, the Bentley Continental was much more in the spirit of the French Grand Routiers of the 1930s though, as will be apparent, it did have a share of Italian influence.

The first significant step towards the creation of the Continental was displayed on the Bentley stand at the 1948 Paris Motor Show, in the shape of a Pinin Farina-bodied two-door fastback body on the Mark V1 chassis, commissioned by Jean Daninos, head of the Pont-à-Mousson-based Facel Metallon, who would create his own Facel Vega Grand Tourer in 1954. With the help of Walter Sleator, Rolls-Royce's man in Paris who played a formative role in the creation of the Paulin Bentley discussed earlier, a chassis was obtained and forwarded to Pinin Farina in Turin, just two months prior to the show. Facel subsequently marketed a special-bodied two-door Mark V1, with distinctive twin headlights, which it called Cresta, although only six were produced. Pinin Farina built a further semi-official two-door fastback body on a Mark V1 in 1950, which was the year in which Rolls-Royce gave the project official backing, and chief project engineer Ivan Evernden and chief stylist John

Blatchley began work on what was internally, and appropriately, coded as Corniche II.

The car that they were to produce would, in Evernden's words, 'not only look beautiful but would possess a high maximum speed coupled wth a correspondingly high rate of acceleration, together with excellent handling qualities and roadability'. The running gear was essentially that of the R-type but the car would feature a two-door fastback body and once Blatchley had completed the design, a quarter scale model was tested at the Flight Test Establishment's Hucknall wind tunnel. Unlike the pre-war semi-official Paulin Bentley, the Corniche and the Pinin Farina-bodied cars, all of which dispensed with the traditional Bentley radiator, the team had orders that the car should be 'recognizably a Bentley' even though Evernden was well aware that 'the front end shape like that of a Bentley is bad, as it acts as a bluff ploughing through the air'. The radiator, however, was allowed to undercut that of the four-door saloon by not more than $1\frac{1}{2}$ in (38 mm).

The standard R-type weighed 37.6 cwt (1,910 kg) and the Continental turned the scales at 33.5 cwt (1,701 kg), a feat achieved by extensive use of aluminium, which was specified not only for all the body panels, but also for the window frames and bumpers.

The prototype, registered *OLG 490*, and forever after affectionately known as 'Olga' was completed in 1951 when it was taken to the Monthlery circuit, near Paris and completed five laps at an average of 118.75 mph (191.10 kmh). This compared with 100 mph (160 kmh) for the R.

The spirit of the pre-war Bentley Corniche was revived in 1952 by the arrival of the R-type Mulliner-bodied Continental. A model in the spirit of the Grand Routiers of pre-war days, this civilized, stylish but expensive 115 mph (185 kmh) car, the fastest four-seater of its day, lasted until 1955.

The Continental, which revived a pre-war Rolls-Royce rather than a Bentley name, had arrived in 1952 and was not only the fastest four-seater in the world, with top speed in the region of 115 to 120 mph (185 to 193 kmh), but was also one of the most expensive at £6,929, as opposed to £4,824 for the standard R-type. Mechanical modifications were minimal, with the compression ratio upped from 6.4 to 7:1, a higher ratio 3.077:1 rear axle, a special exhaust system, which absorbed 25 bhp less than the original, while India produced special tyres to cope with the demands of high speed touring.

A total of 208 R-type Continentals were made, of which H.J. Mulliner built 193, the remaining 15 chassis being bodied by Park Ward, Franay, Graber and Pinin Farina. A 4.9-litre engine appeared in 1954 and was extended to the longer and wider S-type four-door saloon in 1955, which saw the Rolls-Royce marque becoming more closely integrated with the Bentley as the Silver Cloud shared the same standardized coachwork as the S. The Mulliner-bodied Continental was perpetuated though, with 8:1 rather than 7.25:1 compression ratio. The S-type Continental was more popular than its R-type predecessor, and 431 had been built by the time production ceased in 1959.

In 1959 Rolls-Royce introduced its S2, powered by a 6.2-litre V8 engine and, although the Continental name remained, the two-door fastback body was discontinued because there was not sufficient difference between its performance and that of the standard car to warrant the manufacture of two separate bodyshells. However, a slightly higher rear axle ratio, of 2.92:1, featured on the Continental, though it was only available with bespoke coachwork. The model name was perpetuated on the SIII for 1963 though, on this occasion, the specification of the standard chassis, and that of the Continental, were identical. So this special Bentley, in the spirit of its distinguished pre-war predecessors, came to the end of the road.

For Rolls-Royce, the Bentley Continental had been an exclusive but supplementary Grand Tourer. But when the West Bromwich-based Jensen company introduced its GT, the 541 of 1954, it was the company's sole product and was a theme that would endure for the next 22 years.

Alan and Richard, the Jensen brothers, took over a West Bromwich coachbuilding business in 1931 and initially produced bespoke coachwork for Morris, Singer, Standard and Wolseley chassis. Jensen began building cars under its own name in 1936 and, after the war, the firm introduced its low production Six saloon, powered by a 4-litre six-cylinder

The West Bromwich-built, 4-litre Austin-engined Jensen 541 of 1953 pioneered the use of glassfibre grand touring bodywork and lasted until 1963. A total of 845 were built, making the model the best selling Jensen of its day.

Austin Sheerline engine which had powered Austin *and* Morris trucks prior to the 1952 BMC merger. It was also used in the firm's open Interceptor of 1950 and, when Jensen was asked by Austin to design an open sporting body for its A40, introduced in 1951, stylist Eric Neale simply scaled down the big Interceptor's lines.

Jensen obtained the BMC contract to build the Austin Healey 100 bodies in 1953, and it was this financial security which permitted it to launch its own Grand Tourer for the 1954 season. The well proven 4-litre engine was carried over from the Interceptor while a new twin-tubular chassis was employed. Austin A60 independent front suspension was fitted, while the rear axle was cartsprung.

Styling was the work of Richard Jensen and Eric Neale and there was a distinctive driver-operated air intake shutter at the front of the car. In the interests of cheapness and lightness, the firm opted for a mostly glassfibre body for the first time on one of its production cars, though some Interceptor body panels had been made of the material. The 541 was made in three sections; the front, roof and rear, though the doors were light alloy pressings. The use of glassfibre was reflected in an all in price of £1,771, making the 541 the cheapest GT on the British market. It was a 115 mph (185 kmh) four seater and 225 examples were built.

In 1957 came all-round disc brakes, the first British closed car to be fitted with them. For 1958 came the more powerful 140 bhp 541R, with rack and pinion steering, courtesy of the MG ZA saloon, and this proved more popular than the 541 in its original form, as 493 of them were sold. The model endured, in *less* powerful 135 bhp S automatic transmission form, until 1963. In all, 845 examples of the 541 family were built, making it numerically the West Bromwich company's most successful car to date.

Jensen had quite deliberately joined the ranks of the GT manufacturers yet, over at Coventry, Alvis became a member of the Grand Touring community by accident rather than design! It had been building cars since 1920 but, during the 1930s, had diversified into aero engine manufacture, though car production was maintained. After hostilities the firm introduced its pre-war inspired, cart-sprung TA 14 saloon, which lasted until 1950. That year it was replaced by the all-new 3-litre, with very traditional four-door Mulliners of Birmingham saloon bodywork and new 2,992 cc six-cylinder engine, box-section chassis, coil and wishbone independent front suspension and live rear axle. This was an 85 mph (136 kmh) car and a faster 100 mph (160 kmh) TC21/100 version, with bonnet scoops and wire wheels, and known as the Grey Lady, was offered in 1954 to pep up this somewhat dowdy image.

But, in 1954, Mulliners of Birmingham, which built Alvis's saloon bodies, committed all its production to Standard-Triumph, and David Brown's 1955 purchase of Tickford meant its drophead coupés were no more. This left Alvis cars in limbo though the firm was profitably engaged in the manufacture of aero engines and Saracen armoured cars.

There was some surprise, therefore, when Alvis's stand at the 1955 Paris Motor Show featured a magnificent ivory Graber-bodied two-door saloon. This Swiss coachbuilder had transformed the Ugly Duckling from Coventry into a delectable Grand Tourer. Carrosserie Herman Graber of

Alvis ceased to manufacture cars in 1967 but not before it had produced the TC/D/E/F series cars which first appeared in 1956. The years have dealt kindly with the lines of the Park Ward-built, Graber-styled coachwork.

Berne, Switzerland had, in fact, been offering Continental customers Graber-bodied 3-litres since 1951 and Alvis decided to put the car in production in Britain for 1956. Arrangements were made with Willowbrook, the Loughborough-based coachbuilders, which specialized in the production of coach bodies, but a £2,700 price tag, which would have bought almost *two* 2.4 Jaguar saloons, resulted in few buyers and only 16 examples of this TC/108G were built.

Production did not get onto a sounder footing until October 1958, by which time body manufacture had been transferred to Rolls-Royce's Park Ward subsidiary. By then the car's price was £2,993 and improvements were made to visibility and seating. Demand considerably increased. No less than 1,060 TD21s were built between 1958 and 1963 though production gently ran down from thereon and the last, and by then outdated TF21, was built in 1967. Rover bought the company in 1965 and had plans to replace the ageing 3-litre line with a special-bodied version of its V8-engined saloon; this GTS, as it would have been designated, was a new Grand Tourer. One experimental example was built but, in 1967, Rover itself became part of the Leyland Motor Corporation and what might have been a new generation of Alvis cars disappeared overnight.

It is difficult to think of a more diametrically opposed car company to Alvis than Lotus. Whereas the well established Coventry firm specialized in solidly built, traditionally engineered models, the newly created Lotus company produced cars of the 'seat of the pants' variety and Colin Chapman, its restless, engineer/founder, was always in the forefront of technical innovation. Consequently when Chapman launched Lotus's first significant road car at the 1957 Motor Show, he turned his back on the open two-seater, so beloved of his established contemporaries, and unveiled the exquisitely proportioned *closed* Elite. Not only did this GT represent a stylistic *tour de force*, it also had the distinction of being the world's first glassfibre monocoque which did, alas, contribute to an excessive amount of interior noise. Neither did it make money for Lotus, and Chapman once estimated that latterly he was losing the equivalent of £100 on every one produced. But it did pave the way for the profitable Elan sports car which succeeded it in 1963.

Twenty-two-year-old Anthony Colin Bruce Chapman had established Lotus Engineering in stables behind his father's Railway Hotel in London's Hornsey in 1950. The business was reformed in 1953, with £25 borrowed from his girlfriend

Hazel and £100 of his own money. The firm's first car to be offered for sale was the multi-tubular Mark 6, which was offered in 'Do It Yourself' kit form and intended for club racing. In the following year came Team Lotus, which produced sports racers and subsequently Formula 2 and ultimately Formula 1 cars.

Work on what was Lotus's first true road car, the Elite, had begun late in 1955. In 1953 Chapman had sold one of his Mark 6 kits to 23-year-old Peter Kirwan-Taylor, a keen motoring enthusiast, who was studying to be a chartered accountant. When it came to bodywork, he adventurously designed his own open two-seater body for it but, in 1955, by then married with a family, he bought a more practical Swallow Doretti and created his own coupé body for that. Subsequently he got into conversation with two friends, who wanted to enter a car for Le Mans in 1956. They were keen for it to have a closed body, because of its aerodynamic advantages, and Kirwan-Taylor approached Chapman, with whom he had struck up a firm friendship, and proposed that he design a coupé body for the new Lotus Eleven. It so happened that Chapman's own thoughts had been moving towards the concept of a new, closed road car but he was reluctant to use the Eleven for reasons of weight distribution. So the concept of the Elite, designated Mark 14 in the Lotus design register, was born.

'We wanted a minimum of compromise from competition specifications so that an owner could win the Monte Carlo Rally, and then use the car for going to the office!' recalled Kirwan-Taylor, though the reality was that the finished product preferred the open road, or track, to the London rush hour . . .

Kirwan-Taylor started work with remarkably few constraints and, because he was not basing the car on an existing open two-seater, the all important roof looked an integral part of the whole. But there were cost compromises because the windows were curved in plane and would not wind. Thus they were detachable and could be stored in the back of the car when not in use. As the design progressed, Frank Costin, an aerodynamicist with de Havilland, made his contribution to the design, by making alterations to the radius between the bumper and bonnet and deciding exactly where the radiator inlet should go. He also suggested the distinctive cut-off Kamm rear end. Ironically the team's main concern at the time was that the design looked so simple. But it is precisely for that reason that time has dealt so kindly with the Elite, as it is devoid of any contemporary clutter of fins, briefly considered and quickly discarded, or

Lotus's attempt to produce a small British GT in the Italian idiom was a mixed success; the visually triumphant though loss-making and impractical glass-fibre monocoque Elite of 1957/63.

an excess of chrome. Yet further input came from John Frayling of Ford's styling department, who helped transfer Kirwan-Taylor's two-dimensional design into a three-dimensional one and transferred it into a 1/5 scale model.

For the prototype car, the name 'Lynx' had been considered but Elite was chosen because it was alliterative with the Eleven which preceded it and it was displayed at the 1957 Motor Show. Under the bonnet was a 1216 cc Coventry Climax FWE single-overhead camshaft engine, canted to permit a low bonnet line, while suspension was all independent, coils and wishbones at the front, and a long Chapman strut, a combined coil/spring damper layout, with wheels located by drive shafts and a kinked radius arm at the rear. This 115 mph (185 kmh) car turned the scales at a mere 13.25 cwt (673 kg).

However, it would be a further 14 months before, in December 1958, the first production Elite was completed. Prior to that the design had to be 'productionized' and the 60 separate glassfibre parts reduced to just three. But Lotus was outgrowing its cramped north London premises and, in mid-1959, the firm moved to more spacious facilities at Cheshunt, Hertfordshire. Here Elite production could get under way in earnest and by the time the model ceased production in 1963, no less than 988 had been built, though latterly, and perhaps unwisely, later examples were offered to enthusiasts in kit form with attendant falling off in quality.

Ironically it was the Elite's fixed roof that proved unpopular with many enthusiasts and when Lotus introduced the Elan, which succeeded the Elite in 1963, Chapman created an ingenious, and substantial, backbone chassis for it which permitted, in the first instance, open bodywork and therefore the Elan initially falls outside the scope of this chapter.

In 1964 Lotus had held tentative talks with Jaguar about a possible merger but these soon stalled. In the 1960s the famous Coventry company was consolidating its racing and technological successes of the previous decade. In 1961 it introduced one of Britain's most impressive Grand Tourers in the shape of the fixed head coupé E-type. Jaguar had not produced a model to follow directly its original SS sports cars after the war, though, in 1948, came the XK 120, powered by its new 3.4-litre twin overhead camshaft six-cylinder XK engine, destined for the big Mark VIII saloon of 1950. The 120's lines were inspired by one of the open 328 BMWs, which ran in the famous 1950 Mille Miglia, brought to Britain by H.J. Aldington (see page 70). It should not be forgotten that in the XK 120, William Lyons, Jaguar's chairman and chief stylist, deliberately moved away from the concept of the traditional British sports car with its harsh ride, noisy engine and minimum of equipment. It was well-equipped, comfortable, carpeted and the closed version of 1951 was even better. The XK 120 was replaced by the 140 for 1955 and, from the outset, a fixed head coupé was available, though with occasional rear seats. In 1958 arrived the XK 150 and its fixed head variant outsold the open version, a state of affairs that would be perpetuated with the E-type, which made its debut at the 1961 Geneva Show. There nomenclature went awry when both the closed *and* open cars were announced as Grand Touring (GT) models.

The E-type was rooted in the sports racing D-type which was designed to win Le Mans, and did so in 1955, 1956 and 1957. Magnificently styled by aerodynamicist Malcolm Sayer, the D-type had the distinction of looking like no other car, only a Jaguar. It featured a strong monocoque tub, with triangulated front end and these features were transferred to the E-type. Suspension was all independent, with torsion bars at the front and lower wishbones and twin coil springs, fixed-length drive shafts and lower wishbones at the rear. The engine was the triple-carburettored 3.8-litre engine, as fitted to the XK 150s. Although the road test cars were capable of a 150 mph (241 kmh) top speed, production cars had difficulty in attaining this figure.

The engine was notable for its top gear flexibility while its ride was shake free and handling similarly impressive. In 1966 the 3.8-litre E-type was replaced by a 4.2 version. The coupé was perpetuated although it was joined by a longer wheelbase two plus two. The 140 mph (225 kmh) plus top speed remained about the same, though acceleration was improved. The 4.2 model, which was the most popular of the range, remained in production until 1971 when the Series III version was introduced. This dispensed with the long running six-cylinder XK engine, which was replaced by a 5.3-litre V12 unit.

Its ancestry reached back to the mid 1950s when Jaguar was intent on challenging Ferrari's growing supremacy at Le Mans and it appeared initially with twin-overhead cam-shaft cylinder heads in the experimental XJ13 sports racer of 1966 which was, alas, never used in competition. Though it finally appeared under the bonnet of the E-type, it was destined for the 1972 XJ12 salon *and* the more expensive XJ-S of 1975. Acceleration was faster than the six's although the top speed of 140 mph (225 kmh) plus was about the same. The model was discontinued in 1974. Total production stood at 72,507 cars of which 38,515 or 53 per cent, were coupés.

A long-time exponent of the overhead camshaft engine, though in this case the single one, was the AC Company of Thames Ditton, Middlesex, which had been building cars since 1919. It returned to car production in 1947, with its pre-war inspired 2-litre, a dated heavy two-door saloon, though the use of the company's long running 1991 cc single overhead camshaft engine ensured that it was an 80 mph (128 kmh) performer. A total of 1,142 examples were built. Incredibly AC continued to list this elderly, all-cart sprung GT, until 1956.

Jaguar called both its open and closed E-types of 1961 Grand Tourers though the marginally faster coupé was the true GT. But production examples could not equal the 150 mph (241 kmh) of the road test cars.

By this time the firm's considerably more up-to-date Aceca coupé had appeared. This was rooted in the open two-seater Ace of 1953, AC's Charles Hurlock having been much impressed by the sports racing Tojeiro-Bristol. Vincent Davidson, who worked for Tojeiro, had produced his own Lea-Francis-engined example and AC purchased the

car, along with its creator, and transformed it into the Ace, which appeared at the 1953 Motor Show. The open two-seater bodywork was inspired by the Touring-bodied 166 Inter Ferrari, while the faithful AC six engine was employed. The twin-tubular chassis featured, along with front and rear transverse leaf spring independent front suspension.

Its Aceca Grand Touring derivative appeared in 1954, with rear open door in the manner of the Aston Martin DB2/4 of the previous year, and costing £1,722. An uncompromising two-seater, AC went to some lengths to improve on the Ace's slightly spartan specifications, so the differential was rubber mounted to minimize noise and glassfibre bulkhead was introduced between the engine and driving compartment. Supplementary 2-litre Bristol engines were available for both models, from 1956, which made them 115 mph (185 kmh) cars, though when supplies were threatened, the 2.6-litre Ford Zephyr engine was also offered from 1961. The model ceased production in 1963. A total of 727 Aces had been produced though the Aceca was less popular with just 329 sold.

By this time AC had introduced a supplementary GT, the four-seater long-wheelbase Greyhound of 1959, though there were substantial and unseen differences from the Ace. Suspension was still all-independent but with coil and wishbones at the front and triangulated semi-trailing wishbones and coil springs at the rear. Power was courtesy of AC and Bristol, but the model's appearance produced an unfavourable response from enthusiasts, and resulting cosmetic modifications meant that the car did not enter production until 1960. Also, at one ton, (1,016 kg) it was heavy and could just reach 105 mph (168 kmh). It was also expensive at £2,998 and perhaps AC was relieved to stop building it in 1961 after a mere 82 examples had been made. After the demise of the Greyhound, AC built no more four-seater cars.

Down the road from AC at Clapham, South London, Sydney Allard had begun building cars under his own name in 1946. A pre-war racing and trials driver, Allard usually drove V8-engined Ford specials. When car production proper began, inevitably they were powered by 3.6 litre Ford V8 engines while the suspension had considerable Dagenham imput, being transverse leaf front and rear. The former featured an LMB-type divided axle, which produced some degree of independence, while the usual torque tube transmission and radius arms featured at the back. The most popular model of its day, and significant as an early British Grand Tourer, was the P1 two-door, four-seater saloon,

Ironically Sydney Allard's victory in the 1952 Monte Carlo Rally with his Ford V8-powered P1 coincided with a decline in the company's fortunes and it effectively ceased building cars in 1956. Allard is flanked by *The Motor*'s Rodney Walkerley (left) and navigator Tom Lush.

with lengthy 16 ft (4,876 mm) wheelbase, which appeared for 1949. These luxurious but expensive cars, at £1,277, were mechanically similar to their predecessors though, in 1950, twin coil springs replaced the transverse front leaf in the manner of the contemporary J2 sports car. The 80 mph (128 kmh) P1 is best remembered as the model in which Allard won the 1952 Monte Carlo Rally, giving Britain its first post-war victory in the event. A total of 551 P1s were built, making it the best selling of all Allards.

However, for 1953, came a chassis frame with twin side tubes, reinforced by steel plates and all round coil springs. The saloon was accordingly uprated, titled the P2 Monte Carlo, with de Dion rear axle and inboard disc brakes, and the price increased to an eyebrow-raising £2,568. But production was minimal and manufacture ceased in 1954 after a mere 11 had been built.

Dagenham stopped building its V8-powered Pilot in 1951 and Allard responded to the prospect of a new generation of Fords by introducing the smaller Palm Beach model for 1953. This was powered by a 1½-litre overhead valve Ford Consul engine or 2.2-litre six-cylinder Zephyr unit, though the latter was easily the more popular of the two. The car was available with two-seater open bodywork and a Mark II version appeared in 1956. The following year came a GT derivative, though only two were ever built; one was Chrysler V8-powered and the other, Sydney Allard's own car, having a Jaguar XK engine. The Mark II Palm Beach really represented the end of the road for Allard and car production ceased in 1959.

One of the cars that also appeared at the same 1952 Motor Show as the Allard Palm Beach, and represented formidable opposition to it, was the first of the Triumph TR sports car series. The original TR2 was replaced by the TR3 in 1955, which evolved into the TR3A in 1957. Like its predecessor, it was an open two-seater but it was this chassis that formed the basis of a little known Grand Touring variant, the Vignale-bodied Triumph Italia, which entered production in 1959. This followed Giovanni Michelotti becoming Triumph's principal stylist, the Herald saloon of 1959 being the first fruit of the liaison. He, in turn, initiated contact between Triumph and the Vignale styling house in Turin, for which he did work. It was provided with a TR3A chassis to which it fitted an attractive fixed-head body, which was displayed at the 1958 Turin Show, and went into production, with modifications to its front, in the following year. A few hundred Italias were built by the time that the 3A ceased production in 1963, but the contact was not maintained.

The Triumph TR, in this instance, the TR3, formed the basis of the Peerless GT, introduced in 1957. At this time, most of the traditional Grand Tourers cost around the £3,000 mark though the glassfibre-bodied Jensen 541 had pointed the way to a cheaper GT. The Peerless's arrival was welcomed by *The Autocar* when it wrote: '. . . serious British rally drivers have bemoaned the shortage of *gran turismo* type cars on the home market, feeling that in this category we have few cars that can match up to the Continentals.' The Peerless cost only £1,498, making it the cheapest GT of its

The glassfibre-bodied Triumph TR3-engined Peerless arrived in 1957 and survived for three turbulent years until its demise in 1960. Here J.A.C. Kennard drives his in 1962. The make was relaunched in refined form as the Warwick but it only lasted until 1962.

day on the British market and, although it only lasted for three years, it proved a source of inspiration for other manufacturers and pointed the way to the glassfibre-bodied GTs, some, alas of dubious quality, of the 1960s.

Peerless Motors of Slough was so called because it had started life after the First World War selling war surplus American Peerless lorries. Post-1945 Peerless took on a lucrative Jaguar distributorship for Buckinghamshire and John Gordon, who ran the firm, decided to diversify into car manufacture. The Peerless of 1958 was designed by Bernard Rodger and based on Triumph TR3 mechanicals, that is to say engine, gearbox and independent front suspension. A de Dion rear axle was employed. The chassis was a space frame of rectangular and steel tubes, $6\frac{1}{2}$ in (165 mm) longer than the Triumph, as the Peerless was to be a four seater. The two-door body was glassfibre. Despite this the car weighed $18\frac{1}{2}$ cwt (939 kg) but it was still capable of 105 mph (168 kmh).

Unfortunately the firm over-extended itself, and there were the twin problems for any small manufacturer of reliability and finish. The Peerless came to the end of the road in 1960 after 325 cars had been built. Gordon subsequently gave his name to the more ambitious Gordon-Keeble Grand Tourer of 1964 and Rodger went on, briefly, to produce a mildly modified Peerless under the Warwick name, which had been its factory coding prior to production, at nearby Colnbrook. But by 1962 the Warwick had ceased production after only a handful had been made: a version powered by the $3\frac{1}{2}$-litre Buick V8 was produced, prior to Rover taking over the unit in 1965.

One of the first cars to follow in the Peerless GT's wheel tracks was the glassfibre bodied TVR Grantura. Like Peerless, the TVR marque also had its origins in a garage business, this time one established in Blackpool by Trevor Wilkinson in 1946. The following year he founded TVR Engineering, a name derived from his Christian name. Wilkinson subsequently produced a handful of specials and went on to produce his own multi-tubular chassis frame. In 1955 and 1956 Wilkinson built a few open two-seaters, with proprietory glassfibre bodywork. These in turn evolved into a coupé in 1957 which paved the way for the stubby Grantura of 1958, which echoed the Grand Touring name. The, by then, well established tubular chassis frame was perpetuated while the all-independent suspension was by trailing arms and transverse torsion bars derived from the VW Beetle. The choice of engine was up to the individual customers and ranged from the side-valve Ford 100E, via the same manufacturer's overhead-valve 105E four, to the MGA and ultimately, to the over-camshaft Coventry Climax FWE unit. The MGA engine was mostly used in the Mark II Grantura of 1961 while the Mark III of the following year featured a redesigned chassis frame with all independent suspension by coil springs and wishbones. Once again there were Ford, Coventry Climax and BMC engine options though the MGB unit was very popular and made the TVR a 100 mph (160 kmh) car.

Another pioneering recruit to the glassfibre-bodied Grand Touring ranks was the Gilbern GT of 1960, which sold for £978 in kit form. During the late 1950s Bernard Frieze, a German prisoner of war who had settled in Britain, interested himself in glassfibre bodywork and built himself a special which attracted the attention of Giles Smith, a butcher who ran his business from a shop in Llantwit Fardre, near Pontypridd, Glamorgan. The Gilbern name was created simply by using the first parts of the two individuals' christian names. In 1959 they decided to join forces to build a car. A factory was established in Llantwit Fardre and the Gilbern, from 1960 until 1974, was the only car to be built in Wales and, accordingly, used a Welsh dragon as its badge.

The Gilbern was based on the 948 cc Austin Healey Sprite engine and front suspension and its rear axle was coil sprung. But, like the TVR, alternative power units were available and the MGA and Coventry Climax units could be specified, while the car could also be purchased in kit form. In 1964 the MGB engine was fitted, which resulted in the creation of the 105 mph (168 kmh) 1800 GT. This first Gilburn lasted until 1966.

There was thus no shortage of exclusive, well-engineered Grand Tourers available in Britain during the 1950s. But across the English Channel in France there was a positive dearth of such cars. This was because France's newly introduced swingeing tax structure penalized larger-engined models. Owners of cars of below 16 CV, which was about 2.8-litres, paid the equivalent of £23 annual tax while those who opted for larger capacity models, were liable for a formidable £79 per annum. This spelt a slow death for those actual and spiritual successors of the Grand Routieres of the previous decade which survived into the post-war years. Thus the 3½-litre 20 CV Delahaye and Hotchkiss disappeared in 1954, the year in which both firms effectively ceased making cars and merged to concentrate on commercial vehicle production, while Talbot's 4½-litre 26 CV Lago Record was also discontinued in the same year.

This formidable obstacle did not deter Jean Daninos, head

France's swingeing car taxation of the post-war years, spelt death to many of the Grand Routiers of which this 1948 Talbot T 26 Grand Sport coupé by Saoutchik is an example.

of Facel Metallon who, in 1954, introduced France's only significant Grand Tourer of the 1950s, the Chrysler V8-engined Facel Vega. Facel, an acronym of *Forges et Ateliers de Construction d'Eure et Loire*, established prior to the Second World War, had initially produced tools and dies for the aircraft industry. After the war it made stainless steel parts for jet engines, and expanded its product range to include steel parts for scooters and, significantly, car bodies for the smaller French car makers. First came hulls for the Dyna-Panhard of 1946, then the Simca Sport of 1949. Facel's forté was pressed steel but, in the late 1940s, the firm began to make the transition from manufacturer to *carrosserie*. There had been the aforementioned two-door, four-seater body on the Bentley Mark V1, and Brasseur, Facel's stylist, was responsible for the lines of the Ford Comete coupé of 1951, which, for tax reasons, was fitted with a small capacity V8 engine and, accordingly, short lived. Facel Metallon also produced, and styled, the four-door saloon body for the big 3.9-litre Ford Vendome. Then there was the Simca Sport. The firm already built its bodies and Brasseur undertook a partial and highly successful facelift for 1953. Although the firm's headquarters were at Pont-à-Mousson, about 170 miles (273 km) east of Paris, body building work was undertaken at a factory at Colombes, near the French capital. Then, in 1954, Facel lost the Dyna-Panhard contract and Daninos decided to use the resulting spare capacity to manufacture his own car.

His first thoughts centred around a four-door Ford Vendome-based saloon though, fortunately, thought better of it after one example had been produced. Instead Brasseur came up with a well-proportioned two-door, four-seater coupé, in the best *Grand Routieres* traditions, while its distinctive vertically located headlamps had been foreshadowed by the Facel-bodied Bentley Mark V1 and would be widely copied by the end of the decade. Introduced at the 1954 Paris Motor Show, the Facel Vega was based on a straightforward twin-tubular chassis and conventional suspension; coils and wishbones at the front and a live coil sprung axle at the rear.

But the really significant aspect of the Facel Vega was that Daninos opted for reliable and cheap power in the shape of a Chrysler-built $4\frac{1}{2}$-litre V8 Firedome engine, as introduced to the in-house De Soto of the same name in 1952. There was a choice of transmission: a four-speed Pont-à-Mousson-built all-synchromesh four-speed unit, courtesy of the short-lived Ford Vendome or the V8's attendant Powerflite automatic unit. The combination of Old World coachwork concealing New World mechanicals was not new. The most important European exponent of the concept had appeared in 1933 with the British Railton, which used a 4.2-litre Hudson straight-eight engine and its Terraplane chassis which was then fitted with bespoke British bodywork. About 1,400 of these 'Anglo American sports bastards' had been built by the outbreak of war. Post-1945 Sydney Allard and Donald Healey had employed Cadillac and Nash engines in their respective sports cars but these were intended as nationalistic bait in models which were sold on the American market.

The Facel Vega also featured a highly distinctive interior

The Facel Vega's aircraft-type dashboard was a feature of the marque from its 1954 arrival until its demise ten years later and was widely copied.

which was more reminiscent of an aircraft than a car, no doubt reflecting Facel's work for that industry. There were aircraft type controls, while secondary instrumentation was relegated to a console between the front seats, a feature that was widely imitated in the 1960s. Seating was luxurious, the so-called roly-poly squabs having been pioneered in the Facel-built Ford Comete bodies. This contributed to making it an ideal Grand Tourer, for this stylish Franco/American hybrid was a 120 mph (193 kmh) car.

But there were some disadvantages in being solely reliant on America for his power units for, across the Atlantic, the Big Three's horsepower race meant progressive, and regular, increases in capacity. By 1955 the Chrysler unit had grown to 4.7 litres and, again, to 5.4 litres two years later. Hydrosteer power steering became an optional extra in the same year. Also in 1957 came a supplementary four-door model, with wheelbase extended by 19 in (482 mm), and named the Excellence. Despite Facel's experience in the body building field, it opted for pillarless construction, with the result that, on occasions, the big doors refused to shut and, if they did, could sometimes jam closed. The Excellence continued to be built in small numbers; there were 157 in all, until Facel stopped producing cars in 1964.

The two-door model was renamed the HK 500 for 1959 and, by this time, engine capacity had been increased, again, to 5.9 litres. It had been enlarged again, to 6.2 litres, in the facelifted Facel II which appeared for 1962. It boasted new body lines, slightly narrower and lower than its

Facel Vega was the French company which combined the concept of the Grand Routier with an American V8, in this instance a Chrysler unit. The original model of 1954 also spawned this four-door Excellence derivative in 1961. It lasted until 1964 and 157 were built.

Unlike its big Chrysler-engined brothers, the Facel Vega Facellia of 1960 had its own purpose-built 1.6-litre twin overhead camshaft four-cylinder engine. Its unreliability, and the model's resulting failure, proved to be factors in the firm's demise.

predecessor, and all the better for it. A new Marchal headlamp layout helped reduce front end drag and 150 mph (241 kmh) top speed was claimed. But the marque was only destined to endure until 1964, which was when the firm finally went into liquidation. Approximately 1,500 examples of these big cars had been built with about 350 of the original, 500 HK 500s and 180 Facel IIs produced.

But it was not these big, luxurious Facels that brought about the firm's demise. It was Daninos's decision to build a smaller version, the Facellia, which was the firm's undoing. It looked like a scaled down HK 500, a neat two-door, two-seater, and with similar suspension. Selling for the equivalent of £1,500 when announced at the 1959 Paris Motor Show, it aroused considerable interest. But whereas Daninos had relied on the Chrysler V8 for his original line, which, it should be said, gave remarkably little trouble, for the Facellia he decided to produce his own purpose-designed Pont-a-Mousson built four. Carlo Marchetti, formerly of Talbot, was responsible for the 1.6-litre twin-overhead camshaft four-cylinder engine. Unfortunately it was plagued with problems, caused by faulty cooling, which resulted in burnt out pistons. It took two years to resolve the problem, by which time confidence in the Facellia had fallen away and by the autumn of 1962, the firm was facing collapse. In the spring of 1963 came the Facellia-based Facel III, powered by the Volvo P 1800 engine. Then, in October 1963, SFERMA, a subsidiary of Sud-Aviation, took the firm over. While the big cars continued virtually unchanged, though with capacity upped to 6.8 litres, it decided to produce an additional model, also rooted in the Facellia but powered by an Austin Healey 3000 engine, reduced to 2860 cc to circumvent the French tax system. Only a handful were made and the last Facel Vegas were built in 1964.

Because France's taxation system favoured cars below 16CV it was inevitable that what nationally engined GTs that did appear would be based on their small saloon counterparts. One such was the Type A106 Alpine-Renault of 1954 with glassfibre fastback body. It was created in Dieppe by Jean Redele, whose father ran a Renault garage there. When he took it over, he began racing a rear-engined 4CV Renault and recognized that it would form the basis of a sports car. Consequently the A106 Alpine-Renault used its 747 cc engine, with optional five-speed gearbox, platform chassis and all independent suspension; coils and wishbones at the front and swing axle and coil springs at the rear. The 120 mph (193 kmh) model came to prominence when it won its class in the 1955 Mille Miglia and evolved, in turn, into the A108 of 1957, with a new backbone chassis. It boasted an enlarged 845 cc Renault Dauphine engine and the new, purposeful coupé body was to last until 1977. This, in turn, became the Renault R8 956 cc engined GT of 1963, a theme which was to benefit from progressive engine up-dates as the Renault range expanded into the 1970s.

These Alpines were strongly challenged from 1962 on-wards by the Bonnet Djet, also Renault-powered but with the engine mid-located. Its origins are to be found in the visually similar Champigny-sur-Marne built front-wheel-drive DB of 1953, though mechanically diametrically oppos-ed to the Alpine as the engine was front, rather than rear located.

Rene Bonnet and Charles Deutsch had begun building specials in 1938. Up until 1949 they employed a backbone chassis with rear-mounted Citroen 11CV engine and transmission. They then switched allegiance to Dyna-Panhard front-wheel-drive specials and these evolved into the DB, with a 851 cc flat-twin air-cooled overhead valve engine and drive unit attached to the inevitable backbone chassis. Suspension was by transverse leaf at the front and the Panhard torsion bar suspended dead rear axle also featured. The 95 mph (152 kmh) coupé was initially aluminium panelled, though it subsequently sported Chausson-built glassfibre bodywork. In addition to the stan-dard engine, virtually any power unit built by Panhard, up to 1.3 litres capacity was available, while a supercharged op-tion could be specified. A DB won its class in the 1954 Mille

The rear-engined, glassfibre-bodied Alpine-Renault first appeared in 1954 and evolved into the A108 of 1963. Suspension and engine were courtesy of the contemporary Dauphine saloon. It was perpetuated, in various forms, until 1977. This is a 1963 example.

Miglia but Panhard's declining fortunes could have done the model little good and Bonnet and Deutsch went their separate ways in 1961. The DB was no more but, by that time, Bonnet had hitched his star to the more prosperous Renault wagon.

Yet another side effect of France's post-war car taxation policy was that the resulting proponderence of relatively small-engined cars meant that, after the war, it had no makes to field competitively in its own Le Mans 24-hour race. The $4\frac{1}{2}$-litre Talbot which won in 1950 was a pre-war car and it would not be until 1972 that a French make, a purpose built 3-litre Matra, won the event. During the 1950s the race was dominated by the Italian Ferraris and British Jaguars, apart from 1952 when a Mercedes-Benz 300SL coupé took the chequered flag. It was not only the first time that the German company had won the event but it was the first closed car to be victorious in the 24-hour classic. This coupé, the 300SL, was to evolve into one of the most legendary road cars of the post-war years, forever remembered for its novel but essentially functional gullwing doors.

In 1951 Daimler-Benz decided to return to sports car racing. A C-type Jaguar had just won Le Mans and the company was inspired by its success, with its 3.4-litre twin-overhead camshaft six-cylinder engine, economically borrowed from the big Mark VII saloon of 1950. The German company decided to do the same and produce a road car-based sports racer, in this instance its 300 series saloon of 1951. It contributed its 3-litre single-overhead camshaft six-cylinder engine, transmission and suspension; coils and wishbones at the front and a swing-axle rear.

Mercedes-Benz's legendary 300SL of the 1954/63 era, displaying its famous gullwing doors demanded by the use of a space frame chassis. Top speed was nudging the 130 mph (209 kmh) mark.

These components were, not unnaturally, heavy and the small engineering team appointed by Rudolph Uhlenhaut and headed by Franz Roller and consisting of Ludwig Kraus and Manfred Lorscheidt, responded to the problem by designing a light, rigid space-frame instead of a conventional chassis. The load-bearing latticework of tubes had to be as rigid and deep as possible along the cockpit sides which would normally have been occupied by conventional doors. In view of this the Daimler-Benz engineers introduced the famous gullwing doors, hinged along the centre-line of the roof, and thus gave the model its distinctive appearance. Following pre-war Alfa Romeo and BMW and more recent Porsche experience, the firm opted for a coupé body because of its low aerodynamic drag and, when wind tunnel tested, it recorded an impressive 0.25 Cd. The model was titled the 300SL (Sport Light). In its 1952 introductory, and only competitive year, it won the Swiss Grand Prix, Le Mans and an open version was victorious in a sports car race at Nurburgring.

The following year the design was mildly modified, with Weber carburettors instead of Solex units and, ultimately, Bosch fuel injection replacing the carburettors, a slightly shorter wheelbase and low pivoting swing axle. However, these silver coupés were not used in anger in 1953 and it was at this stage that Max Hoffman, the firm's American importer, suggested to Daimler-Benz that it market the 300SL as a road car and said that he would order 1,000. The car entered production in 1954 though modifications to the space frame put the weight up by 181 lb (82 kg) to 22 cwt (1,160 kg) and this spiritual successor of the SSK of pre-war days was built until 1956.

It was one of the fastest road cars of its day with perhaps only the occasional Ferrari able to out-perform it. Top speed was in the region of 155 mph (249 kmh). The 300SL also had a distinguished rallying career. Among its victories were a win in the GT class in the 1955 Mille Miglia and, the same year, privateers also won the Liege-Rome-Liege and Tulip Rallies. But the car did have its shortcomings. Its handling could be unpredictable to the uninitiated and its space frame was expensive and difficult to repair in the event of an accident. After 1,371 examples had been built, the 300SL was replaced by the simpler 300SL roadster of 1957 and, by the very nature of its open body, this did not feature those lovely gullwing doors. The roadster remained in production until 1962.

Mercedes-Benz thus made a triumphant return to competition but, considering the formative role that BMW played in the creation of the sports coupé, its early post-war years were bleak as it struggled to regain its identity. With its Eisenach factory lost to East Germany, car production was centred on the former Munich aircraft engine works, or what was left of it. BMW had lost its 326, 327 and 328 models to Bristol in Britain and, when car production re-started in 1952, it was with the pre-war inspired 1.9-litre 501 with pushrod six-cylinder engine. This substantial saloon endured in uprated 2.1-litre form until 1958. In 1954 the firm introduced its 502-derivative, powered by a new 2½-litre V8 engine, BMW's and Germany's first, with light-alloy cylinder block and overhead valves.

This engine was used in the firm's 503 Grand Tourer, which took BMW foursquare into Mercedes-Benz territory. Introduced in 1956, it was powered by an enlarged 3-litre power unit and the same 9 ft 3 in (2,835 mm) wheelbase as the saloon. Suspension was by torsion bars, independent at the front and a live rear axle, and the gearbox was unusually mounted separately from the engine, although, from 1958, it was conventionally mated to it. Although elegant, the 503 was heavy at 29 cwt (1,500 kg) and expensive, so sales of 412 units were disappointing and the model was discontinued in 1959.

There was also a short-wheelbase 130 mph (209 kmh) 507-derivative of 1956, which was BMW's answer to the Mercedes-Benz 300SL coupé. It also looked like a GT but was in fact an open car fitted with a substantial detachable hardtop and only lasted until 1959, after a mere 253 were built. Both cars were styled by Count Albretch Goertz, who obtained the commission via the same Max Hofmann who initiated the 300SL construction, as he was also BMW's American importer. Goertz was subsequently to be involved in the conception of a very different model: Datsun's best-selling 240Z sports car of 1969.

BMW's life-saving 1500 arrived in 1962 and the same year came the 3200 CS, the last of the V8-engined BMWs. This handsome Bertone-styled Grand Tourer was a 120 mph (193 kmh) car with the same engine as the 3200 S saloon, which was discontinued in 1963. The torsion bar suspension was much the same as the preceding models and the sales story was similar: just 603 cars sold by the time that production ceased in 1965.

If BMW had a somewhat uncertain start in the post-war years, then the same could not be said of Porsche, which was to become Germany's most famous sporting marque, and was born in 1948 with the arrival of the 356 model. The spartan 356 is much more in the spirit of the pre-war sports coupé and its creation is important to our story in two respects. It was directly inspired by the lovely little Pinin Farina-bodied Cisitalia coupé and it paved the way for the 911 of 1965.

It had been while Ferdinand Porsche's son Ferry and engineer Karl Rabe had been in Turin working on the Piero Dusio's over ambitious four-wheel-drive racing car that they had become acquainted with and greatly impressed by the Cisitalia coupé. What particularly appealed was the idea of

Prior to the arrival of the all-important 1500 saloon in 1962, BMW cars were usually high cost, low production models. This Bertone-bodied 3200 CS of 1962/5 was powered by a 3.1-litre V8 engine. But only 603 were built.

using existing components, in this instance, Fiat parts. What better idea than to apply the same principles for producing their own sports car and instead use parts of the Volkswagen which the Porsche Bureau had designed before the war. At this time the Bureau was housed at Gmund, Austria, where Porsche owned land and, in June 1947, work began on a car which was titled 356 in the firm's design register. Like the Cisitalia it had a tubular chassis, although the 1131 cc flat-four air-cooled Volkswagen engine was mounted in the centre of the car, rather than behind the rear axle line in the manner of the VW saloon. All-round independent torsion bar suspension also followed VW precedent. The chassis was completed in 1948. As originally conceived, the 356 would have been first produced in coupé form but the lack of production facilities at Gmund meant that this experimental car was an open two-seater.

Even while it was undergoing trials, Ferry Porsche simplified the design with the construction of a second car, a coupé titled 356/2. This differed from the first one in that the Cisitalia-inspired tubular chassis was replaced by a simpler platform and the engine reverted to its original rear position. It was intended to produce the car in open and closed form and the latter showed a family resemblance with the prewar sporting Volkswagen created for the aborted Berlin-Rome-Berlin race of 1939. Styled by Erwin Komenda, and aided by mathematician Joseph Mickl and Ferry Porsche, an aerodynamically efficient shape was created without the convenience of a wind tunnel. The coupé was covered with tufts of wools and subsequently photographed while on the move. The prints were then carefully scrutinized to confirm that they had all flattened correctly.

Manufacture began in 1948. A batch of 50 cars was laid down though, from 1950, production was transferred from Gmund back to the Bureau's Stuttgart home. In its original form, the 356 was capable of 85 mph (136 kmh) and the model remained in production until 1965. Capacity was progressively increased to 2 litres in the 356's top line 125 mph (201 kmh) twin-overhead-camshaft Carrera.

Porsche is thankfully still very much in production at the time of writing though the Spanish-built Pegaso Grand Tourer enjoyed only a relatively short life, from 1951 to 1955. It was designed by Barcelona-born engineer Wilfredo Ricart, who had been responsible for the high quality Ricart-Espana car, built in the city in 1928 and 1929. In 1936 he left Spain and joined Alfa Romeo, where he had the doubtful distinction of having successfully conspired to oust Vittorio Jano from Portello. In 1940 he became technical director of Alfa

Porsche's first model, the 356 of 1948, was in the tradition of the sports coupés of pre-war days. This is a Gmund-made example, the seventeenth car to be built in 1949. The 356 lasted until 1965.

Romeo though his 3-litre 16-cylinder twin-supercharged Type 162 Grand Prix car never got beyond the prototype stage because of the outbreak of war. He left the firm on the expiry of his contract in 1945 and subsequently returned to his native Barcelona.

There he joined Empresa Nacional de Autocamiones SA, (National Lorry Company) though better known by its ENASA acronym. Created by the Spanish government in 1946, it absorbed the Hispano-Suiza company, which had stopped building cars in 1940, and took over its Barcelona factory. However, Hispano-Suiza withdrew from ENASA in 1956 and took its aero engine business with it. But the Spanish firm's mainline products were commercial vehicles, the first of which were built in 1946. These carried the 'Pegaso' name, the Spanish version of the Greek flying horse, Pegasus.

The Pegaso car, which followed in 1951, was never intended for quantity production but was a prestige vehicle to publicize the company and its products and, although it had no direct connections with the pre-war Hispano-Suiza car, it can certainly be considered as its spiritual successor. Designated the Z102, it was mostly produced in Touring-bodied coupé form, though Saoutchik offered variations. Suspension was by torsion bars and wishbones at the front while the de Dion rear axle, with integral five-speed gearbox, echoed Ricard's complex V16-engined Alfa Romeo. It was powered by a purpose-built light alloy V8 engine, with twin overhead camshafts per cylinder bank. The formidable power unit was available in two sizes: a $2\frac{1}{2}$-litre supercharged version or an unblown option of 2.8 litres capacity. Not surprisingly, the Pegaso was expensive at the equivalent of £3,000 on its 1951 introduction but then the entire chassis, with the exception of its Bosch electrics, had been made in the lavishly equipped factory in Barcelona's Calle de Segrera. Top speed varied according to engine capacity but most Z 102s were capable of 120 mph (193 kmh). Capacity increased over the years and, by 1954, the V8 was a 3.2-litre unit. There was also a lively 285 bhp variant with twin superchargers, which was another favourite Ricart feature.

The Pegaso effectively came to the end of the road in 1955 with the announcement of the original car's Z103 replacement. The costly twin-overhead camshafts were replaced by more conventional pushrods and, although it was offered with the usual choice of capacities, in this instance 4, $4\frac{1}{2}$ and 4.7 litres, only a handful were made. The last Pegaso car was built in 1958 as the firm was becoming increasingly committed to commercial vehicle production, which continues to this day, and in 1959 Ricart departed and became president of the French arm of the American Lockheed company.

If the Pegaso was unexpected then so was the GT that the

Spain was the unexpected host of the V8-powered Pegaso of 1951/8. Capacities ranged from $2\frac{1}{2}$ to 4.7 litres. This is the customary Touring-bodied coupé body.

Volvo introduced its distinctive P1800 coupé in 1960. Built by Jensen in Britain until 1964, production was subsequently transferred to Sweden and the model lasted to 1973.

Swedish Volvo company introduced in 1960. The firm had begun building its robust, no nonsense products in 1927 but, after the Second World War, like the rest of the Old World's motor industry, it was waking up to the sports car potential of the vast American market. Its first excursion into performance motoring was tentative and disastrous. The P1900 of 1954 was an open two-seater, based on the components of the PV444 saloon and its 1.4-litre engine. The body was glassfibre, styled and built by Glasspar in California, USA, of all places, the hulls then being shipped to Sweden for assembly. This somewhat crude offering only lasted until 1957 and a mere 67 were built.

But Helmer Petterson, a freelance engineer, who had a considerable influence with the Volvo company, and played a key role in getting its PV444 saloon of 1947 into production, was convinced of the need for a sports model which could be sold in America and he took his ideas to Gunnar Engellau, who had taken over as Volvo's president in 1956. The latter agreed to this initiative but what he did not know was that Petterson's son Pelle was an aspiring stylist.

Helmer recognized Italy as the aesthetic centre of the motoring world and, armed with some of Pelle's sketches, made his way to the Ghia styling house. Instead of an open car he wanted a closed one, though Frua also became involved when Ghia, because of its contractural obligations to Volkswagen, had to bow out of the project. However, the design finally chosen was by Pelle Petterson. Once again there was a body building problem since no spare capacity existed at Volvo to produce the shells, so the West German Karmann company was approached. This firm agreed to build it, but then withdrew, and Volvo had to look elsewhere. So Volvo came to Britain and the contract was awarded to Pressed Steel, which produced the P1800s' bodies at its plant in Linwood, Scotland. The shells were then delivered to Jensen Motors' West Bromwich factory for completion.

Announced in 1960, the P1800's mechanicals were courtesy of Volvo's P 120/Amazon model. The 1.8-litre four-cylinder engine was coaxed to produce 100 bhp instead of its customary 60 to 85 bhp. Suspension was conventional; coils and wishbones at the front and a cartsprung rear and the P1800 proved itself an effective 105 mph (168 kmh) performer. The car, with its distinctive and well-proportioned rear fins, soon gained international recognition when it provided transport for the 'The Saint' in the television series of the same name.

The cars were built in Britain until 1963 but that year final assembly was transferred from Jensen to Sweden because of quality problems. The car was renamed the P 1800S (for Sweden) though Pressed Steel continued to build the bodies, a state of affairs which continued until 1970, when their manufacture was also moved to Sweden.

Engine capacity was upped to 1986 cc for 1969 and, in 1970, the model was renamed the P1800E (for *Einspritzung*) which is German for 'fuel injection' as the Bosch system replaced the twin carburettors. By this time the engine was developing 130 bhp. A 1972 ES estate version belongs to the next chapter but the coupé ceased production in the same year after a respectable 40,000 or so had been built during an impressive 12-year run; a testament to Volvo engineering and the stylistic abilities of young Pelle Petterson.

CHAPTER FOUR

A GT for Everyman, 1964–70

'The Mustang was an instant hit . . . as a sports car it was certainly deficient in some ways; but as a sporty car it was better than anyone had expected.'

Richard Langworth in *The Mustangs: A Collector's Guide*

The thread of the GT story now moves across the Atlantic to America. Up until the 1960s, the Grand Tourer had invariably been a low-production, high-cost closed car with good looks, excellent performance and handling and the fittings and refinements of a saloon. But in 1964, the entire GT concept changed and what had only been within reach of the few became available to anyone. This shift in emphasis occurred as a result of America taking up the Grand Touring concept, and followed Ford's introduction of its top selling Mustang with its European Capri counterpart, built in both Britain and Germany, from 1969.

There are two discernible strands to the Mustang's evolution. From 1955 until 1975 the Volkswagen Beetle, or Bug as Americans called it, was the country's top-selling European import and by 1959 the VW had sold a record 120,442 examples, or a massive 20 per cent of all car imports. The American Big Three responded by producing what they called Compacts, large cars by European standards and in size placed somewhere between the Beetle and the mainstream American sedans. In the 1960 model year, the American car makers unveiled their responses to the Europeans. Chrysler produced the Plymouth Valiant and Ford offered its no frills Falcon. Both these were traditional front-engine/rear-drive packages, but General Motors' Corvair, with all independent suspension, was totally revolutionary for the American industry, being powered by a rear-mounted 2.2 litre flat-six air-cooled six-cylinder engine.

But there was a second string to the American response

The Ford Mustang, which arrived in 1964, was one of the fastest selling cars in American automotive history. It was initially available in open (top) and closed (centre) forms and was followed later in the year by a fastback GT version (bottom), which greatly popularized the name. The steel wheels and racing stripes between them identifies the GT. This is a 1966 car.

and this initially countered the threat posed by the British open two-seater sports car. In 1953 GM produced its glassfibre-bodied open Chevrolet Corvette. The model continued in this form until 1963 when it was replaced by the Sting Ray. The open version was perpetuated but, significantly, there was an additional coupé version. Styled by William Mitchell, who looked across the Atlantic for many of his design initiatives, it was much more of a Grand Tourer in the low-production, high-cost European tradition, and remained in production until 1968.

In the main, however, the so called American sports coupés of the 1950s had little stylistically and mechanically in common with their European equivalents and would not qualify for a moment as Grand Tourers. About the closest an American company got to the GT concept were the Studebaker Starliner and Starlight coupés, introduced back in 1953. The Starlight evolved into the Hawk of 1956 and when this was reworked for 1962, it was renamed the Gran Turismo Hawk, an early instance of the GT name being applied to an American car though not the first time since it also appeared on the Dodge Lancer hardtop coupé of the same year. By this time Studebaker was fighting for its life and president Sherwood Egbert hoped that a pukka GT, the Avanti, would pull the company round. Styled by the Raymond Loewy organization, like the Corvette, its body was made of glassfibre and lacked the traditional radiator grille, with the air intake positioned below the bumpers. Based on the chassis frame of the Lark convertible, it was powered by Studebaker's long running 4.7-litre V8 engine, but this 120 mph (193 kmh) car only lasted until 1963, the year in which Studebaker ceased its American operations. A mere 4,143 Avantis were made.

Meanwhile how had Ford been responding to the British two-seater sports car? In 1955 it introduced its open two-seater Thunderbird, a 'personal' car which only survived in this form until 1957. Just 53,166 were built, a flea bite by Detroit standards. Robert McNamara had taken over as head of the Ford Division in 1955 and cancelled the project in view of its disappointing sales, though the Thunderbird name was too good a one to die and was transferred to a new four-seater hardtop, which proved a strong seller, and Thunderbird has remained a mainstream Ford model name ever since.

But there were soon changes in the Ford hierarchy. John Kennedy was elected United States president in 1960 and McNamara accepted the post as the administration's Defence Secretary. His place as chairman of the Ford division was taken by 36-year old Lido Anthony (Lee) Iacocca, whose father, Nicola, had emigrated to America from southern Italy at the age of 12 in 1902. Lee Iacocca's appointment coincided with Ford's market research telling it that the post-Second World War baby boom was due to burst in the 1960's and that individuals would invariably remain faithful to the make of car that they bought when they were young throughout their life. As youth and a sporting image are synonymous, Ford adopted what it dubbed its 'Total Performance' profile, which began to take effect from 1962, the high point of which was Ford's first win at Le Mans in 1966 with the Anglo/American GT40, a victory followed by subsequent successes in 1967, 1968 and 1969.

Ford's General Motors rivals had experienced an unexpected success when its initially slow-selling Corvair line was re-invigorated with a sporty variant, hastily introduced late in the 1960 season. Instead of the standard model's somewhat basic interior, it acquired bucket seats, carpeting and floor-mounted rear-change and was named the Monza. Subsequently, in 1965, the Corvette was visually transformed by the stylistic skills of William Mitchell, into a handsome European-type 'GT' and destined to remain in production in this form until 1969. In the same introductory year, the Corvette's original swing rear axle was replaced by a fully independent system, after initial criticisms of unpredictable handling.

Clearly the youth market was going to be an increasingly important one for all manufacturers and the ambitious Iacocca was determined that Ford was going to win that particular race. What he wanted, and it would take a little time for the profile to emerge, was a crisply styled, sporty car, in other words a GT for everyman, and Iacocca had in mind one with a long bonnet and short boot in the manner of the original Lincoln Continental of 1940 vintage. Although ideas came and went in 1962, an experimental car titled Mustang 1, was actually built. An open two-seater with a 1.9-litre mid-located Taunus engine, it was shown to the public at Watkins Glen at the 1962 US Grand Prix. There it received rapturous applause although the car in question did not lend itself to quantity production.

Subsequently, in mid-1962, four styling divisions, Lincoln-Mercury, Corporate Products, Ford Division and Ford Motor Company Advanced Design, were asked to produce rival designs for the proposed car. The parameters submitted to them were that it should sell for less than $2,500, have a length less than 180 in (4,572 mm), four-passenger capacity, front bucket seats and a rear bench one. A floor gear change was also specified, with a peppy six-cylinder engine as standard, room for an optional V8 and a long accessory list.

The divisions were given less than two weeks to produce their clay models. The winning design was a racy looking two-door hardtop, coded Cougar, created by the Ford Division studio under Joe Oros, and the work of executive designer David Ash. The model was approved in September and prototypes were built, including Mustang II, which also received public acclaim, when it was displayed at Watkins Glen in 1963. There had been the inevitable changes of name in the development process and Turino, or Torino (both early possibilities) had strong Italian overtones but eventually the factory Mustang coding was chosen.

Although the bodyshell was new, the Mustang's basic engine, transmission and suspension all came from the Ford parts bins, in this instance the Fairline and Falcon models. Initially the Mustang buyer had a choice of body styles: a hardtop or a convertible. Sales of 100,000 cars per annum were contemplated but, just prior to the launch in April 1964, Iacocca upped the figure to 240,000 when demand looked promising.

It was just as well he did. The 100,000 sales figure was broken within four months and the latter in seven. By the end of the following year of 1965, a record-breaking 680,992 Mustangs had been sold, with the millionth car built in

An Italian/US GT: the American magazine, *Automobile Quarterly*, commissioned Bertone to produce this special-bodied 1965 Mustang. The headlamps were usually covered by extensions of the radiator grille during the hours of daylight.

The GT for Everyman: the European version of the Mustang was the Ford Capri, introduced in 1969. It remained in production for eighteen years. This is a 1979 Series X 3-litre. The last Capri was built in 1987.

March 1966, a sales performance which that year helped Ford to pull ahead of its General Motors' Chevrolet rival in the US sales charts.

As a compact, the Mustang was a small car by American standards and the basic power unit ranged, in the first instance, from a 2.7-litre Falcon six-cylinder engine to a 4.7-litre V8. These were just the first of numerous engine options which grew in range and complexity as the years progressed. Suspension was conventional and predictable: coils and wishbones at the front and a cartsprung rear. In September 1964 the existing body styles were joined by a third, a 2 + 2 fastback, which came closest to the GT concept. It soon outstripped the convertible in popularity, though the hardtop remained the top seller. The first anniversary of the Mustang's announcement fell in April 1965, and Ford took the opportunity to announce the introduction of a 'GT' package though it was only available on the 225 and 271 bhp V8. This boasted front disc brakes, a special radiator grille, five-dial instrument panel and throaty exhaust pipes. This 'bolt on' theme, which was intended to turn a standard car into a 'GT', was to be avidly copied the world over.

A few months prior to the announcement of the GT package, former racing driver Carroll Shelby introduced 'his' Mustang, the GT-350, based on the 2 + 2 fastback finished in white with an optional blue 'Le Mans' stripe, and black interior. This came about when Ford approached Shelby, who had a distinguished sports car racing career, and had decided to become a small scale manufacturer of high performance cars. His first effort was the Ford V8-engined AC Cobra open two-seater of 1962. This established contact between the two and, when Ford wanted someone to challenge the Chevrolet Corvettes in Sports Car Club of America competitions, it was Shelby to whom they turned. Ford was adamant that the cars would be outwardly identical to the production version and to qualify, Shelby-modified Mustangs had to be built for homologation purposes. They soon proved their worth and these Shelby Mustangs were national class champions from 1965 until 1967. Although originally for the track, it was also decided to market the Shelby Mustang as a road model.

These cars were built to specifications similar to the track version and were offered with 271 bhp version of the Hi-Performance option of the 4.7-litre V8 and all-synchromesh close ratio gearbox, although they were heavier than the racing Mustangs. These 130 mph (209 kmh) cars were considerably faster than the 115 mph (185 kmh) of the equivalent road cars.

It did not take the other members of the American 'Big Three' long to respond to the Mustang phenomena. General Motors came up with the Chevrolet Camaro and Pontiac Firebird while Chrysler challenged with the Plymouth Barracuda. Consequently Ford updated the original Mustang for 1967, developing a car both wider and longer than its predecessor, but this shape endured only until 1968. The model was completely revised for 1969 and, from thereon, there has always been a Mustang in the Ford model line up.

As no less than 1.7 million Mustangs were sold between 1964 and 1967, it comes as no suprise to find Ford's British subsidiary developing its own two-door long bonnet/short boot version of the highly successful transatlantic formula. This represented a considerable shift in emphasis from a company that, in the 1950s, had produced sound, value for money but distinctly non-sporting products. The winds of change that blew through Ford's Detroit headquarters did not take long to reach Dagenham. In 1961 Ford had introduced its 1.3 litre Classic saloon, which proved to be a slow selling, underpowered model. In mid-1962 came a 1500 cc version and, in an effort to pep up the model's appeal, the following year, a 78 bhp version of its two-door Capri equivalent was named the GT. It thus became the first car by a mainstream British motor manufacturer to be so described but also marks the starting point of the slow dilution of the initials' hitherto near impeccable credentials.

Meanwhile the Classic had been followed in 1962 by the

Cortina saloon, which proved to be the fastest selling car in the history of the British motor industry, with one million examples being built by the time that the model was replaced by its Mark 2 derivative in 1966. As a private venture, a most unusual state of affairs at Ford, a sporting version was developed and Henry Ford II drove the prototype at the corporate launch of the mainstream Cortina at the Montlhery circuit in June 1962. He personally gave the project the go-ahead as it perfectly complemented Detroit's contemporary thinking. Based on the more robust Australian version of the Cortina, what became the GT in 1963 proved a popular car but the precedent of applying the GT label to a family saloon was firmly established.

With such developments, it comes as no surprise to find Dagenham beginning work on a British version of the Mustang from late 1964 and, appropriately, the project was given the Colt coding. The brief visualized the use of the full British range of existing Ford engines, together with a variety of trim options which echoed the Mustang's requirements. But, above all, this sporting car had to be 'available at a family budget price'.

As in the case of the American car, styling concepts were gathered from numerous sources, from the parent company in America and the firm's still separate German arm. Consumer clinics, where members of the public are invited to see and comment on manufacturers' projected models, were held in London and all over Europe, as far afield as Milan, as well as Geneva, Hamburg, Amsterdam and Brussels, which underlined the company's intention to sell the new model all over the Continent. By June 1966 Ford of Britain was given the go ahead to develop the Colt and the £20 million production and development programme was based on a clay model which had been produced by Ford in America. The new car remained the Colt until November 1967, when it became the Capri, which revived memories of the sporty two-door version of the Classic. The Colt name, by contrast found its way on to Japanese Mitsubishi products from 1965.

As the project developed, it was overtaken by events when Ford's British operations were merged with Germany's to create Ford of Europe in 1967. As originally conceived, it was intended to build the Capri at Ford's new plant at Halewood on Merseyside. But with the integration of Ford's European operation, it was also decided to build the car at the company's Cologne factory. This meant it had to be capable of being powered by Ford Germany's range of V engines.

The Capri made its international debut in January 1969 and the Brussels Motor Show was appropriately chosen to underline its very European appeal. The finished car clearly revealed in-house Mustang associations, as the long bonnet/short boot line had been preserved intact, though a less desirable inheritance were the imitation air scoops, just ahead of the rear wheel arches. Here, at long last, was a mass-produced version of the Grand Touring concept, available at £890 (in its most basic form), that had hitherto been available only to a small, exclusive clientele. Little wonder that Ford proclaimed the Capri as 'the car you've always promised yourself'.

The two-door, four-seater coupé bodywork proved remarkably resilient and enjoyed an 18-year production run, the longest of any post-war European Ford model. It was face-lifted in 1974, making it longer, wider and higher than its predecessors. The phoney air scoops thankfully disappeared and, more significantly, a tailgate was introduced. It was further refined in 1978. The model survived in this form until 1987, by which time 1.8 million had been built. The concept was to be widely copied by other manufacturers.

Mechanically the car was stock Ford with MacPherson strut independent front suspension and a cartsprung rear. The lowest capacity British version was powered by the 1.3-litre engine from the contemporary Escort saloon. This cheapest Capri was a somewhat breathless 85 mph (136 kmh) performer. Next came the by now inevitable GT version, with crossflow cylinder head and 90 mph (144 kmh) though the 1600 GT was just a 100 mph (160 kmh) car. Then there was the V4-powered 2000 GT, although it was not until September 1969 that the top line £1,386 3-litre version with the necessary bonnet bulge as the only indication of its V6 engine became available. This 114 mph (183 kmh) car was, in truth, the only model in the Capri range to really approach the concept of the true Grand Tourer.

The German version of the Capri was available in 1.2-litre to 3-litre forms and, interestingly enough, the model was more popular in that country than in Britain. It was built there exclusively from 1976. The Capri also had the distinction of capturing a greater number of customers from competing makes than any other Ford model.

With its new found enthusiasm for motor sport, Ford attempted to buy Ferrari in 1964, the most famous name in the motor racing world. Up until then the Modena company had remained proudly independent but money was always short and owning the firm would have dramatically complemented Ford's new Total Performance image. The protracted negotiations finally came to nothing, but they did, nevertheless, highlight the vulnerability of Italy's most illustrious marque. Perhaps inevitably, it would be Fiat which acquired a 50 per cent interest in Ferrari in 1969 which gave it effective control of the firm's Gran Turismo road cars. This left Ferrari himself to look after the racing side of the business which was always his first love.

As it happened, Ferrari was having to deal with an unexpected success in the shape of the Dino, introduced in 1967 and the best-selling Ferrari road car of its day. The firm had been toying with the idea of building a small car since the late 1950s. In 1959 the firm had created an 850 cc prototype which developed, in 1962, into the ASA 1000 mentioned in Chapter Two.

Like all Ferrari road cars, the Dino has a strong racing pedigree. In 1956, Ferrari's son Dino had died at the tragically early age of 24. Just prior to his death, he had opted for a V6 configuration for a new generation of Ferrari Formula 2 cars, though perhaps the presence of Vittorio Jano, who had joined Ferrari from Lancia in 1955, and was well versed with V6 engines in the pioneering Lancia Aurelia road car, had a great influence on this decision. The first Jano-designed V6-engined Formula 2 car, named Dino, appeared in 1957 and was also enlarged for Formula 1 events.

In 1960 all Ferrari's Grand Prix cars went mid-engined and the sports racers followed suit. One such was the V6-powered 166P coupé of 1965 and its distinctive, curvaceous bodywork represents the starting point for the lines of the Dino road cars. Displayed on the Pininfarina stand, it was titled the 206S GT Speciale, so anticipating the 206S

The starting point for the Dino line was displayed on Pininfarina's stand at the 1965 Paris show. It was described as the Dino 206 S Speciale, built on a racing chassis so the engine was longitudinally mounted.

sports-racer of the following year. (Ferrari's V6 and V8 engines used a different type of designation from the V12 variety, so Type 206 referred to a 2-litre [20 decilitres] six-cylinder engine). The show car was a sensational mid-engined coupé with distinctive curved rear window treatment. As it was effectively a rebodied sports-racing chassis, its 2-litre V6 twin-overhead camshaft engine was located fore and aft.

A further Dino prototype appeared at the 1966 Turin Show, though the power unit was still longitudinally located. Also at the show was a *Fiat* front-engined Dino model. Ferrari had been intent on using the Franco Rocchi designed 2-litre unit for Formula 2 racing from 1967. But the regulations demanded that the engine be derived from a mass-produced unit. No less than 500 were required for homologation, an impossible figure for Ferrari as a low capacity, specialist manufacturer. So Fiat undertook to manufacture the V6 and also used it in its own car which would also carry the Dino name.

The finished car was revealed at the 1967 Turin Show. It differed from the earlier prototypes in that instead of being longitudinally mounted, the 1987 cc V6 engine was transversely located behind the driver. The chassis was a substantial ladder frame of oval and rectangular tubes and the all-independent suspension was by coil springs and wishbones. Interestingly the car was not badged a Ferrari but a Dino, as there were thoughts about developing the name as a separate marque.

But in reality the 1967 Turin car was little more than another Pininfarina prototype and production proper of this 140 mph (225 kmh) coupé did not begin until the spring of 1969. Scaglietti in Modena produced the bodywork to Pininfarina's design and about 100 examples of the original 206

The production Dino had a transversely-mounted 2-litre V6 engine which was uprated to 2418 cc in 1969, when the model was redesignated the 246. This example dates from 1973, the Dino's penultimate production year.

Perhaps the quintessance of the 250 GT Ferrari line, the 250 GT Berlinetta Lusso is one of the most sought after models in the range. Only about 350 were built between 1962 and 1964. This example dates from the latter year and was Pinin Farina's own car.

GT Dino were built by the end of the year. It was replaced by the larger capacity 246 GT, with 2418 cc engine and slightly longer wheelbase. It was also heavier and the engine had an iron rather than an aluminium cylinder block. External changes were minimal. The Dino remained in production until 1974, so helping to tide Ferrari over the first effects of the 1973 oil crisis. A record 2,732 Dino GTs were built, while an open version of 1972 accounted for a further 1,180 cars. The Dino engine also continued in production in the in-house, rally-winning Lancia Stratos of 1972–9.

But, at the other extreme, Ferrari was continuing to build exquisite, low production V12 Grand Tourers. In 1964 came the first of a new generation of GTs, in the shape of the 275 GTB of 3967 cc. It was technically significant as, for the first time, the five-speed gearbox was rear mounted in unit with the differential and it was also the first Ferrari to feature independent rear suspension. As usual, Pininfarina was responsible for the coupé bodywork. It was the first GT Ferrari to be fitted with cast alloy wheels, in this instance by Campagnolo, in place of the customary Borrani wire spoked ones. This 145 mph (233 kmh) 3.3-litre car could be used for touring or racing and was available with all-aluminium bodywork and six, rather than the usual three Weber carburettors. The 275 went into Series 2 form, with minor body modifications in 1965 and production ceased in the following year, after approximately 450 had been built.

It was replaced that year by the visually similar 275 GTB/4, the significance of the suffix being that it was the first road-going Ferrari in which the engine was fitted with four overhead camshafts, that is to say two per cylinder bank, rather than one as had been the case on the V12s of every

The 2 + 2 Ferrari line began with the Pininfarina styled 250 GTE line in 1960 and was succeeded in 1964 by the longer 330 GT 2 + 2, which lasted for four years and of which this is an example. It was powered by a 4-litre single overhead camshaft V12 engine. About 1000 examples were built.

Ferrari introduced all independent suspension in the 275 GTB of 1964 and, two years later, came the visually similar Pininfarina bodied 275 GTB/4, which reflected that the 3.3-litre V12 had, for the first time, twin overhead camshafts per cylinder bank. This example dates from 1968.

Ferrari road car since 1947. It did, however, enjoy a relatively short production life and lasted only until 1968.

These models were uncompromising two-seaters but, in 1964, Ferrari replaced his 2.9-litre 250 GTE 2+2 with the 4-litre 330 GT 2+2, with similar bodywork to its predecessor but initially with ugly twin headlights. The increased seating capacity meant that this was a popular model, available with power steering and air conditioning, and about 1,000 had been built by the time that the car was discontinued in 1968. It was replaced by the 4.4-litre 365 GT 2+2, with the all-independent suspension pioneered on the 275 GTB, and the rear axle-mounted gearbox. This big 150 mph (241 kmh) car lasted only until 1971.

There was inevitable cross pollination between the 2+2 Ferraris and the two-seater GTs, most notably the 330 GTC of 1966, which was powered by the 330 GT 2+2's 4-litre engine mounted in the 275 GTB's chassis. The bodywork was also something of a cocktail but a very successful one. Ferrari took the 400 Superamerica front and succeeded in successfully combining it with the rear of the open version of the 275 GTB. This civilized, well-appointed Grand Tourer was not as fleet of foot as some of its Maranello contemporaries, but was still capable of well over 90 mph (144 kmh) and, for 1969, the model was fitted with an enlarged 4.4-litre engine and accordingly renamed the 365 GTC. It remained in production in this form until 1970.

The performance of the 365 GTC dramatically contrasted with that of the 365 GTB/4, better known as the legendary Daytona. This appeared at the 1968 Paris Motor Show and at the time was the most expensive, at £8,563, and fastest Ferrari road car ever built. The 174 mph (280 kmh) model was powered by a 4.4-litre version of the twin-camshaft V12. For the Daytona, which was the last of the big, V12 front-engined Berlinettas, Pininfarina produced a magnificently proportioned coupé body with finely sculptured front end and the headlamps covered by clear plastic. Suspension was all-independent, with all-round unequal length A arms and coil springs, as pioneered on the 275 GTB. The gearbox was similarly rear mounted.

Despite its weight at 32.5 cwt (1,601 kgs), the Daytona was an impressive performer with formidable acceleration and, by mid-1971, production had reached the 500 mark, which meant that it qualified for the Group Four Special Grand

The legendary Ferrari Daytona was built between 1968 and 1973. Its engine was a 4.4-litre twin cam, which resulted in a top speed of close on 175 mph (281 kph). The Pininfarina bodywork is still breathlessly impressive. Over 1300 Daytonas were built.

The last of the front-engined, four-cam V12 Ferraris ceased production in 1989. This long-running Pininfarina styled model started life in 4.4 litre form as the 365 GT4 in 1972, was enlarged to 4.8 litres in 1976 and redesignated the 400 GT. By its 1989 demise, capacity had grown again, to 4.9 litres, and the model was known as the 412.

Touring class. This magnificent vehicle endured until 1973 by which time 1,350 had been built.

The 365 GTC was discontinued in 1970 and Ferrari had no two-seater with which to replace it until the arrival of the 365 GTC4 of 1971–2. This was powered by what was, in effect, the Daytona's engine but with sidedraught Webers instead of that model's downdraught units. However, the gearbox was in unit with the engine rather than the differential. The Pininfarina body was perhaps a little uninspired. Power steering and air conditioning were standard fitments, as demanded by the all-important American market.

Mechanically the 365 GTC/4 formed the basis of the 365 GT4 2 + 2 by employing its 4.4-litre engine and, similarly, the five-speed gearbox was mounted in unit with it. Introduced in 1972, derivatives remained in production until 1989, 17 years after it first appeared. This is largely the result of Pininfarina producing an extraordinarily assured, well proportioned coupé bodywork which has proved visually durable over the years. Although its wheelbase was 2 in (50 mm) longer than its 365 2 + 2 predecessor, in overall terms it was 7½ in (190 mm) shorter. This resulted in more passenger and luggage space and consequently the car has enjoyed the longest production run of any road going Ferrari.

Up until the 1960s, Ferrari's position as Italy's premier manufacturer of Grand Touring cars was an undisputed one. But Ferruccio Lamborghini, who had made a fortune as a tractor manufacturer, was determined to challenge the Maranello company's supremacy. He attempted this with the 350 GT of 1963 though it was not until the 1967 arrival of the Miura, the world's first series production mid-engined car, that the challenge became truly apparent. Lamborghini was born in 1916 on his father's estate at Renazzo, only 20 miles (32 km) from Ferrari's birthplace of Modena. Not wanting to follow in his father's agricultural footsteps, he decided on an engineering career and graduated from the Fratelli Taddia Institute near Bologna just before the outbreak of the Second World War. After service in the Italian army and spending time as a British prisoner of war on the island of Rhodes, where he ran the motor pool, he decided to open a garage at Cento, near his birthplace. Soon afterwards he built a tractor from scrap parts for his father who was desperate for mechanization. This represented the starting point of Lamborghini's career as a tractor manufacturer and, in 1949, he established *Lamborghini Trattrici* (Lamborghini Tractors) on his garage site. By the late 1950s he had become one of Italy's largest tractor makers and was also to prove a successful manufacturer of central heating systems. It was then that he turned his attention to fast, expensive cars and decided to enter the business. As a wealthy industrialist, Lamborghini had owned exotic cars aplenty and his stable invariably included the latest Maserati, OSCA, Jaguar and Ferraris. His target was to challenge Ferrari and the car would therefore be powered by a V12 engine but better than anything then being produced at Maranello . . .

A brand new, lavishly equipped factory was built at Sant'Agata Bolognese, just north of the Milan-to-Bologna

The first Lamborghini was the Touring-bodied 350 GT of 1964 and this example is pictured in front of the Lamborghini factory at Sant' Agata Bolognese. It was powered by a purpose-built 3.4-litre V12 with twin-cam heads, unlike the contemporary Ferrari, while the chassis featured all-independent suspension.

autostrada and Lamborghini's first car, the 350 GTV, was revealed at the 1963 Turin Show. Its coupé body was the work of Bertone's former chief stylist, Franco Scaglione, and was an uneasy amalgam of styles. But the V12 engine, displayed alongside the car was its *tour de force*. Designed by former Ferrari engineer Giotto Bizzarrini, it was of 3464 cc and, unlike contemporary Ferraris, used twin-overhead camshafts per cylinder bank rather than one. Similarly the tubular chassis boasted all independent suspension, by unequal length wishbones and coil springs, at a time when Ferrari offered a cartsprung rear axle.

But when the model made its debut proper at the 1964 Geneva Motor Show some changes had been made to the specification. The coachwork, a great improvement on the original, was now by Touring while the V12 was detuned from its original 360 bhp to 270. Consequently the V suffix for *Veloce* (fast) was deleted. Even so the 350 GT had a top speed of 165 mph (265 kmh) but production proper did not begin until the end of the year. In 1966 the 350 developed into the 400 GT 2 + 2 in which capacity was increased to 3.9 litres, though this engine was also available for the original car which continued in production. The 350 had employed a proprietory five-speed ZF gearbox but its derivative was fitted with a Lamborghini-built unit. Ironically, although the 400's engine was a larger capacity than that of its predecessor, the car was about 10 mph (16 kmh) slower at 155 mph (249 kmh) because its bodywork was heavier, Touring having abandoned its celebrated Superleggera body construction for this model. The 350 series Lamborghinis lasted until 1967, after 123 examples had been built, with 23 more cars with the 4-litre engine. The 400 2 + 2 cars remained in production until 1968, by which time 247 had been produced.

Alas, the celebrated *Carrozzeria Touring* finally closed its doors in January 1967 though a group of its employees continued in business in the employ of Mario Marazzi, a former sub-contractor. The Lamborghini 400 2 + 2 bodies were seen through and Marazzi came up with a new body, a slightly anonymous looking coupé, which was built on its chassis. It was called the Islero, after a Spanish fighting bull, as Lamboroghini had been born on 28 April under the Zodiac sign of Taurus and from thereon many of his model names had bull-fighting associations. The 160-mph (257-kmh) Islero was a faster car than its predecessor but it lacked the visual vitality which Pininfarina's bodywork gave the Ferrari chassis.

In 1965, however, Ferruccio Lamborghini found what he

With the arrival of the 4-litre Miura in 1966, Lamborghini found the image he had been seeking. The Bertone-styled model was the first significant mid-engined production car in the world. This example is sharing a Bertone stand with Lamborghini's four-seater Espada of 1968.

wanted in Bertone's chief stylist Marcello Gandini. Sant' Agata had a revolutionary chassis which required sensational coachwork to complement its radical mechanicals. In November 1964 Giampaolo Dallara replaced Bizzarrini and with his assistant Paolo Stanzani and New Zealander Bob Wallace, a test driver who did sterling work evaluating and developing Lamborghinis for the road, tried to interest Lamborghini in producing a sports-racing car. Greatly impressed by the mid-engined Ford GT 40, Dallara wanted to build a Lamborghini with a similar configuration. But the GT 40's V8-engine was mounted fore and aft and locating the Lamborghini V12-engine and gearbox similarly would have resulted in too long a car.

He therefore took a leaf out of Alec Issiognis's book and mounted the unit transversely across the chassis though behind, instead of in front of the driver. And just like the Mini – and there were plenty of Innocenti-built examples around to provide the inspiration – this new Lamborghini had its gearbox located in its sump, so drastically shortening the size of the combined unit.

Lamborghini responded positively to this concept, designated P 400 (*Postiere* [rear] 4-litre) though visualized a road car rather than one for the track. It would therefore be the world's first significant series production mid-engined road car. Furthermore Lamborghini recognized that the P 400 would be an impressive model in its own right and provide the marque with welcome publicity. The resulting chassis was duly displayed at the 1965 Turin Show and, immediately afterwards, Gandini of Bertone began work. The first car, finished in vivid orange/yellow paint, was completed just in time for the 1966 Geneva Motor Show. It was there that the P400 designation was replaced by an official model name: that of Miura, named after Don Eduardo Miura, a famous breeder of fighting bulls.

It was, unquestionably, the car of the show and supercar of the decade, despite inevitable noise and heat problems associated with the mid-engine location and the fact that it was 1967 before the 170 mph (273 kmh) 4-litre Miura became a production reality. In 1968 the factory built a record 184 Miuras. An S variant, with power boosted from 350 to 370 bhp, appeared in 1969 which put an edge on the car's acceleration though its top speed remained the same. What can be considered as the ultimate version of the Miura, the 385 bhp SV, appeared at the 1971 Turin Motor Show, though the following year the model ceased production. A total of 763 examples of this daring, ferocious car had been built.

Marcello Gandini's next sensational body for Lamborghini was displayed on the Bertone stand at the 1967 Turin Show. This was the four-seater Marzal, with distinctive gullwing doors, and a rear mounted six-cylinder engine, in effect half a Miura unit. The Marzal, 'the raging bull of March', never entered production though the four-seater Espada, which appeared at the 1968 Geneva Show, did. It was destined for a production life of ten years, lasting until 1978 and with 1,217 built, this was the most numerically successful Lamborghini car.

In the meantime the 2 + 2 Islero was nearing replacement and, once again, Gandini was requested to style its suc-

The concept of European coachwork combined with an American V8 engine was echoed in Italy by the Bertone-styled Iso Rivolta of 1962. On this occasion a 5.3-litre Chevrolet Corvette engine was employed. The model survived until 1970.

cessor. The Jarama of 1970 was Espada based and shared its 4-litre engine though had a shorter wheelbase. Although the Jarama was Bertone styled, it was built by Marazzi and survived until 1978.

Also sharing the Lamborghini stand at the 1970 Turin Motor Show was a completely new Lamborghini and the first car from Sant' Agata Bolognese not to be powered by the legendary V12 engine. The Urraco was intended to combine the road holding attributes of a mid-engined location *and* four seats. The power unit was new; a 2463 cc V8, with a belt-driven single overhead camshaft per cylinder bank. This was a more cost-conscious design than the big V12-engined cars and was the work of Paolo Stanzani, who had taken over from Dallara as Lamborghini's design maestro in 1968 when the latter left to join the Iso concern. Stanzani dispensed with the unequal length wishbones which had hitherto been used on all Lamborghini models and instead opted for cheaper all round MacPherson struts. Once again bodywork was by Bertone, which also built the hull. However, it would be 1972 before the Urraco entered production and, alas, it soon developed a reputation for unreliability and unacceptably high interior noise levels, all of which suggested lack of development.

In 1974 came the more reliable Uracco P300, with a 3-litre derivative of the original engine, with chain driven twin-overhead camshafts, the belts of the earlier engine having proved troublesome. A 1994 cc version aimed for the Italian market was also offered because a lower VAT rate was charged on cars of less than 2 litres capacity. The original 2½-litre car continued to be produced until 1974 and a derivative was created for the American market though it only lasted until 1976. The 3-litre version remained available until 1979, its potential never fully realized.

There is a link between Lamborghini and the American V8-engined Iso Rivolta, which appeared in 1962. The common factor was that the model's chassis was designed by none other than Giotto Bizzarrini, who completed the assignment prior to starting work on the 350 Lamborghini. Renzo Rivolta's Milan company had begun building motor cycles in 1949 and its 236 cc Isetta of 1953–55 set the fashion for the 'bubble' cars of the 1950s. The Bertone-bodied four-seater Rivolta was in marked contrast to this previous project and was very much in the spirit of the American V8-engined Facel Vega of the previous decade. It featured a platform chassis, coil and wishbone independent suspension and a de Dion rear axle. Power came from the General Motors 5.4-litre Chevrolet V8 as used by the contemporary

Corvette, with automatic transmission or manual four or five-speed boxes. The V8 developed 300 bhp in its basic form though could be had in a more potent 355 bhp state. The performance and reliability of this transatlantic V8 ensured that the Rivolta was a popular model. Output continued until 1970. It was replaced by the mechanically similar Lele, with automatic transmission and new Bertone bodywork.

In 1965 a shorter wheelbase version, the successful and more potent Grifo entered production, powered by the same 5.4-litre V8, though this was a genuine two seater. Engine capacity progressively increased and the 7-litre version pushed the model's top speed up to the 186 mph (299 kmh), making it one of the fastest production cars of its day. The Grifo remained available until 1974, which was when Iso ceased production for the first time, one of the many car companies which came to grief in the financial cataclysm that followed the 1973 Arab/Israeli war. The firm was briefly revived and continued to build the Lele and its four-door Fidia predecessor but finally stopped making cars in 1979.

The hardworking Giotti Bizzarrini was also soon at work on a GT that appeared under his own name in 1965. In 1962 he had established Prototipi Bizzarrini in Livorno, initially to produce prototypes for other manufacturers, though he subsequently diversified into small-scale GT production on his own account. The GT Strada 5300 shared a similar Bertone two-seater body to the Iso while suspension and the 5.4-litre Chevrolet V8 also mirrored those of the Milan car. Although this meant 145 mph (233 kmh) performance, the Bizzarrini GT found few takers and was discontinued in 1967 after only two years' production.

Undeterred, Bizzarrini tried again and the smaller Europa 1900 of 1966 was the result. Styling was once again the work of Bertone and suspension was all-independent by coils and wishbones in the Italian manner. Bizzarrini had used a Fiat 1500 engine in pre-production examples but the eventual power unit was, like his larger car, courtesy of General Motors, though in this instance its German Opel subsidiary. The 110 bhp 1.9 litre 'cam in head' unit made the light and handsome Europa a 125 mph (201 kmh) car. But Bizzarrini had as little success with this smaller GT as the large one and the small Livorno works finally closed its doors for car making in 1969.

Altogether more enduring was the De Tomaso marque, created by Argentinian born Alessandro De Tomaso, who had settled in Italy in 1957. A former racing driver for Maserati and OSCA, during the early 1960s he produced a number of styling exercises and one-off cars which became regular features of every Turin motor show. But in 1966 he astonished the public by unveiling what was destined to be his first production model, the Mangusta, which followed Iso precedent by being powered by an American V8 engine, in this instance a 4.7-litre Ford unit. Adventurously it was mid-engined, in the manner of the Lamborghini Miura. Suspension was by all round coils and wishbones while coachwork was by Ghia, and De Tomaso purchased the Turin styling house in 1967. Performance of this two-door two-seater was 150 mph (241 kmh) plus, thanks to the 300 bhp V8; the Mangusta remained in production until 1971 but was overshadowed by the Pantera, an altogether more practical offering.

This was also mid-engined but more refined than its predecessor. It was, inevitably, Ghia styled but there were structural differences in that the Pantera was built up around a unit-construction bodyshell (though the suspension was effectively carried over). The 5.7-litre Ford V8 engine was a stock unit while the five-speed ZF gearbox perpetuated previous practice.

The car was launched at the 1970 New York Show for reasons that will soon become apparent. On paper this was an impressive 160 mph (257 kmh) GT and De Tomaso succeeded in getting Ford to market the car in North America through its Lincoln Mercury dealerships. Unfortunately there were difficulties. Production took some time to build up and there were quality and reliability problems. Then came the 1973 oil crisis and what had looked like an impressive Supercar almost overnight became a gas guzzling liability. In June 1974 the Ford deal was unscrambled after about 6,000 cars had been imported. Ford purchased Ghia from De Tomaso in 1973, though, amazingly, the Pantera remains in production at the time of writing, an incredible 18 years after it had first appeared.

In the meantime De Tomaso opted for a conventional front-engined model in the shape of Longchamps of 1972. It had its origins in the four-door Deauville, a Jaguar XJ6 lookalike, introduced at the 1970 Turin Show, which falls outside the scope of this study. But its two-door derivative does not. Based on a shortened Deauville floorpan, the Longchamps was powered by the proven 5.7-litre Ford V8 engine and employed all independent suspension. Jaguar-like coils and wishbones were used and three-speed automatic transmission featured, though a five-speed ZF unit was also available. This was a luxury two-seater in the spirit of the Mercedes-Benz 450 SLC, though quality was hardly on a par with Stuttgart. This two-plus-two also con-

The Maserati Mistral arrived in 1963 and its mechanicals were essentially carried over from the earlier Sebring. It was accordingly powered by a 3.6-litre six-cylinder twin-overhead camshaft engine. The coachwork was by Frua and the model continued until 1969.

tinues to be currently listed.

Alessandro De Tomaso would eventually become the owner of Maserati but, in 1968, the French Citroen concern had bought a majority stake in the firm from the Orsi family, consolidated by outright ownership in 1971. But back in 1964 Maserati was building on the success of its 3500 GT, introduced in 1958. In 1962 had come its Sebring derivative, which lasted until 1966, and its Mistral two-seater coupé successor made its debut at the 1963 Turin Show. The engine was Maserati's faithful twin-cam six, available in 3.7 and 4-litre forms and suspension was the established front coils and wishbones and cartsprung rear. The Frua-bodied Mistral remained available until 1970 and was the last Maserati to be six-cylinder powered. A total of 948 examples were built, making it, by Maserati standards, a strong seller. In 1965 had come the supplementary Vignale-styled 4.7-litre V8-powered four-seater Mexico; although capable of 135 mph (217 kmh), it hardly had the acceleration to match and lasted until 1968.

Far more successful was the Ghibli of 1967. This Ghia-styled coupé was the work of Giorgetto Giugario, soon to create his own Ital Design consultancy. Power was once again by the proven four-camshaft 4.7-litre V8, the frame was tubular but, less desirably, the cartsprung rear axle persisted. This good looker was a 165 mph (265 kmh) car and endured until 1973, latterly in 4.9-litre form. With 1,149 examples produced, the Ghibli was the best selling Maserati of its day.

The V8 was reduced in capacity to 4.2 litres for the Vignale-bodied four-seater unitary construction Indy of 1969. Later power was upped to 4.7 and 4.9 litres. It remained in production until 1974 and with 1,136 cars sold in was second only to the Ghibli in sales.

Maserati waited until 1971 to go mid-engined. This was the Bora – like so many of Maserati models it was named after a wind – in this instance the one that blew off the Italian coast north towards the Adriatic Sea. Announced at the 1971 Geneva show, the Bora's lines were the work of Giugario's Ital Design, while its aerodynamic lines reflected Citroen commitment in that quarter. The 4.7-litre V8 was longitudinally located behind the driving compartment and a five-speed gearbox was employed. For the first time on a Maserati, suspension was all independent and by coils and wishbones. Brakes were courtesy of the Citroen SM, for which Maserati had provided a 2.7-litre V6 engine, with its associated engine-driven pump and hydraulic accumulator. In view of its intrusive engine location, the 160 mph (257 kmh) Bora was an uncompromising two-seater. Production lasted until 1980.

It was followed in 1972 by a smaller but similarly mid-engined model, the Merak, which was powered by a 3-litre version of the SM's V6 unit. In view of this more compact engine, two small but impractical rear seats were introduced. The Merak proved to be the most popular model of its day, with about 1,300 cars sold by 1975. That year the model was uprated, the lighter, more powerful SS lasting until 1981.

The Khamsin, which appeared at the 1972 Turin show, although it did not enter production until 1974, was the last Maserati to be produced during the Citroen era. It was a stylish though impractical four-seater and was the first Maserati to be styled by Bertone, and the work of Marcello Gandini, who had the Lamborghini Miura to his credit. The 4.9-litre V8 was front-mounted and suspension all independent. This 140 mph (225 kmh) car was built in small numbers until 1981.

Citroen's ownership of Maserati is echoed in the mid-engined Bora of 1971 with its wind tunnel tested bodywork, styled by Ital Design. Power came from Maserati's proven 4.9-litre V8 engine.

Top The 140 mph (225 kmh) Khamsin was the first Bertone-styled Maserati. Introduced in 1974, it was a 4.9-litre front V8-engined model and was built until 1981.

Above Although the 1971 Alfa Romeo Montreal gives the appearance of a mid-engined car it was, in fact, a front-engined one, in this instance the power unit was the firm's sports racing 2.6-litre V8 unit.

Bertone was also responsible for the lines of the Alfa Romeo Montreal which first appeared as a show car at the 1967 Expo 67 World Fair held at Montreal. The coupé suggested a mid-engine; in fact it concealed conventionally located Giulia running gear.

When the Montreal was unveiled at the 1970 Geneva Show, it perpetuated the Giulia's coil and wishbone front suspension and coil sprung rear axle. However, the engine was much more exciting and was a de-tuned version of the firm's Type 33 2.6-litre V8 engine, with Spica fuel injection and 200 bhp on tap. This resulted in a 135 mph (217 kmh) GT but the Montreal only lasted for six years after entering production in 1971. This was in part due to there being no right-hand-drive version until 1974 but, more significantly, Alfa Romeo's racing department replaced its V8s with a flat-12 in 1975. Production ceased two years later, in 1977.

Meanwhile the evergreen Bertone-styled Giulia coupé continued to be produced in a bewildering number of variations. In 1967 the existing 1570 cc Sprint GT Veloce was enlarged to 1750 cc and remained available in this form until 1972. Even more popular, with 80,623 sold between 1966 and 1972, was its smaller GT Junior variant with only 1290 cc but it still provided classic twin-overhead camshaft Alfa Romeo motoring, a practical GT for the young family man. Capacity was upped to 1600 cc from 1974 and lasted until 1979. A 2-litre GTV version had ceased production two years earlier.

Although Alfa Romeo's Fiat rivals were deeply and successfully committed to the mass market, in 1967 the firm unveiled an upmarket GT in the shape of the Dino. It shared the same name, and 1.9-litre V6 engine, as its Ferrari stablemate, with Fiat building the power unit for both manufacturers. The model had begun life as a Pininfarina-bodied open car in 1966 but the closed model was rather longer. Suspension was coils and wishbones at the front and with single leaf half elliptic rear springs, a first for Fiat. The use of a limited-slip differential was another innovation. In this form, the Dino was a 115 mph (185 kmh) car though perhaps performance did not quite echo its handsome Bertone lines. Consequently, in 1969, the open and closed versions were revised. The main mechanical change was the substitution of the light-alloy V6 with a cast-iron Fiat 130 engine of 2418 cc, which was also a V6. There were also radical suspension changes and the live rear axle was replac-

Alfa Romeo's Bertone-styled coupé enjoyed an impressive production run. It began life as the 1600 cc Giulia Sprint GT in 1963 and subsequently evolved into the 2-litre 2000 GT Veloce, shown here, in 1971 and lasted for a further six years.

ed by an independent layout with coil springs and trailing arms also courtesy of the 130. Both brakes and wheels were uprated and the model continued to be built at the Ferrari factory at Maranello until 1972.

Far more popular was Fiat's Grand Tourer for everyman, the 124 Sport of 1967. Although based on the best-selling 124 saloon of the previous year, it differed radically in being powered by an enlarged twin overhead camshaft derivative of its 1200 cc pushrod engine. However, the concept of a sporting 124 had initially been established with the arrival of the 124 Sport Spider, which first appeared at the 1966 Turin Show.

Produced on a shortened version of the 124 floor pan, suspension was essentially the same, with coils and wishbones at the front while the live rear axle was coil spring suspended with radius arms and transverse location. Similarly disc brakes were fitted all round. But the principal difference was its 1438 cc engine, which had a new cylinder head with twin overhead camshafts, progressively driven by toothed neoprene belts. Not only that. Capacity was enlarged to 1438 cc by upping the bore size from 68 to 80 mm. The 90 bhp unit gave the model a speed of about 101 mph (162 kmh). A five-speed gearbox was fitted, while the car's open body was designed and built in Pininfarina.

The closed Sport version, which followed in 1967, was, by contrast, competently styled in-house by Fiat but reverted to the original wheelbase of the saloon and was therefore heavier than the open car, though this was compensated for by the better aerodynamics of its closed bodywork and it accordingly shared the Spider's top speed, if not its acceleration. Despite this, the 124 Sport handled and performed well and was praised by the contemporary motoring press as very much of a driver's car, happy to cruise all day at 90 mph (144 kmh), well styled and engineered; in short, a thoroughly modern Grand Tourer. A five-speed gearbox was soon made available as an option.

In 1969 this popular model was revised and, while the original 1438 cc engine was retained, a 1608 cc unit, courtesy of the 125 Special saloon, also became available. With the arrival of this large power unit, top speed remained about the same but acceleration was improved. The Sport remained in production until 1972 though the Spider, which preceded it, soldiered on for a further 10 years, buoyed up by American sales where it enjoyed some popularity.

The Dino was a conventional front-engined car but, in 1972, Fiat introduced its first mid-engined GT, the X1/9. However, this particular project hailed from the Bertone concern. Its original brief from Fiat had been to produce an open version of the 128 front wheel drive model. One was accordingly built but Bertone took the initiative and produced a mid-engined closed version which particularly appealed to Fiat's chairman, Giovanni Agnelli. Fiat accordingly gave the project the green light and its engineers were soon at work interpreting the Bertone styling sketches which were the work of Marcello Gandini, best known for the lines of Lamborghini's sensational Miura. The new Fiat was introduced in 1972 and it says much for the competence of Gandini's work that the car is still in production at the time of writing.

The 75 bhp 1290 cc single overhead camshaft engine/gearbox unit from the Fiat 128 Sport 1300 was mounted diagonally behind the driving compartment with all independent suspension by MacPherson struts and coil springs. A detachable top was standard equipment and there was room for it in the front luggage compartment when it was not in use. The road holding advantages of the mid-engine location were apparent even if the driving compartment was a little cramped for the more ample driver! In its original form the X1/9 was a 100 mph (160 kmh) car, though the detoxing equipment demanded for the all-important American market meant that transatlantic examples could just manage 95 mph (152 kmh).

Unfortunately for Fiat, the 1970s were the years of the energy crisis and the disappointing performance of the American version resulted in the car's mechanicals being revised. For the 1979 model year, the 128 engine was replac-

Last of the V-engined Lancias, the Fulvia coupé of 1964 was far more successful than its boxy saloon predecessor. Capacities ranged from 1.2 to 1.6 litres. It survived until 1976.

ed by the 1498 cc Ritmo unit and there were changes to the interior. But in 1981, in the wake of the second energy crisis and the strength of Japanese competition on the American market, annual X1/9 production reached an all time low of 4,619 cars. Such volumes were of little interest to Fiat. But Bertone, which was delivering fully-trimmed shells to the car company, took over full responsibility for the model. In 1982 the Fiat badge was replaced by the Bertone monogram and, as the world emerged from its second oil crisis, X1/9 production has progressively increased and this evergreen model is still going strong, 15 years after it first appeared.

In 1969 Fiat had bought the ailing Lancia company though, ironically, the firm had only recently introduced its best selling Fulvia based coupé. Paradoxically the model's boxy saloon car parent had been a flop. This arrived in 1963 and it was not until 1965 that its coupé derivative, styled by Pietro Castagnero, who had the saloon to his credit, made its appearance. Mechanicals were basically similar with a 1216 cc V4 twin-overhead camshaft engine, transverse leaf and wishbone front suspension and a cartsprung rear. This was a good looking 90 mph (144 kmh) car and during the next three years spawned a host of derivatives: the HF, with output boosted to 88 bhp, the Rallye with enlarged 1298 cc engine, while the 112 mph (180 kmh) 1.6 HF boasted a 1584 cc engine and five speed gearbox. In the meantime Fiat had absorbed the firm and, from 1972, the range was progressively simplified. The coupé endured until 1976 and with its demise went Lancia's last V engine, a feature of the marque since 1922.

Such was the strength and vitality of the Italian Grand Tourers, their influences were all too obvious in the booming British GT market and no more so than with the prestigious Aston Martin marque. In 1966 the firm had introduced its Touring-bodied DB6, its most numerically successful model in its range of DB4-derived cars. A total of 1,575 examples were built. The DB6 was a longer wheelbase version of its DB5 predecessor which improved rear passenger accommodation and there was a distinctive spoilered lip. Power came from the proven Marek designed 4-litre twin-cam six and the DB6 was nudging 150 mph (241 kmh). A Mark Two version, with larger wheels, accompanying flared arches and better rear seats appeared in 1969 and lasted until 1970.

For two years Aston Martin offered its customers a choice of models for, in 1967, the DBS was announced. As Touring had finally closed its doors, this new generation of Aston Martins was styled in house by William Towns. It was very

This picture highlights the problem faced by the world's specialist car makers who wanted to sell their products in America from 1968. Cars had to be driven into a block of concrete at 30 mph (48 kmh) to ensure that they met US safety regulations. Here a new Aston Martin DBS of 1968 passes the all-important test.

much in the spirit of the earlier cars though its 8 ft 6 in (2,844 mm) wheelbase was longer than the DB6's and it was also wider than its predecessors. This was to accommodate a V8 still under development, so the S was powered by the DB6's power unit until 1970, when the new engine finally arrived, though the six remained as an option until 1973. Mechanically, the DBS retained the coil and wishbone independent front suspension of its DB6 predecessor, though the live rear axle was replaced by a coil-sprung de Dion unit.

Tadek Marek had also been responsible for the new 5.3-litre V8 which finally arrived in 1970 and has formed the basis of every Aston Martin since 1973. An alloy block/wet liner unit with twin overhead camshafts per cylinder bank, it developed about 345 bhp in its original Bosch fuel injected form. Performance was a dramatic improvement on the DB6. The DBS V8, as it was originally known, was capable of 160 mph (257 kmh) with acceleration to match. It was instantly identifiable by its alloy rather than wire wheels. In 1972 came another change of name when David Brown sold Aston Martin, which he had owned since 1947, to a property concern, Company Developments. The DB initials were accordingly dropped and the model became the plain V8 with revised front end and its four small headlamps were replaced by two large ones. The following year four Weber carburettors took over from fuel injection. The V8 was to take Aston Martin through the most traumatic period in its history, a survival process that belongs to the next chapter.

Aston Martin had always been a low-production/high-cost car but, in 1965, MG introduced its popular and successful GT, directly inspired by an Aston Martin of 1950s vintage. MG had consolidated its position as the world's leading manufacturer of open sports cars when it replaced its ageing T Series cars in 1955 with the more up to date MGA which endured until 1962. By then over 100,000 examples had been built. A coupé version of the A had arrived for 1957 with the MGB roadster following in 1962.

The MGB GT was an example of a popular nomenclature applied to a coupé in the 1960s though it cannot be considered to be a true Grand Tourer because of its relatively pedestrian performance, 0 to 60 mph (96 kmh) in a little over 14 seconds, or slower than the smaller capacity Ford Cortina GT saloon. But it is relevant to our story because the faster though unsuccessful MGC was derived from it and the coupé version has more claim to GT status than its four cylinder predecessor.

Mechanically the GT was virtually identical to the open car, with 1.8-litre Austin engine and conventional coil and wishbone independent front suspension and cartsprung rear. Top speed was just over the 100 mph (160 kmh) mark, about the same as the roadster, though acceleration was inferior to that of the lighter open car, but redressed by the GT's superior aerodynamics. With the GT, MG's general manager John Thornley achieved his objective of producing a car 'which no managing director would be ashamed to leave in his car park'. The model experienced relatively few changes throughout its manufacturing life though, from 1976, both open and closed cars were disfigured by the fit-

Often likened to a 'poor man's E-type', the Michelotti-styled Triumph GT6 arrived in 1966. Initially criticized for its Herald-derived swing rear axle, this was rectified from 1969 and the model lasted until 1973.

ment of polyurethane bumpers for the all important American market. The MGB remained in production until 1980 by which time over half a million had been produced and, of these about a quarter, or 125,323, were GTs.

But there was an MG derivative which would have been much more in the spirit of its Aston Martin progenitor had it been successful. In the 1960s MG's BMC parent recognized that its long-running open Austin Healey 3000 sports car, which dated back, in essence, to 1952, was due for replacement. MG's Abingdon factory therefore developed a six-cylinder version of the MGB which would also be badged as an Austin Healey. A new engine derived from its original 2.9-litre power unit was produced by BMC but the resulting power unit was unexpectedly 44 lb (19.9 kg) heavier than its predecessor. Donald Healey was sufficiently discouraged to axe the Austin Healey version and the MGC appeared in open and closed forms in 1967.

Although externally similar to its four-cylinder stablemate, the C had undergone structural surgery to accommodate its six-cylinder engine. The B's front suspension had been replaced by torsion bars and larger wheels had been fitted. Outwardly its specifications looked impressive but the reality was that the mass of engine produced understeering problems and the 120 mph (193 kmh) model was discontinued in 1969 after only two years' production. A total of 8,999 cars were built and split almost evenly between roadsters and GTs.

MG's great rival in the sports car market was Triumph and although its TR series continued to be produced in open form until 1975, it had offered a GT in the shape of the GT6 in 1966. This had its origins in the Herald saloon of 1959, styled by Turin-based Giovanni Michelotti with distinctive backbone chassis and all independent suspension with swing axle rear. In 1962 came the similar Vitesse but powered by a 1596 cc version of the 2-litre engine of the soon to be announced 2000 saloon. Also launched in 1962 was a pretty Herald-based Spitfire open two-seater.

It was in 1963 that Triumph's chief engineer Harry Webster and Michelotti began thinking about a closed version of the Spitfire and experimentally produced a hardtop version with rear opening door. Although this was faster than its open equivalent, it was heavier on petrol, so the Vitesse's 1.6-litre six was substituted but, by the time that the GT6 model entered production, it had the 2000 saloon's 2-litre engine under its forward opening bonnet. Although this was a 105 mph (168 kmh) car, there were criticisms of its Herald-derived swing rear axle. This was rectified with the

Bristol was the first British GT to employ an American V8, in this instance a 5.1-litre unit by Chrysler of Canada. It first appeared in the 407 model of 1961 and the make and configuration has powered every subsequent Bristol. This is a 409 car of 1966.

Mark 2 version for 1969 with redesigned more 'independent' layout with lower wishbones used in conjunction with the transverse leaf spring. The GT6 endured until 1973 by which time only about 40,000 had been produced.

In addition to the GT6, Triumph also entered the more exclusive end of the GT market with the Stag in 1970. This had started life as a project by Michelotti, who wanted to produce a sporting version of the best selling 2000 saloon. The project was coded Stag, another instance of a factory designation emerging as a model name. Initially the Stag was fitted with the 2½-litre six-cylinder engine, destined for the TR5 sports car, but it was replaced by a new V8, created by combining a pair of the firm's newly developed overhead camshaft fours.

The 3-litre Stag finally appeared in 1970 as an open two-plus-two though with a substantial hardtop usually in place, hence its GT designation, and distinctive roll over bar. Beneath the surface was the familiar Triumph all independent suspension: coils and wishbones at the front and rear semi trailing arms. Although the Stag was capable of more than 115 mph (185 kmh) there were engine reliability problems which dogged the model throughout its production life. An export demand accordingly failed to materialize and by the time the model was dropped in 1977, a mere 25,077 had been built.

The Stag was powered by a British-designed V8, though Bristol had opted for a more reliable American V8 for its Grand Tourer. It will be recalled that its 407 of 1961 had featured a 5.1-litre Chrysler V8 in place of the BMW-derived six which had featured on every model from the marque's outset. However, the 407 was replaced for 1964 by the 408, easily identifiable by its twin headlights. It was also slightly taller than its predecessors. In 1966 came the 409, with engine slightly enlarged to 5.2 litres. The following year came the 410 with improved road holding along with smaller wheels. It was good for 130 mph (209 kmh) but in 1970 came the even faster 411, with enlarged 6.2-litre V8 under its bonnet. Otherwise it was the ultra-civilized message as before.

Jensen similarly opted for a Chrysler V8 when its Austin engined 541 ceased production in 1963. It was replaced that year by the CV8 and styled in house, like its predecessor, by Eric Neale. Glassfibre was once again the medium and the model featured distinctive twin headlights which produced its famous slant eyed 'Chinese' look. The engine was the aforementioned 5.9-litre Chrysler V8, with manual or automatic transmission, while the twin-tubed chassis was essentially carried over from the 541. Although this was a 130 mph (209 kmh) car, only 496 examples had been sold by the time the CV8, latterly 6.2-litre-engined, ceased production in 1966.

Chief engineer Kevin Beattie and managing director Brian Owen believed that what was required was a new model with steel bodywork to perpetuate the GT theme that Jensen had been so quick to exploit and that, like Aston Martin, the firm should go to Italy for its styling. There was predictable opposition from the Jensen brothers but Beattie appealed directly to John Boex of the Norcros Group, which had own-

In 1962 Jensen followed the trend to American engines by introducing a 5.9-litre Chrysler unit in the glassfibre-bodied CV8 which was built until 1966.

ed Jensen since 1959, and secured his agreement. Beattie then travelled to Italy and approached the illustrious Touring coachbuilding concern which was, alas, in its death throes. Despite this the Milanese Maestros produced a highly distinctive GT with large opening rear window. In view of Touring's precarious position, the drawings of the new car were taken over by Vignale and the first hulls were built in Italy, though production was soon transferred to Jensen's West Bromwich factory.

The Interceptor name had originally featured on a low-production Jensen of 1949–58 and the new car appeared at the 1966 Motor Show. The model's mechanicals were based on the CV8's running gear. The 6.2-litre V8 was perpetuated, though only with three speed Torqueflite automatic transmission. At £3,742, the Interceptor cost almost the same price as the CV8 but with 6,387 sold by the time that production ceased in 1976, it was the best selling Jensen ever made. There was, in addition to the mainstream model, a four-wheel-drive version making the Interceptor the world's first series production car to offer this facility. Built under Ferguson patents, it also featured Dunlop Maxaret anti-skid braking system. At £5,339, however, there were few takers and only 318 FFs were built, the option being discontinued in 1971. The Interceptor proper meanwhile continued as before. A Mark II version had appeared in 1970 with frontal modifications and a new interior. A Mark III car, identifiable by its new alloy wheels, arrived for 1972 and that year came the more expensive 7.2-litre SP version, with bonnet louvres. From 1973 the larger engine was extended to the basic model.

The old established AC company also opted for V8 power

Instead of opting for in-house styling for its next model, Jensen went to Italy for the lines of its steel-bodied Interceptor of 1966. Although in its death throes, Touring produced this memorable shape which endured until 1976 and was revived in 1988. Jensen also offered a four-wheel-drive version, the FF, until 1971, which is shown here.

The Frua-bodied AC 428 also boasted an American power unit, in this instance a Ford V8 of 427 cu in (6989 cc). This good-looking car was only built between 1966 and 1973 and was capable of over 140 mph (225 kmh).

for its handsome 428 Fastback of 1968 but to discover its origins we must briefly return to 1961. It was then that Texan former racing driver Carroll Shelby approached the Thames Ditton company with a view to combining AC's Ace body and chassis with a Ford V8 engine. The outcome was the Cobra; Shelby had literally dreamed up the name. AC produced the complete body and chassis, which were shipped to America with engines being fitted at Shelby's Californian factory. Initially the Cobra used a 4.3-litre Fairlane unit though this progressively increased to 7 litres, but sales were relatively disappointing. Production ceased in 1968 after just 1,078 examples had been built and Shelby had much better luck with his version of Ford's best selling Mustang.

The Cobra was, of course, an open car and in Britain AC had decided to produce its own 'Cobra' though it was not able to call it that since the name by this time belonged to Ford. AC therefore called its version the 428, which echoed the capacity of its 7-litre V8 engine in cubic inches. This was initially produced in open form, with the Italian Frua concern being responsible for the styling. More significant, as far as our story is concerned, was the closed version which was marketed under the 428 Fastback name. The tubular Ford-developed chassis featured and suspension was all independent by wishbones and coil springs. Top speed was a respectable 140 mph (225 kmh) and AC looked as though it had a winner on its hands.

But there were problems. Frua, which also built the bodies, was plagued by labour disputes and the hulls also suffered from premature rusting, an all too familiar failing of Italian built bodywork of the day. Eventually the supply of bodies ceased altogether and there were also engine delivery problems. Alas, this stylish Grand Tourer ceased

When Lotus introduced its Elan model in 1962 it was an open car and it was not until 1967 that the long wheelbase Plus 2 coupé arrived and outlasted its open forebear, surviving until 1974.

production in the summer of 1973, prior to the oil crisis, after just 51 examples had been built.

The 1960s was the era in which glassfibre came into its own as a body building material and in the vanguard of development was the innovative Lotus company of Cheshunt, Hertfordshire, under the dynamic direction of Colin Chapman. It had followed its stylish but unprofitable Elite Grand Tourer of 1958 with the viable but open Elan in 1962. It falls outside the scope of this book in its initial form but, in 1967, came the longer wheelbase Elan Plus 2 which was a closed car and one which was never offered in an open state. As its name suggested, there were two additional small, and rather cramped, rear seats and the car shared basically the same 1558 cc overhead-camshaft engine, gearbox, backbone chassis and all-round coil-spring and wishbone suspension of its open counterpart. The power unit, however, was slightly more powerful, developing 118 rather than 105 bhp. The Plus 2 was therefore faster, aided by its superior aerodynamics and lasted a year longer (until 1974) than the open version.

The Elan had been specifically designed as an open car but, late in 1966, Lotus unveiled a new, closed model. Its arrival coincided with the firm moving to Hethel, near Norwich. The Europa, as its name suggested, was aimed at the export market and was a logical extension of the mid-engined racing car concept in which Lotus had played such a prominent role. The car was built up around a deep backbone chassis in the Elan manner and, with a view to making it as rigid as possible, the glassfibre body was fused to it. Suspension was all-independent, with coils and wishbones at the front and coils, fixed-length drive shafts and radius arms at the rear. The power unit was the 1470 cc aluminium wet liner four-cylinder Renault 16 engine mounted longitudinally behind the driver.

When announced, this 105 mph (168 kmh) 13.1 cwt (665 kg) car featured a sophisticated ventilation system which, less desirably, required fixed windows and also suffered from poor rear visibility. These shortcomings were rectified with the arrival of the S2 in 1967 but three years later, in 1971, the Renault engine was discarded in favour of the Elan's proven 1558 cc twin-cam unit. The final variant, the 126 bhp Europa Special of 1973, boasted a Big Valve version of the faithful twin-cam and gave the Europa a 120 mph (173 kmh) top speed. The last example was built in 1975.

Glassfibre bodywork was also used by the Blackpool based TVR company which, in 1958, had introduced its multi-tubular Grantura coupé. A 150 mph (241 kmh) derivative was the Griffith of 1964, so called because it was made solely for the American market, being sold there by Griffith Motors. As with the AC Cobra, engineless cars were shipped to America where they were fitted with 4.7-litre Ford V8 engines. This model led in turn to the 3-litre Tuscan V6 of 1969, which resulted in a somewhat more manageable car. The chassis followed the usual TVR tubular frame with all independent suspension and the model lasted until 1971.

The Griffith was produced concurrently with the Grantura but, in 1967, it ceased production and was replaced by the Vixen. These coupés could have been mistaken for the earlier model but for their distinctive cut off rear end. It was mostly Ford Cortina GT or MGB powered and remained available until 1973.

The TVR concern was taken over by the Lilley family in 1965 though it took a few years for the new order to manifest

Not perhaps to everyone's taste, the Lotus Europa of 1967 perpetuated the mid-engined location of Lotus Formula 1 cars. Later, in 1977, the rear profile was modified to improve vision and the original 1.4-litre Renault engine was replaced by the 1.6-litre Ford-based twin cam unit.

itself. The first of a new generation of cars appeared in 1972 with the arrival of the M series (for Martin Lilley) of models with open and closed bodywork. There was a new backbone chassis and all-independent coil and wishbone suspension was perpetuated. The engine was the trusty Ford 3-litre V6, as pioneered in the Tuscan. It was these models which were destined to keep TVR just afloat in the turbulent waters of the 1970s.

By the mid-1960s the British Grand Tourer was an established part of the motoring scene. But, in 1968, came yet another variation in the shape of the Reliant GTE (estate) which combined the virtues of a GT with the lines and carrying capacity of an estate. On the face of it, Reliant was an unlikely manufacturer of performance cars. Based at Tamworth, Staffordshire, it had taken over Raleigh's three-wheeler van in 1935 and, after the war, had graduated to glassfibre bodied three-wheeled cars. Reliant was founded by Tom Williams, who headed Reliant until his death in 1964, and introduced Ray Wiggin to the firm. Wiggin, who became managing director on Williams' death, introduced the ungainly glassfibre bodied 1.7-litre Ford Consul-engined Sabre sports car in 1961. It was revised in SE2 form for 1963, with all important modifications to its front end. In addition there was a new model in the shape of the distinctive Scimitar, a $2\frac{1}{2}$-litre Ford Zephyr-powered GT, which represents a demonstrable starting point to the GTE's pedigree.

It was while visiting the 1962 Motor Show that Wiggin noted the Daimler SP 250-based Ogle X250, a stylish GT which was being offered by the Letchworth, Hertfordshire, based David Ogle Associates, but only a few had been sold.

The Blackpool-based TVR company began producing kit cars in 1954 and this is the glassfibre bodied Vixen of 1967 which replaced the earlier Grantura model. Power came from either MGB or Ford Cortina engines.

A GT from Tamworth, Staffordshire, the glassfibre-bodied Ogle-styled Reliant Scimitar was initially available with a 2½-litre six-cylinder Ford engine though this was replaced, from 1967, by a 3-litre V6 unit from the same source. The car was built between 1964 and 1970.

However Wiggin believed that it would be suitable for the Sabre Six chassis. A shell was subsequently delivered to Tamworth and the resulting union both looked and felt right. Consequently a new box section chassis was designed which was fitted with coil and wishbone independent front suspension and a coil sprung live rear axle. The 2553 cc Zephyr six engine was carried over from the Sabre, and when Ford went V6 in 1966, Reliant followed suit for 1967. As this engine took up less room than that of its predecessor, Reliant took the opportunity to revise the Scimitar's interior and the model continued to be built in this form until 1970.

But this model had been dramatically overhauled in popularity by the GTE estate car derivative which made its debut at the 1968 Motor Show. It was an ingenious and pioneering concept which gave buyers 115 mph (185 kmh) motoring with the traditional carrying capacity and opening tailgate of an estate. The shape, with its distinctive up-swept side windows, evolved following lengthy discussions between Ray Wiggin and Ogle's Tom Karen. A completely new chassis was devised which was wider and longer than that of the Scimitar, its wheelbase being 8 in (203 mm) more than the GT's though its overall length was about the same. It just *looked* longer because of its unusual and distinctive

When the Grand Tourer became an estate car: the pioneering GTE, styled by Ogle's Tom Karen, enjoyed a seventeen-year production run, from 1968 until 1985, and has recently been revived.

side windows treatment.

The GTE was initially available with 2½ and 3-litre Ford V6 engine options though the smaller capacity engine was soon discontinued. It was made in this form until 1976 when Reliant answered criticism of its rather cramped interior, particularly noticeable when two broad-shouldered occupants were sharing the front seats! The revised model was both longer and wider than its predecessor, the intention being to make it more of a four-seater than a two-plus-two. The GTE endured in this revised form until its demise in 1985 after about 16,000 had been built.

In 1969 Reliant took over the Bond company, which had produced its own range of glassfibre-bodied GTs from 1963. The previous year Tom Gatrix, of the Preston, Lancashire-based Sharp's Commercials, which had built the Laurice Bond-designed three-wheeled Mini car since 1949, approached Standard-Triumph with a view to producing a Herald-based GT. The attraction of the Herald, and of its Vitesse and Spitfire derivatives, was that they retained a separate chassis frame, making an ideal platform for a glassfibre body. Triumph also agreed that the cars would be sold through its own distributors, a major plus as far as warranty and spares provision were concerned.

The original Bond Equipe GT of 1963 was accordingly Herald-based and although that model's steel doors were retained, the remainder of the bodywork was lighter than the Triumph's and was consequently good for 80 mph (128 kmh) plus. However, the Herald's swing axle rear suspension resulted in a predictably lively tail.

The GT 4S of 1965, although Spitfire-engined, was less

visually successful than its predecessor but it had a claimed top speed of 90 mph (128 kmh). Far more satisfactory was the 2-litre Equipe GT of 1968, with body designed by Specialist Models of Preston. This was a good looking 100 mph (160 kmh) car and was powered by the 2-litre six-cylinder engine, also found in Triumph's own Vitesse 2000 and GT6. But Reliant's acquisition of Bond in 1969 led to the end of Equipe production in 1970 when the firm's Preston factories were closed and three-wheeler production was concentrated at Tamworth.

Meanwhile, over at Llantwit Fardre, Gilbern was continuing to produce Wales' only Grand Tourer. The glassfibre-bodied GT, introduced in 1960, was MGB engined from 1963 though in 1966 the firm began to experience supply problems with its MGB engines, so that year it switched to the ubiquitous Ford 3-litre V6 unit. It powered Gilbern's new model, the Genie, which made its debut at the 1966 Motor Show and was a fair reflection of the steady progress the firm had made since its 1960 inception. The Genie had a completely new body, though the frame was substantially the same, with the MGB front suspension and rear axle perpetuated.

The glassfibre-bodied Gilbern Invader of 1969, built at Llantwit Fardre, Wales evolved from the 1967 Genie and was powered by the Ford 3-litre V6 engine. It was being built when Gilbern closed its doors in 1973.

In 1968 Gilbern's founders, Bernard Frieze and Giles Smith, stepped down and the firm was taken over by Ace Industrial Holdings. In 1969 the Genie was replaced by the 115 mph (185 kmh) Invader. Its body was basically the same though the chassis was strengthened to cope with the V6 and the MGB suspension and steering parts were replaced by more substantial MGC ones. But the same year came yet

another change of ownership, and it is worth recalling that such upheavals were typical of the financial problems that plagued British specialist manufacturers of their day. Ace sold out to the Clubmans Club which, in turn, was taken over by Mecca, who then sold Gilbern to the family of managing director Maurice Collins.

A Mark II version of the Invader arrived in 1971, along with an estate version in the manner of the Reliant GTE, of which about 70 were built. Total Mk I and II output amounted to 394 cars. The year 1972 saw the firm sold once again to Collins' co-managing director Mike Leather and that year saw the arrival of the Mark III Invader, a wider car with Ford Cortina running gear to replace the MGC parts, dwindling following that model's recent demise.

Gilbern itself was near the end of the road, despite having received an order for 150 cars from Holland. Such was the precarious state of the firm's finance that a left-hand-drive version stretched the firm's resources to breaking point. It went into receivership in July 1973 but was briefly revived by Anthony Peters. But by the end of the year the only car maker in the principality was no more, despite the patronage of the Prince of Wales who had bought one for personal use.

Somewhat more enduring was the Fairthorpe's Grand Tourer, the TX GT, which appeared for 1969, the series lasting until 1981. The firm, founded by Air Vice Marshal 'Pathfinder' Bennett, had started life in 1954 with its glassfibre-bodied Atom coupé, powered by a succession of rear-mounted BSA motor cycle engines.

After having had a number of homes, Fairthorpe finally settled in Denham, Buckinghamshire. It was also moving progressively up market and its TX 1 open two-seater of 1965 was so called because it had been designed by Bennett's son Torix. This model formed the basis of the 110 mph (177 kmh) TX GT, an uncompromising glassfibre-bodied two-seater. Its chassis was a modified Triumph GT6 frame and could be had with its original rear suspension or Fairthorpe's unique Torix cross-linked independent rear system, which ensured that the rear track remained constant, an advantage which was particularly apparent during high speed cornering. Its disadvantage was that it showed up the limitations of front suspension and also took up a disproportionate amount of space so the spare wheel had to be carried under the bonnet.

A variety of 2 or 2½-litre Triumph six-cylinder engines were fitted to this TX series of cars, either carburettored, fuel injected or supercharged and the cars soldiered on, with

The long-lived Fairthorpe TX series arrived in 1965 and was listed until 1981. This car dates from 1971. Usually powered by 2 or 2½-litre six-cylinder Triumph engines, the marque's unique Torix independent rear suspension system could be specified.

remarkably little development, for the next 12 years.

Two further recruits to the British Grand Touring market arrived in 1964, one ultra traditional, the other daringly unconventional. But first convention. It will be recalled that John Gordon had inspired the short lived Peerless GT of 1957–60; in 1964 came the Gordon-Keeble. The marque was the result of a visit Gordon had received from Ipswich garage proprietor, Jim Keeble, who had tinkered with producing one-off specials. He had been approached by an American named Nielsen, who raced a Chevrolet Corvette and wanted Keeble to shoehorn its 4.7-litre V8 engine into a Peerless chassis. Gordon not only liked the idea but also saw the potential of producing such a combination for series production. Work soon started on the first car with spaceframe chassis, which echoed Warwick practice, though it featured Armstrong coil-spring suspension instead of a Triumph system, while the de Dion rear end was perpetuated.

Ambitiously Bertone was approached to design the body, the work being undertaken by none other than Giorgetto Giugario, the first body he undertook for the Turin styling house. It also bore a striking resemblance to the body he designed for the 1962 Iso Rivolta! The prototype Gordon-Keeble actually appeared at the 1960 Geneva Motor Show, priced at £3,045 though it would not be until 1964 that the first production car appeared.

Unlike the prototype this was glassfibre-bodied and powered by a larger Chevrolet V8 of 5.3-litre capacity. Consequently the Gordon-Keeble was a 135 mph (217 kmh) GT, though it used a tortoise for its badge. It was much praised for its handling and, in an era of shoddy and poorly finished

The Bertone-styled Gordon-Keeble was yet another exponent of American V8 power, in this instance a Chevrolet 5.3-litre unit and, although it used glassfibre bodywork, it was a good quality product. It was only built between 1964 and 1966.

glassfibre GTs, was a presentable, and well-built genuine four-seater, though underpriced at £2,798. It sold to a privileged, titled clientele which included Britain's ambassador to the United States, Lord Harlech, while a number of hitherto dedicated Aston Martin owners decided to follow the tortoise. The cars were built at Eastleigh, near Southampton, but the firm only lasted until mid-1965. Eighty cars were built by the time that the collapse came. However, Harold Smith, a Gordon-Keeble agent, took the company over and built a further 19 cars which he called IT (for International Tourer) Gordon-Keebles at the old Osram works at Sholing near Southampton. Smith sensibly put the car's price up to a more realistic £3,989 before output ceased in 1966. This made a total of 99 Gordon-Keebles built.

Less conventional was the Marcos, developed from a racing GT of the late 1950s, created by engineer Jem Marsh and aerodynamicist Frank Costin, which featured a marine plywood chassis. This was something of an Ugly Duckling but the Marcos GT of 1964 was a very different animal, with sleek, distinctive glassfibre bodywork styled by Dennis Adams and a wooden chassis like its competition predecessor. Built at Bradford-on-Avon, Wiltshire, the Marcos GT contained no less than 386 chassis parts of West African mahogany and Douglas fir plywood and Sitka spruce. However, from 1969, it was replaced by a more conventional tubular steel one.

Front suspension was essentially Triumph GT6/Vitesse and a type of de Dion axle featured at the rear. As it developed an appetite for half shafts, it was replaced by a live axle from the Ford Mark II Cortina. Initially the 1.8-litre

Volvo engine and gearbox, courtesy of the P1800, was fitted, though it was replaced, from 1967, by the 1½-litre Ford Cortina unit. This in turn made way for the 2-litre Ford V4 although, from 1969, the 3-litre V6 unit from the same manufacturer was employed. This pushed the car's top speed up a good 10 mph (16 kmh) to 120 mph (193 kmh). Finally came another Volvo engine, this time a weighty 3-litre six, already de-toxed for America and adopted by Marcos with an eye to transatlantic sales. However, the firm had over extended itself, following a move to a larger factory in Westbury, Wiltshire in 1970. The same year came the four-seater Triumph TR6-engined Mantis, though only a handful were built. After seven years Marcos came to the end of the road in 1971 though, recently, it has been revived.

Marcos Cars now produce the Mantula, also styled by Dennis Adams and thus closely related to the original model. Available in closed and open forms, power comes from Rover's long-running 3½-litre V8. A top speed of 135 mph (217 kmh) is claimed from this 12.4 cwt (635 kg) car.

These were some of the GTs to be found on the British market at this time, but another phenomenon which manifested itself in the 1960s was the dilution of the GT initials as manufacturers applied them indiscriminately to family saloons. Ford may have begun this trend by initiating a GT version of its top selling Cortina of 1963 — which echoed Ford (USA) Mustang precedent. Ironically the Cortina GT was to develop an impressive rallying career but the die was cast. Perhaps British Leyland's GT version of its popular 1100/1300 front-wheel-drive saloon of 1970 epitomized this approach. The GT was readily identifiable by its black vinyl roof and matching side flashes, twin carburettors, interior reclining seats and a rev counter. Similarly, the 1275 cc Mini appeared in GT guise for 1970 with restyled angular front and winding windows. This pint sized 'GT' endured until 1980.

Across the Channel in France the bleakness of the GT market of the previous decade perked up somewhat as the 1960s progressed. As mentioned in the previous chapter, in 1961 Rene Bonnet began producing Renault-engined cars under his own name, the first being the 1108 cc R8-powered Djet, one of the first road-going mid-engined models. A two-seater glassfibre body was employed. Top speed was nudging the 100 mph (160 kmh) mark and there was also the potent but noisy Gordini version. However in 1964 the firm was taken over by the Matra, the massive armaments concern and the model was sold as the Matra Bonnet Djet until 1968.

The previous year had seen the introduction of its replacement, the chunky M 530A two-plus-two glassfibre-bodied coupé. It was, once again, mid-engined though on this occasion the power unit was a German built 1.6-litre Ford V4, complete with gearbox and transmission from the front-wheel-drive Taunus. Suspension was all independent by double coil springs and wishbones. Ironically, this heavier car had about the same top speed as its predecessor. In any event, sales were not encouraging, the angular lines of the coupé not perhaps being to everybody's taste and production ceased in 1973.

The Bonnet Djet lookalike, the rear-engined glassfibre bodied Alpine-Renault line, which had begun in 1957, progressively evolved and, in 1963, came the A110 Berlinette Tour de France with 956 cc Renault engine. The backbone chassis, with all independent suspension, front coils and wishbones and a swing axle rear, was continued. Performance was considerably pepped up with the introduction of the 1470 cc R16 engine which was later enlarged to 1600 cc. However, road car development took something of a back seat to the firm's sports racing and rallying programme, which gained momentum from 1963 onwards and culminated in the A 110 achieving an impressive 1, 2, 3 Monte Carlo Rally victory in 1971.

Also in 1971 came the first new Alpine-Renault since 1957 in the shape of the A310, a good looking rear-engined glassfibre coupé, powered by a 1605 cc version of the R16 engine. A backbone chassis was employed while suspension was independent all-round by coil springs and wishbones. This was a purposeful 130 mph (209 kmh) GT. In 1974 Alpine-Renault was taken under Renault's corporate wing and the A310 was joined for 1977 by a supplementary version powered by the Peugeot/Volvo Renault 3-litre V6 engine which considerably pepped up the model's top speed to 135 mph (217 kmh) and was soon standardized. The long-lived A310 lasted until 1987.

Back in the early 1970s the French GT scene was greatly enlivened by the Michelin-owned Citroen company decision to produce a prestigious Grand Tourer. But as it had no suitable engine, it was a factor in the French company taking over Maserati in 1968. The Modena firm had introduced a 5-litre V8 engine in 1960 which was also available in 4.7 and 4.9-litre forms. However, this was too large a capacity power unit for the DS-based GT, which Citroen called the SM and Maserati's chief engineer Giulio Alfieri was ordered to lop two cylinders off the eight and have it running within six months. In fact an experimental unit was operational in three weeks! A one-off crankshaft had been machined from solid metal and new camshafts manufactured. This resulted in a 3102 cc V6 but this capacity was still too great and eventually a 2670 cc unit was developed in deference to France's preferential 15CV tax ceiling. But the SM's front-wheel-drive layout required that the engine be mounted back to front which meant that the accessory drives had to be relocated. A five-speed gearbox was employed.

This 135 mph (217 kmh) car entered production in 1970 and had the distinction of being the world's first pukka front-wheel-drive Grand Tourer. The SM offered the traditional hydropneumatic suspension of the Citroen saloons, coupled with the road holding advantages of front wheel drive. Power steering also featured while there were no less than six headlamps, concealed behind a transparent screen, which turned with the steering wheel. Not surprisingly the car was expensive. It sold for 46,000 francs (£3,350) on its announcement, but production got off to a good start with 4,988 cars built in 1971. Thereafter demand began to slow. In mid-1972 the V6 was fuel injected while capacity was increased to 2965 cc for a supplementary version of 1973. But these developments did little to arrest the SM's decline and the already ailing model then suffered the fatal impact of the 1973 oil crisis.

SM production was moved from Paris to Guy Ligier's small factory in Abrest, near Vichy in 1974, which Citroen took over that year, but output ceased in 1975 after 12,920 cars had been built, an impressive figure by Italian GT standards, but disastrous for an already over extended Citroen company. The SM engine was, incidentally, also used in

Citroen's ownership of Maserati was mirrored in its SM model of 1970 for although the hull was pure Citroen, the engine was a 2.6-litre V6 Maserati unit, derived from the Italian firm's proven V8. Capacity was upped to 2.9 litres in 1973 though the model ceased production in 1975.

Ligier's own JS2 mid-engined model of 1971 when it soon replaced a Ford V6 unit and endured until 1976. Meanwhile, Citroen itself was in deep trouble. An association with Fiat was unscrambled in 1973 and in December 1974, as the world economy took a post-oil crisis nosedive, the French firm was taken over by Peugeot. As a result, the Maserati company was left to sink or swim, the consequences of which are considered in the next chapter.

The SM had a relatively brief five-year manufacturing life but, in Germany, the Stuttgart based Porsche company was just getting into its stride with its illustrious 911, introduced in 1964, one of the greatest performance cars of the post-war years and still going strong 25 years later in 1989. Yet despite its longevity, the 911's gestation was by no means straight forward. Work on a replacement for the 356 had begun in 1959 when it was alloted the 695 type number. It was late in the year that Ferry Porsche's son Butzi, head of the firm's styling department, began work on the project and, from the very outset, it was decided that the new model would be a four seater, unlike the 356 which began life as a two seater and had rear seats added. Early on in the project, front Mac-Pherson struts with longitudinal torsion bars rather than bulky coil springs were adopted, though the 356's rear swing axle was retained.

When it came to a choice of power units, Ferry Porsche was insistent that the new car should have acceleration comparable with the 356 Carrera but without its noisy and complicated twin-overhead camshafts. This meant the refinement of a six-cylinder boxer (flat) unit, air-cooled in the usual Porsche tradition. Technical director Klaus von Rucker oversaw the project which culminated in the creation of a 1991 cc unit with pushrod operated overhead valves.

But then, early in 1962, von Rucker, a chief advocate of the four-seater layout, left Porsche and was replaced by Hans Tomola. As a result the entire project was subjected to considerable re-thinking and Ferry Porsche decided to give greater sporting emphasis to the project, though still retaining its GT characteristics.

The wheelbase was reduced to 87 in (2,209 mm), 7 in (177 mm) shorter than previously. Butzi Porsche conceived a new fastback body retaining some of the best features of the four-seater within an evolutionary theme.

In 1963 the 695 became the 901 and while it might be thought that this was the next available number in the Porsche design register, the real reason was somewhat more mundane. In the early 1960s, Porsche was integrating its

In 1964 the original Porsche, the 356, which can be seen in the background, was replaced by the 911. It was also powered by a rear-mounted horizontally-opposed air-cooled unit though was a 1991 cc flat-six rather than a four. This evergreen model is still in production at the time of writing.

parts and service activities with those of Volkswagen and it was found that the only free number batches on the Wolfsburg parts computer were the 900 series: hence 901.

Performance was once more to the fore, so it was decided to dispense with the engine's pushrods and locate the crankcase twin camshafts more positively above the cylinders. The work was assigned to Ferdinand Piech, nephew of Ferdinand Porsche, who was undertaking his first assignment for the family firm. These newly located overhead camshafts were driven by chains rather than the Carrera's noisy gears, the inclined valves being actuated via rockers. Yet another refinement was a change in the layout of the independent rear suspension and the swing axle was replaced by semi-trailing arms.

The Porsche 901 was announced at the 1963 Frankfurt Motor Show though production did not begin until September 1964. There were, however, immediate protests from Peugeot about the new model's 901 name. It pointed out that it had used the central placement of the 0 since the 1920s, 202, 203, 204 and so on and they objected to its use in France. This was an important outlet which the Stuttgart company could only ignore at its peril, so the 901 became the 911 though the engine retained the 901 designation!

In its original form the 911 was capable of 135 mph (217 kmh) but these early cars did suffer from somewhat unpredictable handling, due in part to overly narrow wheels and tyres, while the tail could catch the uninitiated by surprise. Some owners also felt that their cars were suffering from an unduly light front end. Porsche countered this problem by bolting and glueing 24 lb (11 kg) weights at the extremities of the front bumper. However, many of these handling problems were quickly resolved.

As in the case of the 356, engine capacity increased over the years. It started out at 1991 cc, which lasted until 1970, when it was enlarged to 2195 cc; the model's wheelbase was enlarged by 2.2 in (57 mm) to 89.3 in (2,268 mm) in the previous year. In 1972, engine capacity went up again to 2341 cc, lasting in this form until 1973. The development of its turbocharged derivative belongs to the next chapter. In 1965 came a variation of the body lines with the introduction of the open Targa version, which disguised a rollover bar, in conjunction with a detachable roof panel that could be removed and stored in the forward luggage compartment when not in use. Originally it featured a detachable unzippable rear window though this was quickly replaced by a fixed one.

The 911 was an expensive car: it sold in Britain for £3,438 in 1965, so that year Porsche introduced a cheaper version, costing nearly £1,000 less at £2,467, which retained the same body but employed the 1582 cc flat-four-cylinder engine from the earlier 356 model, which had finally ceased production in 1965. The interior and instrumentation were spartan compared with its six-cylinder stablemate. Even so the 912 was good for 115 mph (185 kmh) though it only lasted until 1969, but this was not quite the last to be heard of it.

Although the 911 can be considered a great success for Porsche, the mid-engined 914 of 1969, the result of cooperation between the company and Volkswagen, was less so. Sold as a VW-Porsche in Europe and Porsche in America, it did, however, pave the way for a revival of the 912. It appeared in two forms; as the VW-powered 914/4 and the Porsche 914/6. The VW version used that company's Type 4 1679 cc fuel-injected flat-four engine while the Porsche-engined model used the 911's 2-litre flat-six engine. Only 3,360 examples of the latter were sold by the time that the model was quietly discontinued in 1972, four years ahead of its VW equivalent. However, in America the Volkswagen's engine, which had been increased to 1971 cc in 1973, was fitted to the low cost 912 Porsche which re-appeared in 1975, a rare instance of a model being revived, in this case after a six-year absence. Inevitably acceleration was noticeably inferior to its predecessor and the car was short-lived. The 912 finally ceased production in 1976.

Down the road from Porsche in Stuttgart, Mercedes-Benz was complementing its successful saloon car range with sporting models which retained the looks but not the complexity of the 350 SL of the previous decade. Although obstensibly a Grand Tourer, the 230 SL which arrived in 1963 was actually an open car with a substantial and distinctive 'Pagoda' hardtop. As it seems it was more often than not in place, I am calling it a GT! The model's mechanicals were based on the 220SE saloon of 1961. The six-cylinder overhead-camshaft engine was accordingly enlarged to 2308 cc which guaranteed 120 mph (193 kmh). Suspension was the well-established Mercedes-Benz formula of coil and wishbone front suspension while the rear swingaxle was a low-pivot version to improve road holding. The model was destined for an eight-year production life, and was discontinued in 1971, though engine capacity was increased to 2496 cc in 1967, hence the 250 SL, and again to 2778 cc in 1968, when the model was redesignated the 280SL. Ironically the car's weight also went up, forcing performance down and it could only achieve 110 mph (177 kmh) plus.

The 280SL ceased production in 1971 and was replaced by a pair of sporting models. The 350 and 450 SL were open cars with removable hardtops, but the longer wheelbase 350 SLC and 450 SLC were fixed-head two-plus-twos. Suspension was all-independent with the customary coils and wishbones at the front though the long running swingaxle was, at long last, replaced by semi-trailing arms. Once again the power unit came from a passenger model, in this instance the 280 SE saloon of 1970. In the 350 it was a 3499 cc V8 with single overhead camshafts while the 450 featured an enlarged 4520 cc version with longer stroke. The top line 450 SLC used the V8 stretched, yet again, to 5025 cc but with an aluminium rather than a cast iron block, a true Grand Tourer in every sense of the word. At the other extreme, the arrival of the 1973 oil crisis resulted in the option of a supplementary 2.8 litre six. These refined, purposeful cars endured until 1979.

The 1960s were essentially a decade of consolidation and growth for Mercedes-Benz. But it was also the period in which BMW, which had been searching for an identity since the end of the war, finally found it. The firm had suffered during the 1950s from the loss of its all important 2-litre models to Bristol and, as a result, had tottered between two extremes: the luxurious types 503 and 507 on one hand to the production of the Isetta bubble car at the other. It was not until the all-important 1500 arrived in 1962 that BMW finally found its feet. Here was the long awaited BMW of the middle ground, aimed at the growing ranks of West Germany's young executives. The theme of a single-overhead-camshaft engine, MacPherson strut front suspension and rear semi-trailing arms were to set the BMW engineering pattern from thereon. However, BMW also offered a GT at this time, though the Bertone styled 3200 CS of 1962 represented an older generation of corporate thinking, being powered by the firm's 3.1-litre V8 engine. The established tubular chassis and torsion bar suspension were employed. Sales of this expensive 125 mph (201 kmh) car amounted to a mere 603 units and with its 1965 demise went the last of V8 powered cars.

Its spiritual successor was the 100 bhp 2000 C of 1965–9, along with its more popular twin-carburettored 120 bhp CS derivative. Styled in house by William Hofmeister, the rear of the car was judged a triumph, though the front, with its distinctive wrap around headlights, quickly dated. The 1990 cc engine was being used for the first time and had evolved from the 1500 cc's four. As this was a low production model, its manufacture was entrusted to Karmann. Sales amounted to a little over 11,000 of both types in four years.

In 1968 this was replaced by the 2800 CS, with the controversial front end dispensed with. Rather than a four, this had a 2.8-litre six-cylinder engine developed from the overhead-camshaft four under Alex von Falkenhausen's direction that had appeared in that year's 2500 and 2800 saloons. But, once again, the coupé was a low production model. Just 9,399 were built before it made way for the 3.0 CS of 1971. This vehicle was visually similar to the 2800 but represented a 130 mph (209 kmh) capable car in its most basic form. But the same year came two even more potent

The impressive BMW coupé line, which first appeared in 1965, was updated in 1971 as the 3.0 CS model. The top line 135 mph (217 kmh) CSL boasted a lighter body and wider wheels and survived until 1975. Only 1,039 were built.

derivatives in the shape of the 3.0 CSi with D-Jetronic Bosch fuel-injection and 200 bhp, rather than the basic model's 180, and the sports racing CSL, which was ultimately enlarged to 315 cc. From 1972 this lightweight model was available with a distinctive aerofoil wing though it was essentially a Group 2 car for the race track rather than the road.

The 2000 C/CS 1990 cc engine was to form the basis of the 2002 saloon of 1968, which was to prove to be the best selling BMW of its day with nearly 340,000 examples built by the time that production ceased in 1976. This had started life in 1966 when BMW introduced a new two-door 1600. It was initially powered by a 1.6-litre single-carburettor engine though, in 1967, came the twin-carburettored TI derivative. Impending safety and emissions regulations on the all-important American market which would have adversely affected its performance were a problem, so BMW decided to employ the 2000 coupé's 1990 cc engine and revert to a single carburettor. There was also a twin-carburettored 'ti' version which lasted until 1971. This was replaced by a fuel injected car, the tii, enduring until 1975. The 2002 was Germany's equivalent of the Alfa Romeo Giulia, a well-priced, stylish two-door saloon which offered lively though practical motoring. BMW was back.

The company was also growing by acquisition. In 1966 BMW took over the Glas company, which had over-extended itself during the 1960s by producing a range of bubble cars, saloons and GTs. Glas was an old established manufacturer of agricultural equipment, based in Dingolfing, which in 1955 had begun the production of the Goggomobile bubble car. Initially powered by two-stroke, two-cylinder motors, these progressed to four-strokes and, in 1961, came Glas's first four-cylinder, four-stroke-powered saloons. These were available in no less than four variations, with capacities ranging from 993 to 1682 cc and distinguished by being the world's first series production engines to employ an overhead camshaft driven by a toothed rubber belt — features which are commonplace today. In 1963 Glas introduced 1300 and 1700 GTs, with bodies styled by Frua and built by Maggiora in Italy. These were unitary hulls, with coil and wishbone front suspension and live rear axle.

Despite Glas's relatively low production, it introduced a completely new model, the 2600 V8 of 1966. Styling was, one again, by Frua and showed a similarity to the contemporary Vignale-bodied Maserati Sebring. Accordingly it was dubbed as a 'Glaserati' in Germany. Although front suspension perpetuated previous practice, a de Dion axle

In 1965 the Glas company announced its 2.6-litre Frua-bodied GT car. The engine was a V8 unit with single-overhead camshafts per cylinder bank prophetically driven by cogged belts. But BMW took the firm over in 1966 and the model ceased production in 1968.

with inboard disc brakes was employed. The 2576 cc V8 was completely new and consisted of two 1300 cc GT units, with their attendant belts, mounted on a common crankcase. Unfortunately this 120 mph (193 kmh) GT was only destined for three years' production.

The long-running Goggomobile and the saloon range were discontinued, though the GTs were briefly perpetuated in the shape of a single model as the BMW 1600 GT with BMW grille, 1600 TI engine and semi-trailing arm rear suspension in place of the original live axle. This hybrid continued until 1968, as did a 3-litre derivative of the larger 2.6-litre model of which 400 were built. All Glas production ceased in 1968 and the Dingolfing factory converted into a BMW plant employing 10,000.

By contrast, Opel, as Germany's largest car maker after Volkswagen, had fought shy of the performance market. It came as some surprise therefore when it exhibited a so-called 'dream car' at the 1965 Frankfurt Show. This evolved into the GT model, introduced in 1968, a strict two-seater available in 1100 and 1900 cc forms, with the latter 115 mph (185 kmh) version in greatest demand. Suspension was traditional with coil and wishbone front suspension and a coil-sprung live rear axle. In view of the relatively small production envisaged, body manufacture was contracted to the French Brissonaeau and Lotz company with sales of 100,000 or so cars in six years, 60 per cent of output being exported to America.

The Frankfurt show also saw the announcement of a new luxury Grand Tourer, the Swiss built Monteverdi 375, that made its debut there in 1967. Basle-born Peter Monteverdi inherited his family's garage in 1954 at the age of 21 on the sudden death of his father. He was an enthusiastic competitor on road and track, and his business was deeply committed to Ferrari sales and he later held the franchise for the whole of Switzerland. In the late 1950s he undertook limited car production in the shape of his Formula Junior MBM racer. His firm subsequently took on a Bentley and Rolls-Royce franchise though this only lasted for a year, and he switched to become one of Switzerland's leading BMW importers. But Monteverdi was beginning to turn his attention to creating a GT that combined the performance of a Ferrari with the refinement of a Rolls-Royce.

Switzerland had produced remarkably few cars over the years and Monteverdi was responsible for the car's basic design which was built up around a strong chassis of square-section tubing, with his own purpose-made coil and wishbone independent suspension, and a de Dion rear axle. The bodywork, designed with assistance from Frua, was built by Fissore in Turin and then transported to Basle where it was united with the chassis. The car's engine was a 7.2-litre Chrysler V8 developing 375 bhp, which was reflected in the model's title, though it could also be had in 400 bhp 400SS form. Torqueflite three-speed automatic transmission was employed. It was a 150 mph (241 kmh) car but in 1971 this two-seater was joined by a 375 L (for long) which was fitted with two rear seats.

Monteverdi followed in the wheel tracks of the Lamborghini Miura by developing a mid-engined car, the Hai (or shark), which made its debut at the 1970 Geneva Motor

The 1968 Opel GT was derived from a 1965 'dream' show car. Based on the Kadett floorplan and engines, it was available in 1.1 and 1.9 litre forms and the GT survived until 1973. The model can be considered as Opel's first sporting product of the post-war years.

Show. Once again a tubular frame was employed but the big 7-litre 'Hemi' was mounted longitudinally at the rear of the car with the seats either side and slightly forward of it. Monteverdi claimed that this mighty power unit developed 450 bhp, so the model was accordingly named the Hai 450SS. A five-speed ZF gearbox was employed and air conditioning was a standard fitment. In spite of the car's impressive performance and 160 mph (257 kmh) potential top speed, customers baulked at sharing their driving with the omnipresent V8 and the model was withdrawn in 1976 after only a handful had been built. The 375 was discontinued in the following year and the firm concentrated on its Chrysler V8-powered Sierra saloon.

If Switzerland appeared an unlikely recruit to the ranks of the GT manufacturers, the same might probably be said of the Swedish Saab company which introduced its Sonnet II model in 1966. It was based on the Saab 96's floor pan, 841 cc three-cylinder two-stroke engine of German DKW ancestry and the usual coil and wishbone front suspension and live rear axle. It was, accordingly, front wheel drive and glass-fibre bodywork was fitted, but the model proved something of a disappointing performer despite a claimed 100 mph (160 kmh) top speed. In 1968, acceleration was improved by the use of the German-built Ford V4 1½-litre engine. Output continued at rather a pedestrian rate, however, until what had been renamed the Sonnet V4 was replaced in 1970 by the greatly improved Sonnet III.

This was a low production car, like its predecessor, the work of Italian stylist Sergio Coggiloa, with input from Saab's own design department. It was a good looking coupé, with opening hatchback. Suspension was similar to the previous model but on this occasion the V4 was enlarged to 1.7 litres with a guaranteed 100 mph (160 kmh) top speed. But the model only endured until 1974 after all-important American sales had been hit by that country's increasingly stringent emission regulations.

Volvo, Sweden's other car maker, had built the last of its P1800 coupés in 1972, but that was by no means the end of the story because, the same year, Volvo introduced its 1800 ES estate derivative. This was a car very much in the traditions of the Reliant Scimitar GTE of 1968 though Volvo has archive photographs to prove that it was conceived in 1967, a year before the GTE's announcement! Although the fuel-injected 2-litre overhead-camshaft engine meant that the 1800ES was capable of 115 mph (185 kmh), the reality was that the body lines essentially dated back to 1960 and the model was phased out in 1973, after 8,078 had been built.

CHAPTER FIVE

Japan in the fast lane, 1970-80

'Datsun has created a real sports GT which, with very few exceptions, combines good performance with a maximum of comfort. What is more important is that it has been done for a price of $3,601, an admirable job indeed.'

Motor Trend on the Datsun 240Z

During the 1970s Japan established itself as the world's leading manufacturer of performance cars, a position it holds to this day. But, significantly, it followed German and Italian precedent and opted for closed, rather than open cars. Japan, or more particularly, Datsun aimed its 240Z model straight at the lucrative American market and sales were undoubtedly aided by the public's desire for smaller cars that came in the wake of the recession that followed the 1973 Arab/Israeli war and the rise in petrol prices that resulted from it.

The waves of economic depression were soon lapping at the gates of the motor manufacturers. In Britain, British Leyland, which built MG and Triumph sports cars, toppled in deficit and was nationalized in 1975. Jensen ceased production in the following year and Aston Martin nearly went out of business but managed to survive in a reconstructed form in 1976. Across the Channel in France, Peugeot snapped up Citroen in 1974 and the latter divested itself of its ownership of Maserati. That famous firm was taken over by Alessandro De Tomaso and the Italian government. By contrast, Ferrari, along with Lancia, were safe within the Fiat compound though Lamborghini was less lucky and plagued by financial uncertainties as petrol prices soared. Iso went to the wall. Even in Gemany, the mighty Volkswagen concern suffered the first deficit in its post-war history in 1974, and

With the arrival of Datsun's 240Z coupé in 1970, Japan began to challenge Britain as the world's largest producer of performance cars. This is its 260Z's successor of 1973, powered by 2565 cc six-cylinder overhead camshaft engine, which lasted until 1978.

Porsche picked up an aborted VW performance car project which emerged as its best selling 924 of 1976.

Germany was also in the vanguard of a technical development which swept through the ranks of the GT manufacturers during the 1970s. This was the race-proven turbocharger which, unlike the engine-driven supercharger of pre-war days which itself absorbed power, was driven by the power unit's exhaust gases and consequently absorbed none. BMW pioneered the system on a short-lived version of its 2002 saloon. But despite the economic chill, the turbocharger grew in popularity, having been revived by Saab in 1979 on its 99 sports saloon. In the same year Datsun introduced the turbocharger to its ZX model, a derivative of the 240Z coupé of 1970 which, during the decade, had emerged as the world's best-selling performance car.

Ironically, Nissan, which built the Datsun, had virtually no long-standing tradition for sports car production. Although the firm had been building cars since 1912 it did not enjoy real expansion until the 1960s. Its first significant performance car was aimed at the all-important American market and sold against such British evergreens as MGs, Triumph TRs and Austin Healeys. The Fairlady SP 310 of 1962 was a rather dumpy looking offering with separate chassis, all round drum brakes, coil and wishbone independent front suspension and a cartsprung rear. It was powered by a 1488 cc four-cylinder overhead valve engine and about 7,000 were produced, around half of which were sold in America.

Then, in 1965, the model became the SP 311, with larger capacity 1595 cc engine, gaining front disc brakes and an all synchromesh gearbox, the car being titled the Fairlady 1600. By the time that the model was discontinued in 1970, about

40,000 examples had been produced. It was replaced that year by the aforementioned 240, a presentable though slightly anonymous 125 mph (201 kmh) hatchback coupé, powered by a 2.3-litre six-cylinder overhead camshaft engine with all-independent suspension. In the United States, it slipped effortlessly into the gap that existed between, at one extreme, the pricey Porsche 911 and Chevrolet Corvette, and at the other, the MGB and Triumph TR6.

Yet the 240Z, as the model was known in America, had decidedly un-Japanese parentage; the concept had been laid down by a German-born Count, who was by then an American citizen, named Albert Goertz. Having first worked for industrial designer Raymond Loewy in the 1950s, he had designed the prestigious low-production BMW 503 and 507 models and also had a spell with Porsche during the 911s gestation. In 1961 Goertz decided to go to Japan, where he was retained by Nissan. His first assignment was a two-plus-two coupé launched in 1965 as the Silvia and subsequently titled the Coupé 1600.

But what Datsun required was a completely new sports car, specifically designed for the vast American sports car market, where British open two-seaters held sway. Goertz came up with the concept of a roomy two-seater and, as he was steeped in German performance car traditions, he suggested a closed car rather than an open one. This dialogue took place in 1963 when Jaguar's sensational E-type was a mere two years old and Goertz has subsequently acknowledged his debt to Sir William Lyons' masterpiece. He therefore based his design on the lines of the fixed head E-type, but sized closer to the newly-introduced Porsche 911 with which he was so familiar. Initially the power unit was a sophisticated twin-overhead camshaft unit, which proved troublesome, and Nissan decided to abandon the project.

In the meantime, the rival Toyota company had announced its 2000 GT, a model similar to the aborted Goertz design, with a near identical 2-litre six-cylinder twin overhead camshaft engine and all independent suspension. However, it proved to be a pricey offering and only about 1,000 examples were built. But its appearance had a catalytic effect on Nissan which, once again, returned to its Z car and refined Goertz's styling, the lines having been resolved in late 1967. In that year Nissan introduced its 510 Bluebird saloon, powered by a new 1600 cc four-cylinder overhead camshaft engine. The Z car's six evolved from this unit and shared pistons, conrods and valve gear with it. The all-round independent suspension featured front MacPherson struts but with lower wishbones. Front disc brakes and rack pinion steering rounded off a robust specification.

Introduced to America in October 1969, the 240Z was competitively priced there at $3,500 and, in the first two years, an impressive 50,000 cars were sold there. Interestingly, the Japanese home market for such cars was small at the time with only 5,000 examples of the 240 sold there annually. These, for tax reasons, were marketed with a slightly smaller capacity 2-litre engine, related to but not the same as the American version. By the end of 1971, no less than 190,000 examples of the 240 had been sold in three years. Of these, 135,000 or 71 per cent, found American owners.

The 240 was followed in 1974 by the 260Z, with two-plus-two seating, and engine capacity upped to $2\frac{1}{2}$ litres. But weight went up too and top speed was down by about 5 mph (8 kmh) to 125 mph (201 kmh) and sales fell briefly in the wake of the oil price rises. In America the 260 was only destined to last a year when the 280Z took over in 1975. Engine capacity was increased once again, to 2.7 litres, and Bosch fuel injection was standardized. Externally, the model was similar to its predecessors but was becoming progressively more refined. The optional air conditioning had come in for fulsome praise while automatic transmission also proved to be a popular extra. The 280Z, discontinued in 1978, was destined to be the best-selling of all the Z cars. While the original 240 accounted for 156,076 examples, the 260 sold a mere 80,369, but the larger capacity and better equipped 280 sold 230,128. In a mere eight years, Datsun had built some 550,000 cars, which was roughly the same amount the British MGB had sold during a 18-year manufacturing life. Datsun would now build on the success of its Z sports car range with the 280 ZX in 1978, which was to endure until 1983.

The ZX was the most sophisticated sports Datsun yet. Although the bodywork superficially resembled that of the earlier car, it was both wider and longer than its predecessors and was the first Datsun to have been wind tunnel tested during its gestation. Although the coil and wishbone front suspension was essentially a carry-over from the previous model, the rear unit was new with semi-trailing arm taking the place of the struts previously employed. The 2.7-litre six-cylinder engine was extensively re-designed and, in the case of the two-plus-two version, the interior was particularly luxurious with electric windows, air conditioning and optional power steering. First year American sales were impressive, with 78,000 ZXs sold.

A popular two-plus-two option was the ZX T of 1979 with T-bar roof, consisting of removable smoked glass roof panels on either side of the car, leaving a T-shaped centre section. It was also available with a turbocharged engine when it was designated the ZX TT. When a Garret AiResearch unit was added, power was upped from 130 to 180 bhp and top speed to 129 mph (207 kmh), making it the fastest of all the Z series Datsuns. The model remained substantially unchanged until it was discontinued in 1983.

As will have been readily apparent, this Japanese advance was achieved in the face of a retreat by Britain from the world's sports car stage with its proven though progressively ageing products. And tragically, when a new concept emerged, as in the case of the Triumph TR7 sports car, it proved to be badly engineered and built which compounded the decline of Britain's industry.

The country's principal manufacturers of open and closed performance cars, MG and Triumph, were contained within the rambling British Leyland empire, the fragile finances of which were fatally knocked off course by the decline that followed the oil crisis, culminating in nationalization in 1975. Thereafter the renamed Leyland Cars drifted under a succession of chairmen and did not once feel the smack of positive direction until the arrival of Michael Edwardes in 1977. He initiated essential plant closures and a slimming down of the labour force. But a casualty of this rationalization was the ending of the corporate sports cars, the last of which, the Triumph TR7, ceased production in 1981.

The proven and successful MGB had been scheduled for replacement in 1970 but the creation of British Leyland in 1968 meant these plans were sidelined. However, B produc-

Although the MGB GT cannot be considered to be a pukka GT, its 3½-litre V8 powered derivative can. Arriving in 1973, its appearance virtually coincided with the Arab/Israeli war and the model only lasted until 1976.

tion actually peaked in 1972 when 39,366 cars were delivered. Although the six-cylinder MGC came to the end of the road in 1969, four years later, in 1973, another large-engined version of the B made its appearance. This was the MGB GT V8 and, as its name implies, was only available in closed GT form. It followed in the wheel tracks of enthusiast Ken Costello, who had shoehorned the ex-Buick 3½-litre V8 — by then powering the Rover 3500 saloon and Range Rover cross country vehicle — under the bonnet of a GT. The creation of the V8-engined MG was made all the easier, for by then both Rover and MG were in common British Leyland ownership.

The resulting car, that was engineered at MG's Abingdon factory, was virtually identical to the B GT, apart from its special alloy wheels and discreet V8 badges on the nearside front wings and tailgate. This was a 120 mph (193 kmh) car, but was expensive at £2,294, and its arrival was badly timed because in a matter of months of its announcement came the Arab/Israeli war. In addition to this, MG had supply problems and the V8 only lasted until 1976, by which time a mere 2,591 examples had been built.

Despite this the MGB proper continued in production although demand dropped slightly in the wake of the world depresson. But the 17-year-old design was beginning to show its years and the adoption of energy-absorbing bumpers from 1976, demanded by the all important American market which took 80 per cent of output, did little to improve the car's appearance. By 1979, the rising value of the pound began to play havoc with the B's life-giving American sales and BL Cars, as Leyland's successors, were faced with mounting losses. The decision was made to close MG's Abingdon factory, its home since 1929, and discontinue the B. This was duly undertaken, in the face of considerable public protest.

But the reality was that MG's fate had been sealed in the early 1970s when the Triumph TR7 was designated as British Leyland's corporate sports car. Ironically, the Triumph was a closed, rather than an open model, and was the outcome of an in-house competition in 1970 between MG and Triumph. MG came up with a sensational Maxi-engined coupé while Triumph opted for a more conventional front-engined car, coded Bullet. Triumph emerged as the winner but the resulting TR7 was effectively a combination of its front-located engine with the MG's adventurous styling, which was accordingly modified to accommodate it, which perhaps explains why its lines never looked quite 'right'. On paper the TR7's specifications looked competent

Ancient and modern. After a generation of producing open sports cars, in 1975 Britain bowed to what, at the time, was demanded by American safety regulations and introduced the Triumph TR7 coupé. The more traditional open Spitfire from the same manufacturer, which had arrived back in 1962, is in the background.

enough. It had a unitary hull and a 2-litre four-cylinder overhead camshaft engine, derived from that used in the Triumph Dolomite Sprint saloon. Front suspension was by MacPherson struts while a live coil sprung rear axle was employed with radius arms. In theory this was a 100 mph (160 kmh) car and the TR7 was launched on the American market in the spring of 1975 though the model did not go on sale in Britain until spring of the following year.

The original four-speed gearbox did not prove up to its original job and a five 'box was introduced for 1977, but was withdrawn and re-appeared in 1978. Alas, the model was acquiring a reputation for unreliability, which contrasted with the regard America held for the ageing but respected MGB, though the GT version had been withdrawn from the US market on the TR7's introduction. The Triumph was built at an unprofitable plant at Speke on Merseyside, which was closed by Michael Edwardes in May 1978. TR7 production then moved to the Triumph factory at Canley, Coventry and ultimately to the Rover factory at Solihull. But it was destined to be this unhappy model's last move. The final example was built in October 1981, by which time 111,648 had been made. In numerical terms, it had been the most successful TR ever built, though it tarnished the hitherto respected initials and the Triumph marque followed it into obvilion in 1984.

These were also difficult years for the Lotus marque which moved progressively upmarket when it announced its new Elite in 1974, just as the world economic crisis was beginning to bite . . . And at £6,255, the new Elite was the most expensive four-cylinder car in the world. Work on the project had begun in 1971 and carried the M50 coding. Like its Elan predecessor, the new car was built up around a backbone chassis that instantly identifies Colin Chapman's road cars. Suspension was, of course, independent all-round, with coils and wishbones at the front and coil springs, fixed-length drive shafts and radius arms at the rear. Prior to this new generation Elite, Lotus had relied on proprietory, or modified, engines but this model was the first Lotus to be powered by a purpose-built power unit, though it was initially made available by the firm for use in the Jensen-Healey sports car of 1972. This was a 166 bhp twin-overhead-camshaft 1937 cc four, which had started life as a modified version of the overhead-camshaft Vauxhall Victor engine but was subsequently developed by Lotus into an alloy unit of its own.

The glassfibre body perpetuated the concept of the Elan two-plus-two in that the Elite was a four-seater, styled in house by Oliver Winterbottom, though Ital Design was responsible for the interior. The Elite was a distinctive wedge shape, with opening tailgate, and theoretically capable of 125 mph (201 kmh). But there were reliability problems and an unfavourable economic climate meant that the model never reached its production targets. Then, in 1975, came its cheaper Eclat derivative, with fastback styling instead of the Elite's hatchback and more of a two-plus-two than a genuine four-seater. Mechanically similar to its more expensive first cousin, the Eclat was lighter and consequent-

Lotus introduced its mid Esprit model in 1975. Styling was by Ital Design and a revised 2.2-litre turbocharged version arrived in 1980. Here Roger Moore, as James Bond in the 1980 film *For Your Eyes Only*, is about to sample its delights.

ly faster, being capable of 130 mph (209 kmh).

The flagship of this new generation of Lotus cars also appeared in the autumn of 1975: the mid-engined Esprit, although its claimed top speed of 135 mph (217 kmh) was seldom realized. Unlike the Elite and Eclat, which were styled in house, the Lotus flagship's lines were the work of Ital Design. It had been at the 1971 Geneva Motor Show that Lotus's Colin Chapman and Ital's Giorgetto Giugario decided on the shape of the new Lotus and the latter's first public thoughts were revealed and the Esprit featured the longitudinally located Lotus engine mated to the five-speed gearbox of the short lived Citroen SM. There were disc brakes all round, the Esprit becoming the first Lotus road car to employ them throughout; earlier models had retained rear drum brakes.

But much more exciting was the Esprit Turbo with a 210 bhp version of the Lotus four, now enlarged 2.2 litre. Performance was dramatically improved and top speed pushed up to about 145 mph (233 kmh). The chassis was also redesigned and galvanized and subsequently used in the normally-aspirated Esprit and made ready for a V8 version of the four which never came. Selling for close on £17,000, the Esprit Turbo was offered with air conditioning and luxuriously appointed leather upholstery as standard. The model received some welcome publicity for its appearance in the James Bond film *For Your Eyes Only*. In May 1980 the larger 2.2-litre capacity engine was extended to both the Eclat and the Elite, though in 1982 the slow-selling latter model was discontinued.

A Lotus in everything but name though with a rear, as opposed to a mid-engined location, was the DeLorean of 1981, the brainchild of John Z. DeLorean, a former chief engineer of Pontiac and vice-president of General Motors. After leaving the Corporation in 1973, DeLorean dreamed of producing his own car. The Ford V6 engine was first considered as a power unit though a prototype of 1976 employed a rear-mounted four-cylinder Citroen CX unit. The resulting vehicle proved to be somewhat underpowered, so it was decided instead to use the Renault/Peugeot/Volvo 2.7-litre V6. Like the Alpine A310, which used the same engine, it was also rear-mounted. By 1975, Ital Design, which was responsible for the styling, had finalized the body lines which at DeLorean's request had gullwing doors in the manner of the 1954 Mercedes-Benz SL and a stainless steel finish. Although there were thoughts about building the car in Puerto Rico, it was finally produced, with considerable financial assistance from the British government, at a new factory in the Dunmurry region of Belfast in Northern Ireland.

With development of the car now centred on the United Kingdom, in November 1978, DeLorean commissioned the Lotus company to undertake an intensive development programme, which involved the introduction of a Lotus-type backbone chassis with coil and wishbone independent front suspension, *a la* Esprit. At the rear were coil springs, fixed-length drive shafts and wishbones. There were further holdups when, in 1979, DeLorean decided that the car's styling, by then four years old, was in need of an update and it wasn't until January 1981 that the first cars were built. Regrettably the car had not been worth the wait, for DeLorean's dream had turned into a nightmare. There were problems relating to build quality but, more significantly, despite the V6 being enlarged to 2.8 litres, the car could barely reach 110 mph (177 kmh) and acceleration was accordingly disappointing. In addition, the high rear-mounted V6 engine inevitably presented handling problems. Some examples reached America but the onset of the post-1979 oil crisis provided a new set of problems. A receiver was appointed in February 1982 and the last cars left the factory in December after a mere 8,000 examples had been built. The exercise had cost the British tax payer an estimated £40 million.

As already mentioned, another company with Lotus associations was Jensen which, in 1972, had introduced its Jensen-Healey sports car. The firm had passed through a number of reconstructions since Norcros, which had owned it since 1959, sold out in 1968, and by 1970 Kjell Qvale, an enthusiastic Norwegian-born Californian and long time Austin Healey dealer, had taken an 80 per cent interest in the firm. Donald Healey became chairman. The intention was to build the Jensen-Healey sports car, which was the first recipient of Lotus's new 2-litre four-cylinder twin-overhead-camshaft engine. This was a two seater intended to fill the gap resulting from the withdrawal of the Austin Healey 3000 from America though, as an open car, this falls outside the scope of this book.

But Donald Healey had relinquished the chairmanship of the company in 1972 and there were teething problems both with the new Lotus engine and the car itself. However, in 1975, came a closed version, the *Jensen* GT, an altogether more upmarket model than the original sports car with wooden dashboard, better trim and opening rear windows. A top speed nudging 120 mph (193 kmh) was common to both models. The GT cost £4,198, compared with £3,342 for

The 1970s were switchback years for Aston Martin, which changed hands in 1974/5. The William Towns-styled DBS of 1967 received a new 5.3-litre V8 engine in 1969 and it soldiered on until 1989 when it was replaced by the new Virage.

the open car and, with the benefit of hindsight, was pro-bably what the firm should have built in the first place.

Jensen was in a desperate position as the repercussions of the first oil crisis saw sales of the big Interceptor tumble and, in September 1975, a receiver was appointed. Production continued for a time but finally ceased in May 1976, and after 40 years of building cars under its own name, Jensen was no more. Only 459 Jensen GTs had been built, compared with 10,453 roadsters. The firm continued to operate a spares service from West Bromwich, though in 1987 the Interceptor reappeared, with the announcement that it was going to be built at the very bespoke rate of 12 cars a year.

Not that Jensen was the only British specialist car maker to feel the economic chill of the mid-1970s. Aston Martin had been owned by Company Developments since 1972 but, at the end of 1974, a receiver was appointed. The hiatus that followed produced a flurry of round-the-world interests and, after 18 months, Aston Martin had new owners in the shape of George Minden, a Canadian restaurant owner and Rolls-Royce distributor, and 'company doctor' Peter Sprague, though both men were known to each other prior to their interest in the company. This association, under the chairmanship of company developer Alan Curtis, lasted for five years until 1980 when Aston Martin acquired new owners in the shape of Victor Gauntlett of Pace Petroleum and Tim Hearly of CH Industrials.

In view of these corporate upheavals, the company's V8 mainstay continued much as before, apart from the arrival

The 5.3-litre V12-powered XJ-S Jaguar coupé surprised the public on its 1975 arrival by being an upmarket Grand Tourer rather than following in the wheel tracks of its E-type predecessor. It is still in production at the time of writing (1989).

in 1977 of a more potent Vantage version only available in manual gearbox form. This was theoretically capable of a startling 170 mph (273 kmh) top speed. The firm had also used the 5.3-litre V8 to power a new four-door Lagonda saloon, announced in 1976 and essayed in dramatic style by William Towns. This remains in production at the time of writing.

At about the same time that Aston Martin called in the receiver in late 1974, British Leyland, as the country's leading car maker, announced it was seeking financial assistance from the government, which culminated in its nationalization the following year. In retrospect, it is difficult to think of worse circumstances for Jaguar, as part of Leyland, to launch its XJ-S, the expensive and thirsty Grand Tourer, which it introduced in September 1975.

The XJ-S Model could not be considered as a replacement for the E-type, which had ceased production in 1974: at £8,900 the XJ-S was Jaguar's most expensive car ever and inflation would help push the price up to close on £16,000 by 1979, the firm having decided to turn its back on the sports car market and move up market where the profit margins were greater. Consequently the XJ-S was only available in closed form. Perhaps one of the least visually successful of the modern Jaguars, it was, nevertheless able to eat up the miles with turbine-like efficiency. This was because under the bonnet was the firm's 5.3-litre fuel-injected 285 bhp V12 engine, which had first appeared in Series III E-type of 1971. Although obstensibly available with a choice of four-speed manual or three-speed automatic gearboxes, in reality virtually all examples were fitted with the latter option.

Suspension was all independent, with coils and wishbones at the front and double coils, fixed-length drive shafts and lower wishbones at the rear.

Despite these impressive credentials, the reality was that the XJ-S averaged about 14 miles per gallon and Jaguar's image became sullied through the corporate upheavals plaguing its Leyland parent. These only began to be resolved when BL Cars' Michael Edwardes appointed John Egan as Jaguar's chairman in 1980. By this time XJ-S production was almost non-existent and an HE (high efficiency) version of 1981 came not a moment too soon. This featured a more economical version of the V12, with new cylinder heads developed by Michael May which accordingly improved the S's consumption but, even then, the model came under threat as the effects of the second oil crisis began to bite. For 1984 the XJ-S became the first recipient of Jaguar's newly-developed AJ6 single-cam engine, which came complete with five-speed manual gearbox. This was even more economical, returning an improved 16 mpg though, inevitably, top speed was down to about 140 mph (225 kmh).

If 1975 was a bad year for Jaguar to launch its XJ-S, then the same has to be said for Rolls-Royce, which introduced its £32,128 Grand Tourer, the Camargue, in March, In reality, we are not talking here about one car but two: the Corniche of 1971 and the Camargue which followed four years later. First the Corniche. In 1966 Rolls-Royce introduced a two-door version of its Silver Shadow saloon of the previous year, which was uprated as the Corniche and named in memory of the experimental Grand Touring Bentley of pre-war days. The 120 mph (193 kmh) 6.7-litre V8 model, with automatic transmission, was the fastest Rolls-Royce of its day, with 10 per cent more power than that of its predecessor, whatever that might have been, for in the

Rolls-Royce returned to the Grand Touring concept with its 1975 Camargue. Styling was by Pininfarina, air conditioning was standard, as was automatic transmission, while the engine was the firm's long running 6.7-litre V8 unit.

usual Rolls-Royce traditions, outputs were not disclosed. It had a slightly lower roof line than the Silver Shadow and a deeper radiator. Suspension was all-independent with coilsprings and wishbones at the front and semi-trailing arms, coilsprings at the rear along with the Rolls-Royce self-levelling hydraulic system introduced on the Shadow. Power steering was a standard fitment.

The heavier Camargue followed in 1975, the financial turmoil that culminated in the Rolls-Royce company being bankrupted in 1971 having delayed the model's launch. For the first time, Rolls-Royce used an outside consultant for styling its bodywork, in this instance, the Italian Pininfarina company. The model was an uncompromising four-seater with two-door bodywork, and some echoes of the Fiat 130 coupé, but with a rather angular front, though like the Corniche, the famous Rolls-Royce radiator was tilted gently forward. Production was scheduled at one car a week at Rolls-Royce's London-based Mulliner Park Ward works with interior and exterior finish up to the usual Rolls-Royce standards. Two-level air conditioning was a standard fitment, as was power steering and automatic transmission. The Camargue's engine was the company's customary 6750 cc V8 engine, as fitted to the Corniche, and suspension was also similar.

The 6.2-litre Bristol 411 of 1969 enjoyed a seven year production run though, from 1974, it was fitted with an enlarged 6556 cc engine. This is a 1975 car and the model was replaced in the following year by the 603.

The Camargue was capable of effortless 120 mph (193 kmh) motoring though acceleration was slightly inferior to that of the Corniche, on account of the model's greater weight and, unhappily, fuel consumption was around 12 mpg. Perhaps, not suprisingly, the economic climate was such that production stopped briefly and subsequently the

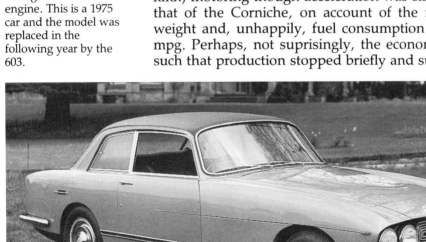

Coventry-based Motor Panels took over the Camargue's construction, with the car being completed at Rolls-Royce's Crewe factory. The model lasted until 1986, by which time about 500 examples had been built. Meanwhile the Corniche was listed until 1981, though it continues to be available in open form, an option from the outset.

Despite the global financial turmoil of the 1970s, Bristol, under the direction of managing director Anthony Crook, continued to produce its three cars a week throughout the decade, much as it had done since the 1950s. However, the body style, introduced for the 407 in 1961, continued, in essence, in the 411 of 1969. Capacity of the Chrysler V8 engine was increased to 6.3 litres while a limited-slip differential was fitted and externally the body, at long last, lost its tail fins. A Series II version of 1971 had automatic rear levelling suspension while the Series III of the following year was easily identified by its new radiator grille and painted coachlines. The Series IV model for 1973 had an enlarged 6556 cc engine and the Series V of 1975 had a modified front end, though with a Bristol-designed self-levelling suspension system. By 1975 the 15-year-old body lines were replaced by two new designs: the 412 and the more expensive 603.

In May 1975 came the new 412 Convertible Saloon, with detachable Targa top. This featured the original, and progressively refined chassis, now graced with new, distinctive, rather angular but aerodynamically efficient bodywork by Zagato. Otherwise the specification was much as before. Steering was power-assisted while the front suspension comprised the customary coil springs and wishbones, with a live axle, torsion bars, radius arms and Watts linkage at the rear. Top speed was in the region of 140 mph (167 kmh) and, under the bonnet, was the 6½-litre Chrysler V8 engine although, as American power units reduced in size in the face of spiralling petrol prices, from 1978 Bristol adopted a smaller 5898 cc engine in 412 Series 2 form. For 1980 came the turbocharged Beaufighter version which lasted until 1981.

The 412 cost £16,924 on its introduction, though Bristol's new 603 of 1976 was a £19,360 car. The 603 wore a new fastback four-seater coupé body even though the 411 chassis was effectively carried over. There were two engine options for the 603, for the 603-S had the 5.9-litre Chrysler V8, later used in the 412, while the 603-3 used a more economic (!) 5.2 unit though this was subsequently withdrawn.

Diametrically opposed to the Bristol's consistency throughout the 1970s was AC's protracted development of a new British GT which finally appeared in 1979, after a nine-year gestation period. It had been back in 1970 that Peter Bohanna and Robin Stables had produced a one-off glassfibre-bodied mid-engined coupé. This was built up around a platform chassis with all independent coil and wishbone suspension and a $1\frac{1}{2}$-litre transversely-mounted Austin Maxi engine, with drive being transferred via a Hewland five-speed gearbox. It was duly displayed at the 1972 Racing Car Show and AC, on the point of discontinuing its low production 428 model, took the model over. Once at Thames Ditton, the Austin Maxi engine was removed and replaced by a 3-litre Ford V6 unit, a new five-speed gearbox was developed and the car renamed the AC 3000ME. But these were difficult post-oil crisis years for all motor manufacturers, let alone small ones, and it was not until 1979 that anything like a production line was built up. Then came the second and far more serious oil crisis. Despite this, AC persevered and spoke optimistically of building five cars a week. Production of this 120 mph (193 kmh) model was limited and, in 1984, the design was sold to AC (Scotland) plc, a Glasgow-based company. The ME was discontinued and replaced by an Alfa Romeo V6-engined AC Ecosse prototype which never entered production.

One firm which responded to the ups and downs of the 1970s in a different way was the TVR company and in 1975 it became the first British manufacturer to offer a turbocharged model. In this instance it was the Ford V6 powered 3000M, to which tuning specialist Broadspeed fitted a Garrett or Holset turbocharger, which boosted power from 142 to 230 bhp, each engine being carefully rebuilt prior to installation. This resulted in a car with a top speed of 140 mph (225 kmh)

The glassfibre-bodied mid-engined 3-litre Ford V6-powered AC 3000ME was the subject of a protracted six-year gestation, finally entering production in 1979. It survived until 1984.

The first British turbocharged car came, surprisingly, from the small TVR concern, which introduced its Broadspeed developed 3-litre Ford V6 turbo-engined chassis in 1975. The unit was available in the M Series and later Taimar coupé and convertible forms but was discontinued in 1979 after 63 had been built.

and one which could reach 60 mph (96 kmh) in under six seconds. But the car was inevitably expensive. In normally-aspirated form, the TVR M series coupé cost £3,686, yet £6,903 in turbocharged state. In addition, the option was offered on the Taimar hatchback, and also in convertible form, but the Turbo was dropped in 1980 to make way for a new generation of TVRs, after just 63 cars had been built.

The car that had inspired TVR to produce its Turbo model was the Porsche 911 Turbo, announced at the 1974 Paris Show. This was instantly identifiable by its larger tyres and distinctive rear spoiler. The normally-aspirated 911 was powered by a 2.6-litre engine though the 260 bhp Turbo used a 3-litre unit, the firm having experimented with turbocharging technology of a Beetle derivative during the Second World War and developed it through racing experience. This transformed the 911 into a 150 mph (241 kmh) plus machine and able to reach 100 mph (160 kmh) in under 15 seconds. But if that was not enough, for 1978, Porsche enlarged the engine to 3.2 litres and introduced an intercooler to the KKK turbocharger. This pushed the top speed up beyond the 160 mph (257 kmh) mark and in 1989 the model is still going strong.

Meanwhile the basic 911 was continuing to evolve. From 1974, capacity was increased to 2.7 litres, bringing it into line with the top-of-the-range revived Carrera model, though it was 1978 before the engine was enlarged again, this time to 3 litres and again to 3.2 litres in 1983. But for all the 911's success, Porsche, although it had experienced some growth, was still essentially a relatively small manufacturer of

specialist cars. In 1963 the firm had built 9,672 cars and a
decade later, in 1973, the figure had risen to 15,415. But 10
years on, in 1983, the firm produced no less than 48,288 cars.
The reason for this considerable growth was that Porsche
espoused the concept of the GT for everyman, as pioneered
by the Ford Capri, which appeared as the 924 model of 1975.
But, as will emerge, there was more than an element of
chance in the change of manufacturing philosophy.

Up until 1975 the Porsche name was synonymous with
sports and GT cars powered by rear-mounted air-cooled
flat-four or six-cylinder engines. But that year the Stuttgart
company introduced a model which broke every rule in its
design canon. It would also come to be the best-selling
Porsche ever built. But as it happened, the 924 Porsche
started out life as a Volkswagen. Heinz Nordhoff, the ar-
chitect of VW's post-war renaissance, had died suddenly in
1968 and was replaced by Kurt Lotz. At this time Porsche
had EA 266, a Beetle replacement, under development and
powered by a liquid cooled four-cylinder engine tucked
away under the car's rear seat. However, in 1971 Rudolph
Leiding, who took over from Lotz, cancelled the project.

But Leiding did give Porsche the go-ahead to design a new
sporting model, under the EA 425 coding, but using the
house 2H litre single-overhead-camshaft four-cylinder Audi
engine from the front-wheel-drive 100 model. By this time
Porsche had laid down the specification of its own 928
model and its front engine/rear drive configuration was mirrored in the layout of the new Volkswagen. In the interests
of good weight distribution, the Porsche design team
separated the engine from its front-wheel drive gearbox,
which was mounted in the back of the car, and separated by
a torque tube. Most of the running gear came from the

Volkswagen/Audi parts bin. The MacPherson strut front suspension was courtesy of the 1302 Super Beetle, while lower A arms came from the Golf. The rear trailing arms were also from the Beetle, though its torsion bars were Porsche's own with half shafts from VW's Type 181 off-road car. Porsche also supplied the seats, which were 911 ones, while the speedometer was from the 914 and switches and instruments from the Golf. Door handles also originated with the Beetle. The two-plus-two bodywork was, however, completely new and was the work of Porsche's Harm Lagaay, giving an aerodynamically creditable Cd of .36.

Although the concept was completed in the mid-1970s, Volkswagen was wrestling with the first deficit in its history and decided not to proceed with the project. Porsche then offered to buy back the design, for DM 100 million (£16.2 million), plus a royalty on the first 100,000 cars built, though a pivotal part of the agreement was that it build the new car at the Audi, former NSU factory at Neckarsulm, about 24 miles (40 kms) from Stuttgart, which was facing closure. The 125 mph (201 kmh) two-plus-two model was introduced in November 1975 and output was such that the 50,000th car was built in 1979 and the all-important 100,000th in February 1981. Automatic transmission arrived for 1977 while, the following year, came a much needed five-speed gearbox, standardized in 1979. But, above all, the 924 brought Porsche ownership to a section of the motoring community who would never have dreamt of aspiring to it. A 170 bhp turbocharged version arrived in 1979, pushing the top speed up to the 140 mph (225 kmh) mark and lasted until 1984. The 924 proper, available in S 2.5 litre form from 1986, remained in production until 1988 when it was discontinued after 150,951 examples had been built.

Reference has already been made to the 928 Porsche, which was developed prior to the 924, but did not appear until after it. Its origins can be traced back to 1971 when Volkswagen cancelled project EA 266. This meant Porsche had no possible mechanical basis to replace the long run ning 911, though in 1988 that evergreen celebrated its 25th anniversary and shows no sign of flagging. The 1980s also saw the arrival of ever more stringent emissions regulations. Porsche recognized that strong transatlantic sales were an essential ingredient of any new model, which tended to mitigate against rear-mounted air-cooled engines. In addition there was a need for automatic transmission, which also pointed to a front-mounted water-cooled engine. The firm also understood that the days of the out and out sports car were numbered with the public requiring greater degrees of comfort and refinement. The result was the 928 of 1978 with front-mounted engine and rear-located gearbox, like the 924, to provide the best possible weight distribution. But unlike the earlier model, here was an expensive, low-production Grand Tourer in the best pre-war traditions.

The 928 was completely new with a 240 bhp 4474 cc V8 engine with single-overhead-camshafts per cylinder bank. Like the 924, the engine and rear-mounted five-speed gearbox were connected with a tubular backbone, though it contained a flexible drive shaft located by no less than five bearings. A three-speed Mercedes-Benz automatic transmission was also available. Suspension comprised the traditional coil springs and wishbones – even if they were not so for Porsche, long wedded to its own patent torsion bars – while at the rear were coil springs and semi-trailing wishbones. This was an integral part of what Porsche called its Weissach axle, named after the Porsche Research and Development facility opened in 1972, and designed to alleviate a possible spin that could occur when an erring 928 driver lifted his foot off the accelerator while cornering.

These sophisticated mechanicals were complemented by a visually impressive two-plus-two body, which ironically had inferior aerodynamics to the cheaper 924. With weight an ever present consideration, the minimum amount of steel was incorporated in the structure with the doors, bonnet and front wings made from aluminium. A revolutionary feature was the apparent lack of bumpers which were concealed *under* the bodywork. They were aluminium beams mounted on collapsible tube or hydraulic rams, depending on local legislation. What was not so apparent was that the 928's front and nose sections were made of a soft plastic, carefully matched to the body colour, which bounced back into shape after impact.

The 928 was launched at the 1977 Geneva Show to a host of accolades, including the 1978 Car of the Year award, the first occasion on which a sports or Grand Touring car had been a recipient. Yet for all the 928's accomplishments – it was capable of 140 mph (225 kmh) – there was a feeling that the new model somehow lacked the traditional Porsche performance formula, exemplified by the 911. These criticisms were met, to some extent, with the arrival, in 1979, of the 4464 cc 928S, which pushed the car's top speed beyond the 145 mph (233 kmh) mark. There was a new front spoiler and rear lip. For 1984 came the Series 2 car, with ABS brakes, and for 1987 the model was effectively re-launched as the 928S4 with aerodynamically improved nose and enlarged 5-litre 320 bhp engine with new heads and four valves per

Conceived prior to the 924, the 928 appeared two years after it in 1977. An all-new model, it was initially powered by a 4470 cc V8 engine though capacity was subsequently enlarged to 4664 cc. In the background are, left to right, 924, 911 SC and 911 'Martini Turbos'.

cylinder. The 928 remains in production today.

In 1981 Porsche unveiled the third of its GTs, in the shape of the 944, based on both the 924 and 928. This was a 160 bhp 2479 cc single-overhead-camshaft four though it would be too simplistic to dismiss it as just one half of a 5-litre 928, had it existed. It retained the V8's 78 mm stroke though the bore size was increased to 100 mm. To combat the customary roughness associated with a large capacity four, Porsche introduced twin balance shafts to counteract these secondary forces. Once again, the gearbox was located at the rear of the car while the bodywork was closely related to that of the 924, though it was 2 in (50.8 mm) wider and able to accommodate wider wheels. The all-independent suspension was effectively that of the 924, suitably uprated. Here was a model that could be considered a genuine Porsche which lacked the noise and harshness of its Audi-engined 924 first cousin. A turbocharged engine was also inevitable and this appeared in 220 bhp form in 1985 and Porsche took the opportunity to rework the front end of the bodywork, along with changes to the rear spoiler. Developing 220 bhp, the Turbo was good for over 150 mph (241 kmh) and is still very much in production.

As will be apparent, Porsche was well to the fore in turbocharger development, although the concept had been first introduced to the European market in 1973 by BMW in the racing 2002 from 1969 onwards. (The first turbocharged road car was American: between 1962 and 1964, Chevrolet offered one as an option on its Corvair Monza Spyder). Unfortunately the BMW's arrival coincided with the 1973 Arab/Israeli war so the concept was shortlived and production ceased in 1974 after only 1,672 had been built. As a two-door saloon, the 2002 perhaps lacked the style to be associated with its performance. The same could not be said, however, for a new generation of BMW coupés which appeared in 1976.

In that year BMW replaced its successful 3-litre coupés, which dated back in essence to 1965, with the 6 Series coupés which did not display any revolutionary features, but purely represented an evolution of the theme. In its most basic 630 CS form, the engine was the proven 3-litre 185 bhp single-overhead-camshaft unit, while there was a choice of transmissions: a four-speed manual 'box or a three-speed automatic unit. There was the usual MacPherson-strut front suspension and semi-trailing arms at the rear. Unlike the earlier coupé, this one incorporated a built in rollover bar but the central roof pillar it required was painted an unobtrusive black. These BMWs were capable of 130 mph (210 kmh) and there was a choice of power units. The 3.2-litre 633 CSi was available from the model's announcement. Capacity was enlarged to 3.4 litres for the 635 in 1978, which was based on the engine of the firm's potent M1 sports racer. By 1985 this had evolved into the M 635 CSi with 24-valve competition-proven cylinder head. After a 13-year production life, these handsome, conservative but expensive GTs still continue to attract a select, loyal clientele.

But the 1970s were difficult years for any specialist manufacturer and this particularly applied to a new one, in this instance the Stuttgart-based makers of the Bitter CD which appeared in 1973. Back in the late 1960s Opel designers, working under the redoubtable Charles (Chuck) M. Jordan, were keen to show the public that they were more than capable of producing exotic cars, as well as their mass-produced saloons, and unveiled two designs at the 1969 Frankfurt Show in the shape of the Aero GT and Open CD.

The Aero was the less interesting of the two concepts and was essentially a GT model with a removable roof. But with the CD (Coupé Diplomat), Jordan and his team had begun with a clean sheet of paper and produced an aerodynamically efficient coupé with flush fitting windows and direct front and rear glazing. The car was built on a shortened Opel

Diplomat floorpan and under the bonnet was a 5.4-litre Chevrolet V8 engine with power transmitted to the de Dion rear axle by Turbo Hydramatic transmission. Suspension was all-independent by coils and wishbones. Although there was no question of putting the CD into production, its appearance interested Erich Bitter, a well known amateur racing driver, who managed to convince the Opel design staff to lend their professional services and the result was the Bitter CD, which appeared in 1973. The handsome two-plus-two bodywork came from the Stuttgart coachbuilding firm of Baur while the mechanicals closely followed those used in the 1969 show car. Power-assisted steering also featured.

In truth, the Bitter could not have appeared at a worse time. Despite this, no less than 463 examples of this 130 mph (209 kmh) car had been built by the time that a new smaller Bitter appeared late in 1979. This was based on the 3-litre overhead-camshaft Opel Senator engine with all independent suspension. This time there was the option of a five-speed gearbox and the interior was leather trimmed for those who wanted it. Ferguson four-wheel-drive was subsequently listed with convertible and saloon versions also available.

All these German GTs are notable for their conventional front engine/rear drive configuration. France, by contrast, opted for a mid-location for the power units of its GTs. The two principal specialist manufacturers were Alpine Renault, which continued with its rear-engined A310, introduced in 1971, and Matra, which, it will be recalled, had joined the ranks of the motor manufacturers when it bought the Bonnet concern in 1964. In 1973 the chunky M 530A was replaced by the Matra Bagheera, a more conventionally styled glassfibre coupé but with three abreast accommodation in rather aircraft-like seats, made possible by the lack of instrusive transmission tunnel because of its mid-located engine. In 1969 Matra had established design and sales links with Simca and the new model was accordingly named the Matra-Simca Bagheera, the latter name being derived from the black panther in Rudyard Kipling's *Jungle Book*. The model's 1294 cc power unit, drive shafts and suspension were courtesy of the front-wheel-drive Simca 1100 saloon. There were all-round torsion bars, with front wishbones and rear trailing arms.

In truth the Bagheera did not initially live up to its good looks. It managed a rather pedestrian 100 mph (160 kmh), so in 1977 the 1442 cc version of the original power unit, as used in the Simca 1308 and Chrysler Alpine models, was

Another evergreen. In 1974 Alfa Romeo introduced a coupé version of its Alfetta saloon. This Guigiaro-styled model was powered by 1.8, 1.6 and, ultimately, 2-litre four-cylinder and 2½-litre V6 engines. It survived in GTV form until 1987.

employed and, from 1979, was the sole fitment. Although top speed remained about the same, acceleration was noticeably improved. The Bagheera continued in production until 1980.

So much for a representative French GT. But what of Italy, home of the Grand Tourer, in the 1970s? Alfa Romeo, which had been in the forefront of the GT revolution, began to replace its long running Giulia Sprint coupés in 1974 with a range of Alfetta-based coupés which enjoyed similarly long production runs and were not finally discontinued until 1987. In 1972 Alfa Romeo unveiled its new Alfetta saloon, which retained its traditional twin-overhead-camshaft engine of 1.8 litres. However, its remaining mechanicals were notably adventurous and a new five-speed gearbox was mounted in unit with the differential, in the manner of its illustrious racing forebear of the same name. Suspension was by wishbones and torsion bars at the front though at the rear were coil springs, semi-trailing arms, Watts linkage and de Dion rear axle, the latter also echoing that of the 1951 Alfetta single-seater.

The GT coupé, which appeared in 1974, had completely new bodywork by Giugario's Ital Design, as opposed to Bertone which had the highly successful Giulia coupés to its credit. The GT was based on a shortened Alfetta floorpan and it was originally powered by the saloon's 1.8-litre engine. This was discontinued in 1976 and replaced by a more economical 1.6-litre unit and, simultaneously, came the 2-litre GTV. The range proved immensely popular, combining performance, a maximum speed of close on 120 mph (193 kmh) and the good looks coupled with the surefootedness which reflected the weight distribution of its mechanical components.

In 1971 Alfa Romeo introduced its first front-wheel-drive model, the 1198 cc Alfasud saloon. The engine was an advanced flat-four unit, with a single-overhead-camshaft per bank and it seemed logical that a sporting derivative would follow in the usual Alfa Romeo traditions. The Alfasud Sprint of 1976 bore a family resemblance to the Alfetta GTV, which was not surprising because Giugario was also responsible for styling the smaller car. The resulting Sprint was based on the Alfasud's floorpan. Similarly suspension comprised MacPherson struts at the front and a coilsprung live rear axle. The engine was an enlarged version of the saloon one and increased to 1286 cc. A five-speed gearbox, pioneered in the Ti saloon, was employed. Alfa Romeo claimed a top speed of 103 mph (165 kmh) but in 1978 capacity was increased — to 1490 cc. Maximum speed remained about the same though acceleration improved noticeably, and the following year came the 95 bhp Sprint Veloce. The model continued in 1490 cc form until 1988 with the arrival of a 1.7-litre engine and, for 1989, there was a 16-valve cylinder head. After 13 years in production, the Sprint is still going strong, long after its saloon parent, which was discontinued in 1984.

The Alfasud was followed in the front-wheel-drive tracks of Lancia, which had introduced the concept to the Italian industry in 1961. In 1969, it will be recalled, the firm had been taken over by Fiat and it was its twin-overhead-camshaft four-cylinder engine, though transversely mounted, which was used in the Lancia Beta saloon of 1972. This was followed in 1974 by the Beta two-plus-two coupé,

One of the great GT survivors, the Ghia-styled 5.7-litre Ford V8-powered De Tomaso Pantera first appeared in 1971 and, incredibly, remains available to this day. This is a 1975 example.

available with 1592 and 1756 cc power units. Suspension was independent all-round, with MacPherson struts front and rear. This meant that both models were capable of 110 mph (177 kmh) with varying degrees of acceleration. In 1975 came the HPE, which stood for High Performance Estate, with similar engine options, plus a 1995 cc one, and sharing the same wheelbase as the saloon. This was a 115 mph (185 kmh) estate very much in the spirit of the Reliant Scimitar GTE. Both models lasted until 1985.

As already noted, Fiat's mid-engined X1/9 arrived in 1972 and in 1975 it unveiled its 'own' mid-engined model in the shape of the Monte Carlo, which was given the in-house Lancia badge. Like its mid-engined Fiat brother, the Lancia was aimed at the American market. Styling was the responsibility of Pininfarina while the 1995 cc engine was the same transversely-mounted Fiat twin-cam unit used in the Beta. Suspension was by all-round MacPherson struts. All this combined to produce a 115 mph (185 kmh) GT, though American versions were called the Scorpio to avoid confusion with the Chevrolet Monte Carlo series. The Beta saloon was boosted to 100 bhp in 1976 and the Monte Carlo stayed ahead with a 120 bhp unit, though the model was withdrawn from America in 1978. Lancia returned in 1980 and also to the British market where the model was sold as the Monte Carlo. Production lasted until 1983.

Fiat kept itself in the Grand Touring field with the 130 coupé of 1972. The 130 saloon was introduced as Fiat's top line model in 1969, with all-independent strut suspension

The mid-engined Montecarlo (Monte Carlo in Britain) began pre-production life as a Fiat and emerged as a Lancia in 1976. A Fiat 2-litre twin overhead camshaft engine was employed and the model lasted until 1983, latterly in more powerful 100 bhp form.

and the 2.8-litre engine was a V6 in the Dino manner though with belt-driven single-overhead-camshafts. This was fitted with an undistinguished four-door body. However, in 1972, came an impressively styled Pininfarina coupé, with an enlarged 3235 cc engine like the saloon, and similarly available with three-speed automatic transmission or a five-speed manual gearbox. Although this was a relatively heavy model and road tests spoke favourably of its comfort, performance was not in the BMW class. However, it was a 115 mph (185 kmh) car which finally ceased production in 1977.

Fiat had also effectively taken over Ferrari in 1969 and it seems likely that had this not occurred, the Maranello company would have suffered the financial problems which plagued Maserati and Lamborghini in the wake of the 1973 oil price rise. Despite the poor economic climate, the Ferrari range continued to evolve. In 1973 the original 246 series Dino was replaced by the 308 GT4 one. The model was notable for a number of Ferrari firsts; it was the first production Ferrari with Bertone bodywork, rather than the customary Pininfarina, and its first mid-engined two-plus-two. A multi-tubular chassis was employed and the engine was new, a 90-degree V8, rather than V6, of 2927 cc and with twin-overhead-camshafts per cylinder bank. These were driven by toothed belts rather than chains which was another milestone for the firm. The engine was transversely-mounted and mid-located in the manner of its illustrious predecessor. This was a two-plus-two though the reality was that the rear seats were only suitable for carrying luggage. This did not prevent the model being capable of 150 mph (241 kmh). Not that it was badged a Ferrari at the outset: the Dino name sufficed until 1976 when suddenly the 308 became a Ferrari. The 308 endured until 1980.

For 1976 came the 308 GTB two-seater short-wheelbase version, initially with glassfibre Pininfarina body, with lines like those of the 246 Dino. It had about the same performance and top speed as the two-plus-two model but looked a lot better, which was a factor in it remaining in production for rather longer, in twin overhead camshaft 3185 cc GTB form from 1986, and still currently available.

So much for the smaller Ferraris but what of the original 12-cylinder line? In 1971 Ferrari introduced its top rank 365 GT4 BB or Boxer, but production did not begin until 1973. This took its name from the fact that its 12-cylinder 4.4-litre engine was horizontally opposed, a design initially featured on a 1964 Ferrari Formula 1 racer though this was the first time it had been used in a road car. The engine was mounted longitudinally in the mid-position and the Boxer was the

The small Ferrari line, which began with the Dino in 1969, was perpetuated in 1975 by the mid-engined 3-litre 308 GTB. Styling was once again by Pininfarina. Handling was up to the usual Ferrari standards and production ceased in 1989.

first road-going Ferrari so powered, the Dino not being badged as such. Power was transmitted by chain drive to the five-speed gearbox. There was a multi-tubular frame with the customary all-round coil and wishbone suspension. Bodywork was the traditional Pininfarina styled/Scaglietti built combination. Despite these impressive credentials, this car was 'only' capable of 170 mph (273 kmh) plus rather than the 200 mph (321 kmh) spoken of when the model was announced, perhaps on account of its weight. It was replaced in 1976 by the similar but longer, wider and larger capacity 4.9-litre 512BB version which, although it had a claimed 188 mph (302 kmh) top speed was actually slower than its predecessor and initially could only manage a little over 160 mph (257 kmh). This Boxer was discontinued in 1984.

But down the road at Sant' Agata Bolognese, all was far from well with the rival Lamborghini company. For during the late 1960s, Ferruccio Lamborghini had become increasingly disillusioned with the company he had created. Strikes throughout the Italian motor industry compounded his problems and, in 1972, he sold a controlling interest in his firm to Georges Rossetti, who ran a Swiss Lamborghini distributorship. Two years later, in 1974, Ferruccio disposed of his remaining share to Rene Leimar, a Swiss businessman. This arrangement came to an end in 1978, when the Italian government stepped in to prevent the firm from closing and culminated in the Swiss/French Mimran group taking over Lamborghini in 1981.

It is ironic that one of Lamborghini's most sensational models, the Countach, was created and sold during these corporate upheavals. In 1970 Lamborghini's chief engineer, Paolo Stanzani, had begun work on a Bertone concept car which was destined to be a successor to the already legendary Miura. Stanzani decided that, instead of placing the Lamborghini V12 transversely, as he had done with the Miura, he would mount it longitudinally. But rather than position the gearbox and differential in the traditional location at the rear of the car, he came up with the ingenious, but costly, alternative of placing the 'box at one end of the engine, alongside the driver, with the differential at the other end of the unit. The drive was taken, via a sealed tube, through the engine's sump. This made for a more balanced car, for the Miura had a tendency to be nose light. The engine itself was enlarged to 4.9 litres. Next, Bertone's Marcello Gandini, who had the Miura's sensational bodywork to his credit, came up with an even more extraordinary and utterly distinctive bodywork which turns heads to this day. In 1968 he had been responsible for a special body on the Alfa Romeo Tipo 33 sport racer with doors which opened upwards like a beetle's wings. It was accordingly named the Carabo (scarab beetle). Taking this theme, the Lamborghini was displayed at the 1971 Geneva Show. Just prior to its completion, one of the Toronese workers is reputed to have exclaimed: 'Countach!' which is local slang for praise and astonishment. The name stuck. The extraordinary wedge-shaped body was only 40 in (1,016 mm) high and the Countach received much the same reception that had greeted the Miura five years previously.

There had never been anything like it before, the Bertone-styled Lamborghini Countach of 1974. The V12 engine was longitudinally mounted and the model was built in this original 4-litre LP 400 form until 1978.

In view of this, the factory decided to put the Countach into production but, unwisely, withdrew the Miura in 1972, though it was to be 1974 before the first production car left Sant' Agata. This differed in some important respects from the show car. The original chassis had been a simple sheet metal and tubular one but this was replaced by a more complex spaceframe and the engine capacity reverted to its original 3.9 litres. Minor changes were made to the bodywork though the extraordinary lines remained intact. Suspension was by coils and wishbones all round and, once on the road, the Countach proved itself a 170 mph (324 kmh) performer though it was hardly the car which the suddenly energy-conscious world wanted.

Despite this, the Countach remained in production throughout a difficult decade. In 1975 Stanzani departed and, in 1978, Giulio Alfieri, formerly Maserati's chief engineer, joined Lamborghini. Faced with uprating the Countach, he decided that, rather than turbocharge the engine, which he believed might make the unit unreliable, he would opt instead for new four-valve cylinder heads and at the same time increase the V12's capacity, already upped to 4754 cc in 1982, to 5167 cc. This appeared in 1985 and pushed power up from 375 to 455 bhp and made the Countach a 180 mph (289 kmh) car. This fabulous model is still in production, with a facelifted version waiting in the wings.

Alfieri's appearance at Lamborghini had followed his sudden departure from Maserati, resulting from Alessandro de Tomaso's 1975 takeover of the firm. It will be recalled that Peugeot's successful bid for Citroen had culminated in Maserati being left to its own devices and, in August 1975, the firm once more became Italian owned. This was the outcome of an agreement whereby the Italian government put up 70 per cent of the necessary capital through GEPI, the State Capital Corporation, and also loaned de Tomaso his 30 per cent stake. However, responsibility for the design of Maserati cars was switched to De Tomaso Automobiles, which prompted Giulio Alfieri's stormy departure. De Tomaso decided on a change of strategy to concentrate on the production of closed performance cars in the Mercedes-Benz manner which fall outside the scope of this book. The 145 mph (233 kmh) Kyalami of 1977, however, does not.

This was effectively a re-skinned De Tomaso Longchamps though with Maserati's 4136 cc V8 engine in place of the customary Ford V8. Suspension, by coils and wishbones, was all independent. In 1978 a 4.9-litre engine became available and the Kyalami lasted until 1982 by which time the significant four-door Quattroporte had appeared.

CHAPTER SIX

Postscript: the Grand Tourer supreme, 1980 to date

'Getting back into an ordinary car feels like stepping back into the past'

Autocar after road testing the Audi Quattro

The car that created the four-wheel-drive revolution: the Audi Quattro of 1980 was based on the firm's GT model and its engine was a turbocharged 2.1-litre five-cylinder unit. The Quattro gave Audi the world rally championship in 1982 and 1984.

By the early 1980s the British sports car was effectively no more. The last MGB had been built in 1980 and the Triumph TR7 ended its ignominious career in the following year. Although Aston Martin, Bristol and Lotus continued to uphold Britain's Grand Touring presence, it was Japan, following Datsun's pioneering Z series car, that took up the concept with greatest enthusiasm, with many of its leading manufacturers offering GTs.

This should be seen against the growing world dominance of that country's motor industry. As the world's economies buckled under the impact of the second, and more damag-

ing, oil price rise or 1979, Japan began to overtake America as the world's leading car manufacturer, something it achieved in 1981. Although the United States subsequently regained the initiative, Japan, as the manufacturer of smaller, more fuel-efficient cars, was back on top again in 1987.

The energy crisis had a profound effect on the appearance of these cars because, as fuel prices rose, the car makers once again began to look to the use of aerodynamic bodywork as a fuel-saving aid. Thus the work, particularly in Germany, of such inter-war pioneers as Rumpler, Jaray, and Kamm, as set down in Chapter One, again became fashionable. Wind tunnel testing, once confined to the development of the racing car and sports coupé, became an obligatory part of automobile technology, as the world gradually recovered from the trauma of 1979.

Another factor in the demise of the European GT has been the arrival of the so called 'hot hatchback' in the wake of the immensely successful Volkswagen Golf GTi of 1979. By 1988 it accounted for over 26 per cent of VW's total sales and other manufacturers have found that their 'GTis' are selling just as well. Ford's XR2 is responsible for 18 per cent of all its Fiesta sales and, significantly, Ford have not yet replaced the long running Capri, its GT for every man, which finally ceased production in 1987.

The American Big Three returned to profitability in the 1980s and looked expansively to Europe's prestigious but vulnerable specialist manufacturers. General Motors set the pace in 1986 when it bought Lotus and today Ford owns Aston Martin, AC and Jaguar while Chrysler is Lambor-

Despite the fact that the Japanese have been setting the GT pace in recent years, in 1989 Vauxhall announced the Calibra which boasts the world's lowest drag factor (of 0.26). There is a choice of 2-litre engines; with eight or 16-valve units and front or four wheel drive. The Calibra was awarded *Autocar & Motor* magazine's Design of the Year award in 1989.

ghini's new master. The 1980s were also years of technological development. Audi pioneered a cheap and practical four-wheel-drive system, which first appeared on its 1980 Quattro. Although originally conceived for rallying, the facility has spread beyond these relatively narrow confines, and found its way, not only to GTs, but also family saloons. Audi is a firm with something of a chequered history. Founded in 1909, it became, along with Horch, Wanderer and DKW, part of the Auto Union combine in 1932, and produced both front and rear drive cars until the outbreak of war. Although the DKW two-stroke car was perpetuated at Ingolstadt in West Germany after hostilities, Audi remained in abeyance. Daimler-Benz took DKW over in 1958 but in 1965 sold out to Volkswagen. They reactivated the Audi name and reintroduced a new series of four-stroke, front-wheel-drive models which echoed pre-war Audi precedent.

In 1972 Ferdinand Piech, nephew of Dr Ferry Porsche, joined Audi from Porsche, as head of Research and Development and initiated a policy of technical innovation by introducing a five-cylinder engine in 1976 in the 100 saloon. When the same model was revised for 1983, it was offered with aerodynamically efficient bodywork and distinctive flush-fitting windows, a feature used by Kamm in the 1930s. Three years previously, in 1980, Audi had introduced its celebrated four-wheel-drive system.

The Quattro's origins are to be found in the four-wheel-drive Volkswagen Iltris, a cross country model, built to a German army brief at Ingolstadt from 1978, to replace the firm's long-running DKW Munga. It was while testing a pre-production Iltris in Scandinavia during the winter of 1976–7 that Jorg Bensinger, Audi's chief chassis engineer, conceived the notion of applying the Itris's ingenious, permanently engaged four-wheel-drive layout to a road car. Significantly it dispensed with the heavy and costly transfer box previously employed.

On his return to Ingolstadt, Bensinger suggested the idea to Ferdinand Piech, who soon gave the idea his blessing. Although four wheel drive was almost as old as the motor car, its roadholding advantages, particularly across country, had been greatly popularized by the war-time Jeep, while the Land-Rover of 1948 underlined its use as an optional facility for an off-road car. As already mentioned, Jensen had offered four-wheel-drive on its FF of 1969–71 but only 318 were sold. Later the Japanese Toyota and Subaru companies produced four-wheel-drive vehicles, though the drive was not permanently engaged.

By the spring of 1978 an Audi prototype was showing its

worth, both in deep snow and on dry test track. That year's 80 model was used to test components and the Quattro made its sensational debut at the 1980 Geneva Motor Show. Based on the 80 floorpan, the body was the yet-to-be-announced GT version, which appeared in 1981. The engine was essentially that of the Audi's five-cylinder 2144 cc unit, intended to combine the economy of a four with the smoothness of a six. It had been turbocharged for use in the Audi 200 of the same year but, when used in the 200 bhp Quatto, an intercooler was employed, which gave 30 bhp more. The four-wheel-drive system was a conversion of the 100's front-wheel-drive layout. There was the usual front-wheel-drive differential located between the engine and gearbox which also contained an all important second grapefruit-sized differential within an enlarged gearbox housing. There was a third differential conventionally positioned in the rear axle. A key feature of the Audi system was a hollow gear cluster within the 'box, with an inner shaft transmitting power forward from the central differential. Suspension was all-independent, by MacPherson struts borrowed from the Audi 200T and 80.

Although competition had not been uppermost in Bensinger's mind when he proposed the Quattro to Piech, it was an obvious natural competitor on the rally field and, for three years, the Quattro dominated the rallying scene. Audi was placed fifth in the World Championship of Makes in 1981, the first year it fielded the model; it won in 1982 and was only just pipped to the post in 1983 by Lancia. But the Quattro was also a road car. Costing £17,052 in 1982, compared with £8,391 for the visually similar front wheel drive GT, the Audi more than lived up to expectations. Acceleration was close to that of the Porsche 928 and 100 mph (160 kmh) came up in less than 20 seconds. This would have been impressive enough without its pioneering mechanicals, but it was on narrow, twisting roads that the system really proved its worth as it could be negotiated a good 20 mph (32 kmh) faster than a conventionally driven car, and proved to be little short of sensational. Top speed was 115 mph (185 kmh).

On the rally field, Peugeot, Citroen, and MG all followed in the Quattro's wheel tracks. Then came the road cars. In 1985 BMW offered its 325i with four-wheel option and, the same year, came news of the Porsche's fabulous 911 related four-wheel-drive twin-turbocharged 959. Production was limited to 200 cars as it was to have been originally homologated for the aborted Group B competition. With a theoretical top speed of 205 mph (329 kmh), making it one of the fastest road cars ever, the sophisticated four-wheel-drive system was operated by spin detectors and micro processors which permitted the driver to select the combination according to the road conditions.

It was, however, the Japanese who applied the system to its performance cars with greatest enthusiasm. No car more sums up the vitality of the Far East's Grand Tourers than the XT from Fuji Heavy Industries' Subaru, a firm which had been producing conventionally engineered four-wheel-drive off-road vehicles since 1973. By 1985 it had extended the system to a range of turbocharged saloons and, that year, introduced a futuristic four-wheel-drive turbo. This sleek, low-drag paper dart of a coupé concealed equally advanced mechanicals. The 1781 cc flat-four engine was turbocharged, while four wheel drive was optional. There was push-button control on the manual gearbox cars while computer assistance was a feature of the versions equipped with automatic transmission. The pneumatic suspension had height adjustment and automatic levelling and, as if this was not enough, the instruments moved with the tilting steering column! The XT was a 120 mph (193 kmh) performer, though the lines were updated in 1987 and four wheel drive permanently engaged. But on the debit side was a cramped interior.

Meanwhile Japan's mainstream sports car grew in stature and sophistication as the decade progressed. Toyota introduced its much praised 120 mph (193 kmh) mid-engined MR2 (for 'Midship Runabout') in 1985. It was offered with a choice of power units: a single-overhead-camshaft 1500 cc engine from the current Corolla saloon or the 1600 cc four-valve version of its GT derivative. With all-round strut suspension, the model received worldwide praise for its superlative handling, good ride and neat gearchange, which is sometimes a weak point on transversely-mounted mid-engined cars.

1983 saw the arrival of the Nissan (as Datsun cars had been known since then) 300ZX replacement for the Datsun 280ZX, which had grown in weight and size over the years. This was a completely new car, with nothing carried over from previous models, a two-plus-two body and opening hatchback, and the long running six replaced by a 3-litre V6 with single-overhead-camshafts, available with or without turbocharger. In the later form, 0-60mph (96 kms) in less than seven seconds became a reality, as did a 140 mph (225 kmh) top speed. Other current Japanese offerings on a similar theme are the rotary-engined Mazada RX, and the Toyota Ceilica and Supra and Izula Piazza.

The Nissan 300 XZ has been available in Britain since 1984, where the Grand Touring scene was little changed from the previous decade. The long-running Bristol continued as before. The 603 line was discontinued in 1982 and replaced by the Britannia, with lower and sleeker body lines, and by 1989 was still a 5.9-litre Chrysler V8-powered £80,000 Grand Tourer. In 1981 Bristol had introduced its turbocharged Beaufighter convertible, which remains in production alongside the Britannia, and for 1983 turbocharging was offered in that model and also remains available.

Like Bristol, Aston Martin initially produced much the same models throughout the 1980s but, in 1986, came news of the Vantage Zagato, limited to 50 cars, in memory of the DB4-based GT from the same styling house of 25 years previously. This is a 187 mph (300 kmh) Grand Tourer; the shortened chassis was built in Newport Pagnell and then shipped to Italy and transported to Milan where the aluminium bodywork and luxury interior were fitted. The chunky, purposeful Zagato bodywork was echoed by the model's impressive mechanical specifications and Aston Martin broke its customary silence over power outputs. The Zagato's engine is a 432 bhp high compression V8, with high lift cams, special Cosworth pistons and five-speed ZF gearbox.

Then, in 1988, Aston Martin announced its new Virage model for the 21st century. Not only did this mean the long running V8 model would be discontinued after a 20-year manufacturing life, it also boasted a brand new chassis, as the V8's dated back, in essence, to the DB4 of 1958. Styled by John Heffernan and Ken Greenley, the Virage is testimony to the vitality of the British Grand Tourer. The V8 is fitted with a new four-valve cylinder head and there is a choice of a five-speed manual or three-speed automatic

Intended to take Aston Martin into the 21st century, the Heffernan and Greenley-styled Virage of 1990 is powered by the firm's long running 5.3-litre V8 but with new 32-valve cylinder heads.

There was a change of emphasis for Maserati with the 1982 arrival of the Biturbo, a luxury GT intended to challenge the BMW and Mercedes-Benz markets. The 2-litre V6 engine boasted two IHI turbochargers though capacity was later increased to 2.8 litres.

gearbox. Suspension is similar to that of its predecessor, but is lightened, with coils and wishbone at the front and a de Dion rear axle. The model is scheduled to begin production this year and it is expected to be capable of in excess of 150 mph (241 kmh). Aston Martin, owned by Ford since 1987, and with a long history of financial uncertainty behind it, now has a more secure future.

In France, the Alpine Renault GTA of 1985 was demonstrably a 1980s product, this glassfibre bodied coupé having a drag coefficient of only 0.28, compared with 0.35 of its predecessor. A replacement for the long-running A310, the new model sold simply as the GTA in Britain – the Alpine name being owned here by Peugeot Talbot. It was longer, wider and higher than its predecessor though the concept of the backbone chassis and rear mounted V6 engine was perpetuated. Suspension was all independent by coils and wishbones. The model was available in conventionally aspirated or turbocharged form, with respective capacities of 2849 and 2458 cc. In the latter form, the GTA was capable of speeds in excess of 145 mph (233 kmh).

A V6 engine and turbocharging were also the key ingredients of Maserati's Biturbo model, though there the resemblance ended. This was an expression of Alessandro de Tomaso's new strategy for Maserati and this new model, a small one by Modena standards, took it into BMW and Mercedes-Benz territory. The Bora and Merak, which dated back to Citroen's period of ownership, were discontinued in

Perhaps only the Italians could produce the daring and extraordinary Countach. By 1988 the V12 had evolved to a 48-valve 5167 cc unit. The rear wing did not contribute to the model's already limited rear visibility!

1980 and 1981 respectively and replaced in 1982 by the Biturbo. Styled in house by Maserati, it was a luxuriously-appointed two-door four-seater coupé which, at the time of its introduction, was the world's first twin-turbocharged road car, with each cylinder bank employing its own Japanese built water-cooled IHI unit. As a result the Biturbo could reach 60 mph (96 kmh) in just over seven seconds and achieve a top speed of about 125 mph (201 kmh), although the latter was a disappointing figure and perhaps a reflection of the model's relatively poor aerodynamics. Engine capacity was increased to $2\frac{1}{2}$ litres for 1984 while the following year came the supplementary and faster 228 coupé, with 2790 cc V6 and twin Garrett turbochargers.

De Tomaso and Chrysler's Lee Iacocca are old friends and the Corporation took a 37 per cent share in Maserati, with a view to it eventually taking the firm over, though the deal was subsequently unscrambled. One firm which, in 1987, Chrysler did buy was Lamborghini, inheriting two models: the Countach and the Jalpa. The origins and development of the long running and fabled Countach have already been chronicled but, in 1982, Lamborghini introduced its supplementary model in the shape of the mid-engined Jalpa, which was a successor to the earlier Silouette convertible and its mechanics were essentially carried over from it. The transversely-mounted V8 was enlarged from 2995 to 3485 cc, with belt-driven twin-overhead-camshafts. Suspension was by all-round coils and wishbones. The Jalpa was fitted with new Bertone bodywork. with a detachable roof panel, visually similar to the Countach's but less costly, selling for £26,000 in 1983, compared with £54,000 for the larger car. And it as capable of 'only' 150 mph (241 kmh). The Jalpa remains in production in 1989 and, like the Countach, is also notable for the fact that its rear-driven wheels have wider tyres than the front ones!

The Lamborghini factory at Sant 'Agata is not far from the Ferrari works at Maranello near Modena. In the 1980s Ferrari has shown it has lost none of its skill and vitality in producing some of the finest Grand Tourers in the world. In 1980 came the two-plus-two Mondial 8, a replacement for the 308 GT4 of the previous decade, but with distinctive and impressive Pininfarina bodywork. Mechanically the model was much the same as its predecessor, with the 2927 cc V8 mounted ahead of the rear axle line, although the wheelbase was 4 in (101 mm) longer to permit more practical rear accommodation. Heavier than the GT4, it was accordingly slower and could not manage more than 143 mph (230 kmh). In 1983 came new four-valve cylinder heads and the model continued substantially unchanged until 1986 when the engine was enlarged to 3185 cc. The Mondial remains in production in 1989.

But what better note on which to end this book than with the magnificent Testarossa. Introduced by Ferrari in 1985 as a successor to the Boxer 512 BB, it is perhaps today the ultimate expression of the GT theme and costs £91,915.

The ultimate Grand Tourer? The Ferrari Boxer was replaced in 1986 by the Testarossa, and was powered by its 4942cc flat 12 engine. For its sensational coachwork, Pininfarina has drawn on expertise which goes back to the dawn of motoring.

Powered by its predecessor's 4943 cc flat-12 engine, with twin-overhead-camshafts per cylinder bank, the cam boxes are painted red, so giving the model its Testarossa name, meaning 'red head' in Italian, and reviving the name of the famous Ferrari sports racer of 1957–61 vintage. The engine is longitudinally located in a tubular frame while suspension is, naturally, all-independent, with coils and wishbone at the front and a similar layout at the rear though with twin spring units.

These magnificant mechanicals are complemented by an equally sensational two-seater Pininfarina wind tunnel-tested body dominated by finned air intakes, introduced on the Mondial but extended to incorporate part of the door panels, as the flat 12 boasts twin radiators located either side of the engine. But, unlike some of its predecessors and con-temporaries, the Testarossa is, in *Autocar & Motor's* words, 'not only . . . one of the world's most capable supercars but also one of the easiest to live with.' The magazine's testers found that it had 'a comfortable cabin . . . good visibility, and sound ergonomics complement an excellent ride' though, on the debit side, its handling 'lacked sharpness'. Although the mighty flat-12 was capable of propelling the big Ferrari at 180 mph (289 kmh) and reaching 60 mph (96 kmh)in 5.2 seconds, it was also 'fabulously flexible'. The Ferrari Testarossa is living testament to the fact that the Gran Turismo car is alive and well in Italy, the country which was, after all, its birthplace.

Bibliography

Aston Martin V8 by Michael Bowler (Cadagon Publications, 1985)

Bodies Beautiful: A history of car styling and craftsmanship by John McLellan (David and Charles, 1975)

From Chaindrive to Turbocharger by Denis Jenkinson (Patrick Stephens, 1984)

Cisitalia by Nino Balestra and Cesare De Agostini (Automobilia, 1980)

Classic Italian Marques by Jonathan Wood (Hamlyn, 1987)

Classic Sports Cars by Cyril Posthumus (Hamlyn, 1980)

The Complete Encyclopedia of Motor Cars, edited by G.N Georgano (Ebury Press, 1982)

An Encyclopedia of European Sports and GT Cars 1945 to 1960 by Graham Robson (Haynes, 1981)

An Encyclopedia of European Sports and GT cars from 1961 by Graham Robson, (Haynes, 1980)

The Ferrari Legend: The Road Cars by Antoine Prunet (Patrick Stephens, (1980)

The Sporting Fords Volume 3, Capris by Jeremy Walton (Motor Racing Publications, 1983)

The Mustangs by Richard M. Langworth (Motor Racing Publications, 1984)

Forty Years With Fiat by Dante Giacosa (Automobilia, 1979)

Land Speed Record by Cyril Posthumus (Osprey, 1971)

Le Mans 24-hour race by David Hodges (Temple Press, 1963)

Mille Milgia 1927-1957 by Giovanni Lurani (Automobile Year 1981)

Mercedes-Benz Racing Cars by Karl Ludvigsen (Bond/ Parkhurst Books, 1971)

Pininfarina 1930–1980: Prestige and Tradition by Dieter Merlin (Edita, 1980)

Streamlining and Car Aerodynamics by Jan Norbye (TAB Books, 1977)

Stromlinienautos in Deutschland (Streamline Cars in Germany) by Ralf J.F Kieselbach (Kohlhammer, 1982)

Stromlinienautos in Europa und USA (Streamline Cars in Europe/USA, 1900–1945) by Ralf J.F.Kieselbach (Kohlhammer, 1982)

Touring Superleggera by Carlo Bianchi Anderloni and Angelo Titio Anselmi (Autocritica, 1983)

The Story of Volvo Cars by Graham Robson (Patrick Stephens, 1983)

The Z Series Datsuns by Ray Hutton (Motor Racing Publications, 1982)

Magazines and publications
Autocar
Autocar & Motor
Automobile Quarterly
Classic Cars
Motor
World Car Catalogues 1962-1971
World Cars 1972-1985

INDEX